CONNECT

CONNECT

A YEAR OF DAILY DEVOTIONS & PRAYER STARTERS

Josh Barnett

Connect
© Copyright 2019 by Josh Barnett

Published by Blue Springs Publishing, LLC
bluespringspublishing.com

All rights reserved. No part of this publication may be reproduced, stored in a retrieval system, or transmitted in any form or by any means – for example, electronic, photocopy, recording – without the prior written permission of the publisher. The only exception is brief quotations in written reviews.

Scriptures are taken from the New King James Version®. Copyright © 1982 by Thomas Nelson. Used by permission. All rights reserved.

ISBN 978-0-578-57681-7

Publisher: Clay Young
Cover and interior design: Marc Whitaker / MTWdesign.net
Typesetting: PerfecType / Nashville, Tennessee
Copy Editing / Proofing: Rachel Ryan

Printed in the United States of America

In honor of a special, godly woman whose life brought two men together to create a devotional book focused on prayer. Rest in peace,

Ginger Young.

Your works and influence still continue today.

FOREWORD

Everyone believes they have experienced true suffering, but often our day-to-day challenges are simply challenges that thought and prayer can help us endure. After practicing medicine for more than thirty years, I can truthfully say prolonged, intense, life-threatening illness always causes suffering that is often very difficult to bear. Faced with the great unknown (why did it happen, and will I survive?), suffering causes many people to question their faith. Yet the Bible tells us that God does not cause suffering or tempt His creations with suffering. Suffering is the consequence of our imperfect world, and God promises to carry us if necessary during our journey through it. We also know Jesus suffered an unimaginable fate, which He foresaw, and so, unlike the people who tell us they know just how we feel when we suffer, Christ does know exactly how we feel.

I watched Josh Barnett as he suffered through a very difficult illness where he was helpless to improve his situation and could only wait for the results of surgeries and other treatments. He faced the loss of his ability to care for his family and his congregation and faced the possibility that he might lose his vision or his life due to the illness. I saw him "sweat blood," and while he was on his knees, he looked up to the great Healer, and he was given everything he needed to survive and to return to his life's work. This book is the fruits of his suffering and a gift to anyone who is faced with a great challenge. When you are too tired and confused to seek the answers yourself, these devotionals will guide you through your journey. Always remember that God moves in mysterious ways, His time is not our time, and if we ask, it shall be given.

Terri W. Jerkins, MD

INTRODUCTION

If given the opportunity to ask Jesus anything, what would it be? Would it be about your life? Would it be one of the big questions of the world? Would it be a question on why something happened to you? The disciples were given the opportunity to ask Jesus questions. One particular occasion, they asked Jesus about prayer. "Lord, teach us to pray, as John also taught his disciples" (Luke 11:1). The disciples were given the power to cast out demons and cure diseases. Yet they still wanted to know more about prayer. I find it interesting that there is no place in the written record of them asking, "Lord, teach us to preach." We have a number of schools that teach homiletics. It's not written that they asked, "Lord, teach us to sing." We have music education in grade school and college. Do you know of any schools that provide a major in prayer? Do they offer a degree in praying? I'm thankful for the education with both preaching and singing. What about prayer? I believe prayer is just as important for us to know and understand.

The disciples desired to know more about prayer. They were not satisfied with what they already knew about prayer. I hope you also feel unsatisfied when it comes to prayer. This devotional book is to honor the privilege of praying to God. It includes a thought to pray for each day of the year. Each day has a couple prayer starters, a thought surrounding a lesson to pray, and examples of specific ideas to pray along with scripture to support those thoughts. Please understand that I'm no authority on the topic of prayer. I'm constantly challenged to know more about prayer. It's my hope that you come away with a closer relationship with God through your daily prayers. I hope you will feel more comfortable talking to God as you use this book daily. I hope you are open and honest with yourself and God. May the Lord bless and keep you.

In Him,
Josh Barnett

LORD, TEACH ME TO PRAY WHEN ...

Our school takes a high school group to New York City to serve in June. One of the activities we do is a "Prayer Walk." This is done by walking, stopping, looking around, listening to what's around us, and praying a specific prayer. The guide of our group gives certain facts about the area we are in. The facts could be about poverty, violence, and drug usage. Students are asked to pray about specific problems and for God's help with those involved. We prayed at Grand Central Station for the problem of trafficking. We prayed at Wall Street to be more benevolent. We prayed at Bryant Park for the problem of homelessness. We prayed at the 9/11 Memorial. We prayed for the problem of terrorism and hate. We walked around quietly, observing what we saw. I was moved by a single white rose placed in honor of a person who died at the North Tower. It was a moment of deep reflection in a busy city. It was a picture of serenity in a place of sadness and loss. The rose was a symbol of living but never forgetting. The person who placed that white rose experienced an awful tragedy. When I see what others are going through, it helps me put my struggles in a better perspective. I'm not alone in what I face.

DEAR LORD, HELP ME ...

1. Pray for the ability to live by faith and not by sight.
2. Pray for the wisdom to put your struggle in the right perspective.

"God is our refuge and strength, a very present help in trouble." **(Psalm 46:1)**

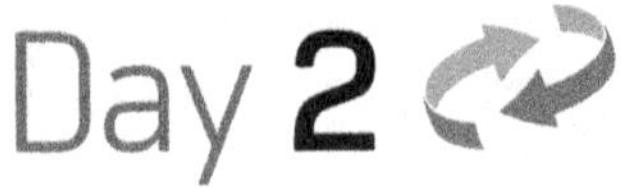

Day 2

DEAR LORD, TEACH ME TO LOOK AHEAD ...

My oldest son and I were playing a friendly game of chess. No, I wasn't going to let him to win. I was helping him with each piece and how to use it. He wanted to play aggressively to attempt to put me in check. In doing so, he left his most important piece, the king, open. Life is like a game of chess. You must think before you move. Every piece has a part to play. Sometimes sacrifices have to be made. It's not what you have but how you use it. The most unlikely can become something greater. I look at the pawns and how we can easily overlook their importance. They can reach the end of the board and become a different piece. The pawns can provide a barrier for the other important pieces. The pawns can represent the little things we do. It may not seem like much, but in the long run it matters greatly. What if we applied these things more to our lives? For example, what about looking ahead by thinking about what we do and say today. Sometimes we can get so caught up in the moment that we don't think about the consequences ahead. Life catches up. This is true physically as well as spiritually. May we take the necessary time today to see what really matters. It starts, continues, and ends with Jesus.

DEAR FATHER, HELP ME ...

1. Pray for wisdom to focus on matters of eternal weight.
2. Pray for patience to see beyond the present circumstances.

> *"Let your eyes look straight ahead, and your eyelids look right before you."* **(Proverbs 4:25)**

Day 3

DEAR LORD, ALLOW ME TO HELP ...

My youngest son loved to set up dominoes and watch them fall. Each time, we took the time needed to set up the dominoes and then knocked them down. We would do it again and again. My son strategically placed his dominoes according to his own design. It's so true to life. He spent more time setting up than knocking down. We would assess the mess and, together, build again. The most important lesson is for him to know that we will be there to help him back up. It's not about falling down. This will happen by his choices in a broken world. It's about having faith and being supported by his loved ones to get back up. He will not be alone when he falls. We will be there to encourage, love, and support back up. We all need the same support and to be that support for others. Are you that person for someone? It's the difference in getting back up or staying down.

DEAR FATHER, LET ME BE ...

1. Pray to be helpful for someone who has fallen because of life.
2. Pray for the ability to be a presence rather than telling someone what to do.

"For a righteous man may fall seven times and rise again." **(Proverbs 24:16)**

Day 4

DEAR LORD, HELP ME TO REALIZE ...

Why do you pray? I find it interesting what Paul prayed for. He prayed for the people to know God better. Wow! He didn't say, "I pray that your circumstance changes." He didn't ask for a change in government, protection from invading armies, or financial security. The ones Paul prayed for lived in a time of harsh treatment, death from disease, and oppression by powerful forces. Paul didn't pray for the goods we have at the top of our priority list. He prayed for the people to know God better. He used prayer to have a better sense of God and all His glory. Have we ever prayed to know God better? Can you imagine in all things of life asking God to have a better understanding of Him rather than a change in your circumstances? Others asked to know God better. Maybe we should take their example and follow.

DEAR LORD, I PRAY TO APPRECIATE ...

1. Pray to know God better through all circumstances.
2. Pray to be in line with God's will and not your own.

"... that the God of our Lord Jesus Christ, the Father of glory, may give to you the spirit of wisdom and revelation in the knowledge of Him." **(Ephesians 1:17)**

Day 5

LORD, ALLOW ME TO THINK BEFORE …

I passed by a marquee sign recently that said, "Go to God before you go to Facebook." I would add Instagram, email, Twitter, and so on. It made me think of what I have posted, emailed, and said through social accounts. It's too easy in the heat of the moment to type a few words and press send without facing someone. The words we type carry tremendous weight. What if? What if we go to God first before we post? If someone makes me mad, I go to God with my anger and hurt first. I confess my feelings to Him and realize whom I'm talking to. I remember in my prayer to God that I have hurt and disappointed Him. If we do to someone what has been done to us, we wouldn't be here because of our actions against God. It's hard to unleash anger and frustration after an open and honest prayer before God. I believe going to God first will put the brakes on my angry words and actions. I need to draw near to Him more so my words and actions don't come back on me.

DEAR FATHER, GIVE ME THE PATIENCE TO REMEMBER MY MISTAKES …

1. Pray for strength to keep your fingers from sending something in anger.
2. Pray for the remembrance of how you have offended God.

> *"Draw near to God and He will draw near to you."* (James 4:8)

Day 6 

DEAR LORD, HELP ME TO IDENTIFY WITH YOU ...

Who are you? Are you a husband or a wife? A father or mother? A CEO or CFO? We like to be identified by who we are and what we do. We can strive to become people of status or titles. We build portfolios to advertise who we are. We begin conversations with new people by establishing who we are; however, maybe we are more than this. Who am I? I'm a husband, father, preacher, and teacher. I'm grateful for each role, especially with family. However, the greatest and most precious role is a servant. I humbly bow in the shadow of the cross. There is no greater privilege than to be branded in my heart with the name of God's precious Son. I take up the daily cross of my health and gladly follow the King. There is no higher position than for me to be on my knees in adoration for my Lord. I say all of this with complete humility. I am a sinful/forgiven servant.

DEAR LORD, HELP ME TO SEE MY VALUE IS IN YOU ...

1. Pray for humility to know that nothing compares to your identification in Christ.
2. Pray to be more mindful that your identity is in Christ and for Christ.

> *"A disciple is not above his teacher, nor a servant above his master."* **(Matthew 10:24)**

DEAR LORD, HELP ME TO UNDERSTAND THE VALUE OF WORK ...

I took two of my boys to a local restaurant in Nashville. The manager of the restaurant is a nice person and hard worker. We talked a bit about what we do for jobs. I was curious and asked if the turnover rate was high in his line of work. He laughed and said yes. He said they were short four workers that night due to people not showing up. One employee worked that morning and promised to come back to close. Well, the person never called or showed up. I thought of a couple things when he said that. Be committed to your words. Remember the time when your word meant everything? I don't, but I try to let my "yes" be "yes" and "no" be "no." If you don't work, you don't eat. If we are able, we need to be go-getters. Make life happen instead of waiting for life to happen. Here's to the go-getters in life who get up and do their jobs.

DEAR LORD, HELP ME TO DO WHAT I DO WITH ALL MY MIGHT ...

1. Pray to follow through with your words and commitments to others.
2. Pray to be mindful that all you do is for God and not just yourself.

"And whatever you do, do it heartily, as to the Lord and not to men." **(Colossians 3:23)**

Day 8

LORD, HELP ME TO UNDERSTAND THAT BEING ...

> "It is hard to have patience with people who say, 'There is no death' or 'Death doesn't matter.' There is death. And whatever is matters. And whatever happens has consequences, and it and they are irrevocable and irreversible." (C. S. Lewis, *A Grief Observed*)

When it comes to the death of a family member or friend, it's tempting to want to say something to help the pain of the grieving survivors. I want to say the magical words that will comfort them. It's a strong desire for many to want to fix those who are hurting. We need to be reminded that each life and death is different. There are no magical words to say to someone in their great loss. I believe greater than our words is our presence. We show up, listen, and support the family. What we do by being there says enough to the family. With the presence of people and the comfort of God, it helps make the reality of death somewhat bearable. However, death matters. It bears more consequences than most things we face in life. May we be present and supportive to those directly affected by death.

DEAR LORD, HELP ME WHEN IT COMES TO DEALING WITH DEATH ...

1. Pray for the understanding that being there in death matters to the survivors.
2. Pray for the comfort that you have received to be there for those who are hurting.

> *"Blessed be the ... God of all comfort, who comforts us in all our tribulation, that we may be able to comfort those who are in any trouble."* **(2 Corinthians 1:3-4)**

DEAR LORD, HELP ME TO HAVE GRATITUDE IN MY HEART ...

Our parents took our four-year-old son to a pizza and game place. His grandparents wanted to treat him because they love him. When they were done, they got into the car to go home. Before they did, my son's grandmother buckled him into his car seat. She reminded him, "Make sure you thank Papa." Silence. No response. She said again, "Did you hear me? Make sure you say thank you to your papa." There was still no sound from my son. (Let me break and say it was a real proud moment as his father.) His grandmother then said, "You know, Papa enjoys doing nice things for grandchildren—when they say thank you." The grandson continued to say nothing. "Do you hear me?" said his grandmother. The grandson finally said, "I'm thankful, Papa. I just don't want to say it!" We can struggle with gratitude. We sometimes can go through a day without giving thanks to God. We can go through moments in life only thanking God after it's over. Our whole lives should be one great big thank-you to God. He is the reason for physical and spiritual life. He is the sustainer of life. May we learn to be more grateful to God even in ungrateful times. Why? This is the will of God in Christ Jesus for us.

DEAR LORD, I THANK YOU IN EVERYTHING ...

1. Pray for gratitude for every day regardless of what happens.
2. Pray for a great appreciation for the moments in your day you take for granted.

"In everything give thanks; for this is the will of God in Christ Jesus for you." (1 Thessalonians 5:18)

Day 10

DEAR LORD, HELP ME TO BE THANKFUL IN HARD TIMES ...

During one of the times I was in the hospital for low sodium, I took a picture of my hands and arms to remind myself of how helpless I was at that time. I'm thankful that God gave me other hands to help me in my helpless state. I'm thankful for the hands that drove me to the ER. I'm thankful for the hands that gave me pain medication and IV fluids to correct my low sodium. I'm thankful for the beautiful hands of my wife rubbing my head and back. I'm thankful for my doctor's hands that knew what I needed medically. I'm grateful for the hands that taught in my place. I'm thankful for the teaching hands at school while my body took the time to recover. I'm indebted to all the hands clasped together in prayer on my behalf. I am most thankful for God's hand, which orchestrated all the right people in place to help me in my set-back. God is so good even in all my pain and suffering. He gave me the hands of others to help me. How can I be angry, resentful, or upset? I'm far from feeling that because of the love of God and His people.

DEAR LORD, HELP ME TO APPRECIATE THE GOOD AND BAD ...

1. Pray for the good that God can do in a tough situation.
2. Pray for the wisdom to see beyond the pain to all the help of others and to be grateful.

"Both riches and honor come from You, and You reign over all. In Your hand is power and might; in Your hand it is to make great and to give strength to all." **(1 Chronicles 29:12)**

Day 11

DEAR LORD, HELP ME TO BE AN ENCOURAGER TO OTHERS ...

Every person has a story. Do we take the time to stop and listen to it? I met a person in a local nursing facility for rehabilitation. My intention was to encourage him, but he was an encouragement to me. I found out through our conversation that we went to the same middle school at different times in Indiana. This person shouldn't be smiling with what he has been through, but he is. He is a victim of a hit-and-run while walking. He was in a coma for a while with multiple broken bones. He is fortunate to be alive. He is laid up in a neck brace and has other braces on him. I asked about his family. He had a girlfriend, but she was killed in a tragic accident by a mail carrier. He spoke at her eulogy almost one year away from his accident. Shouldn't he be angry and resentful because of what has happened to him? He's not. I was humbled by my encounter with him. If he can only move his feet to the sound of music, I can get through my day. May his story encourage you as it has me.

DEAR LORD, LET ME TAKE THE OPPORTUNITY TO VISIT ...

1. Pray for the examples of people that God has placed in your life.
2. Pray to be the same source of encouragement for others.

"Let us run with endurance the race that is set before us." **(Hebrews 12:1)**

Day 12

DEAR LORD, HELP ME TO BE AN EXAMPLE FOR OTHERS ...

I gave my boys "the best outline challenge" while I was preaching. My lesson was on David and Goliath. I had my own introduction, three points, and conclusion. I wondered what they would gain from it. I challenged them to deliver the best notes from my lesson. My oldest son turned in a cursive outline of my entire lesson. I was impressed. The middle son turned in a mixture of writing, illustrations, and homemade emojis. I loved his creative approach. The youngest son turned in what looked like Dante's *Inferno* with PAC-MAN ghosts as angels. Who knew the ghosts chasing PAC-MAN were angels to gather you to heaven? I had to decide on a winner. So, the winner was ... all three. Each of them in their own way gave their own outline of what I had said. I hope they will continue to listen closely to what their mom and dad have to say. I hope we can continue to give them instruction worth listening to. I know they are always watching us. Let us leave an example of how to follow in His steps. There is nothing greater than to pass down our faith to them.

DEAR LORD, HELP ME TO TAKE ADVANTAGE OF THE DAY ...

1. Pray to be a positive influence on those around you.
2. Pray to be a worthy example in Christ.

> *"My son, keep your father's command, and do not forsake the law of your mother. Bind them continually upon your heart."* **(Proverbs 6:20-21)**

DEAR LORD, THANK YOU FOR YOUR AMAZING GRACE ...

I'm blessed by the godly example of my grandparents. My dad's parents have passed on, but their influence still impacts me. My grandmother wanted me to be a preacher when I didn't want to. I think she saw something in me before I did. My mom's parents are still here. They are spiritual giants in my life. My grandmother graduated from high school in 1951. My grandfather joined the military the same year. They were married and raised a home with four children. My grandfather was a butcher, and my grandmother worked in the home and school cafeteria. Their greatest work has been passing along their faith to children, grandchildren, and great-grandchildren. They continue to read the Bible daily. One visit with them, my grandmother surprised me with a painting she had. The painting is an old white church building. The painting is called "Amazing Grace." God's grace is so amazing in a lot of ways. One of the reasons it's so amazing is family. I'm thankful for His amazing grace in godly grandparents who have shown the love of God to their children, grandchildren, and great-grandchildren.

DEAR LORD, THANK YOU FOR THE EXAMPLE OF GRANDPARENTS ...

1. Pray with thanksgiving over God's grace shown in family members with godly character.
2. Pray for the wisdom to learn from their years of experience and go the same way.

"Each one has received a gift, minister it to one another, as good stewards of the manifold grace of God." (1 Peter 4:10)

Day 14

DEAR LORD, GIVE ME THE PATIENCE TO RISE ABOVE ...

The critics fade away. The doers are remembered. In 1796, George Washington appeared before a joint session of Congress. A congressman from Virginia bitterly condemned Congress for praising Washington, saying, "Nobody remembers his name!" Oh, how that critic was wrong about Washington! The list of things named in his honor is long. The critics fade away. The doers are remembered. The people of Jesus' hometown of Nazareth couldn't believe that He was the Messiah. They struggled with the carpenter—son of Joseph and Mary and brother of James, Judas, Joses, and Simon—being the One prophesied. They were offended and rejected Him. Did this stop Jesus from doing what He came to do? He was committed to God's plan despite the naysayers. We can learn from history. We need to be strong in our principles and not back down from the critics. We cannot please everyone, but we can please God. You choose!

DEAR LORD, HELP ME TO RISE ABOVE THE NOISE ...

1. Pray for strength to live for God and not everyone else.
2. Pray to be a doer.

"But be doers of the word, and not hearers only." (James 1:22)

DEAR LORD, GIVE US THE STRENGTH TO PERSEVERE ...

Our thirty-second president of the United States, Franklin D. Roosevelt, was once asked if he ever worried. He replied by referring to polio that had left him disabled. "If you had spent two years in bed trying to wiggle your toe, after that anything would seem easy." I don't know why bad things happen to people. I don't believe in "the answer" to all suffering. I don't believe in blaming God for it. We are a culture that wants to know why. Many times, we don't know why. We don't need to know in order to do what we need to do. What about asking questions like "What have I learned from this?" or "What can I do with my life now?" I don't know about you, but I wouldn't want to go back and do some tough things in my life. Those difficult times have helped me learn who I am today. Some things we learn from education. Other things we learn from experience. We can learn from what life brings us both good and bad.

DEAR LORD, MAY I SEE BEYOND THE MOMENT ...

1. Pray for the endurance to go through the difficult moments of life.
2. Pray for an openness to learn from both good and bad circumstances.

"Not that I speak in regard to need, for I have learned in whatever state I am, to be content." **(Philippians 4:11)**

Day 16

DEAR FATHER, THANK YOU FOR THE GOOD ...

I came across a comic strip that was talking about being good for Christmas. Calvin was nervous about Christmas. He didn't know Santa's definition for being good. We can relate to that as we remember being a child around December. We didn't want to be on the naughty list. Calvin rationalized within his mind what being good meant. He hadn't killed anyone or committed any felons. We too can easily rationalize things by looking at something far worse than what we have done. Calvin's friend, Hobbes, suggested that good is more than the absence of bad. Calvin said, "So, that's what worries me." A rich, young ruler approached Jesus thinking being good was the absence of bad things. He asked Jesus about eternal life. When asked by Jesus, He proudly said that he had followed the rules since he was a youth. Jesus told him to sell what he had and follow Him. Jesus didn't want his things. He wanted his heart. The spiritual heart is the one thing that we struggle to give. The person who had followed God's rules failed to give what Jesus asked. He walked away sadly. Good is more than the absence of evil. It's a life in the Son.

DEAR LORD, THANK YOU FOR THE GOOD ...

1. Pray for the presence of Jesus rather than the absence of wrong.
2. Pray for gratitude in what you have and have gained by being in Jesus.

"For by grace you have been saved through faith, and that not of yourselves; it is the gift of God." (Ephesians 2:8)

Day 17

DEAR LORD, ALLOW ME TO ENCOURAGE OTHERS ...

I don't ask why. I ask what. What can I do now? What can I contribute? This is my approach with my health. I was blessed recently with a "what" moment. I was able to pay it forward. My doctor had my permission to tell a patient about my health condition of having a brain tumor. This person was going through what I went through, and he wanted to meet me. I visited him in the hospital. At the time, he was twenty-two years young and dealing with complications from brain surgery. He had been in the neuro ICU for months. I visited him on his second day out of neuro ICU and in a regular hospital room. I encouraged him with the encouragement I wanted in that situation. I was thankful I was able to be that person to him. Someone who knows what he is going through. Are you someone who can empathize with someone else? We can take the things we have experienced and help those who are experiencing the same. We experience things in life maybe for the reason to learn and share with others. We can do that with losing someone. We can do that with facing surgery. We can do that with losing a job. The list goes on with what we have faced. The opportunity is there for us to share and encourage others facing similar situations.

DEAR LORD, I PRAY FOR OPPORTUNITY ...

1. Pray for God to open a door of opportunity to encourage someone by your story.
2. Pray for your eyes and ears to be open to those around you in need of encouragement.

"As we have opportunity, let us do good." **(Galatians 6:10)**

Day 18 

DEAR LORD, HELP ME TO KEEP THINGS IN THE RIGHT PLACE ...

Has God ever gotten your attention? If so, you don't forget it. I believe sometimes God gives us a little more exposure to those who have it worse than us. It's an opportunity to keep us both grounded and humbled. We can get in a rut of feeling comfortable and picking apart people, ideas, and things. Then, BAM! We are hit with the unexpected. I visited someone celebrating their last few months. This person would have loved to live longer for the sake of family. However, the physical body was in such a state that it was inoperable. I was brought to my knees by their situation. We prayed together. God, You have my attention. I will keep the main things the main things. I will do better to stay away from the many distractions of life. I know these things don't mean much in the end. "Come now, you who say, 'Today or tomorrow we will go to such and such a city, spend a year there, buy and sell, and make a profit'; whereas you do not know what will happen tomorrow. For what is your life? It is even a vapor that appears for a little time and then vanishes away" (James 4:13-14).

DEAR LORD, I PRAY FOR THE RIGHT PERSPECTIVE IN LIFE ...

1. Pray for your heart to be humbled enough to place your priority in Him.
2. Pray to God for the right heart and mind and to focus on the main thing.

> *"Do not boast about tomorrow, for you do not know what a day may bring."* **(Proverbs 27:1)**

Day 19

DEAR LORD, HELP ME TO APPRECIATE WHAT I HAVE ...

My middle son surprised me with a handwritten card. Let me say that dads like cards too. He wanted me to remember that I'm a part of his life and how much he loves me. Don't worry, son! You have no idea how much I love you. You will not know until you are blessed to have a family. Only then will you understand the love I have for you. The thought of not having you hurts too much to think about. When I see you, it's like my heart has jumped out and started walking. My wife feels the same. It's these little, unexpected moments that I cherish the most. My day was busy, and a lot was going on. However, I was reminded of the important things by this out-of-the-blue card from my son. There is something special in a child's innocent love given freely. My cup runs over. Children are precious gifts from the Lord. God, help me to remember that when I'm frustrated and stressed.

DEAR LORD, THANK YOU FOR CHILDREN TEACHING US ...

1. Pray to God with thanks for those unexpected moments of love demonstrated.
2. Pray to God for a remembrance of the things done in love so you can remember when life is hard.

"Behold, children are a heritage from the LORD." (Psalm 127:3)

Day 20

DEAR LORD, HELP ME TO APPRECIATE EVERY DAY ...

I was waiting patiently at the MinuteClinic. (They should change the name to the "HourClinic." The wait was longer than a minute.) Thankfully, I tested negative for strep, but I had a crummy virus. This came with aches, sore throat, and my head hurting. Would anyone like to have it next? "Under the weather" never comes at a convenient time. I guess there is no good time to get a virus. On days like that one, I think about someone I know who has several health issues. Every time, the person says, "I can't complain. There are others worse off than me." What a great attitude! We could complain when we don't feel good. What good will that do? I've never found complaining to be beneficial. In fact, it makes me feel worse. If there is one person who earned the right to complain, it was Jesus. He didn't complain. Are we any better? "Do all things without complaining and disputing, that you may become blameless and harmless, children of God without fault in the midst of a crooked and perverse generation, among whom you shine as lights in the world" (Philippians 2:14-15). The next bad day you have, don't complain and see what happens.

DEAR LORD, THANK YOU FOR JESUS' EXAMPLE ...

1. Pray to God for a heart that is filled with gratitude and not complaints.
2. Pray for the attitude to rise above the moments and situations that you don't like in life.

> *"Let no corrupt word proceed out of your mouth, but what is good for necessary edification, that it may impart grace to the hearers."* **(Ephesians 4:29)**

DEAR LORD, MAY I NEVER FORGET THE GREATEST DEAL ...

During the World Series between the Dodgers and the Astros, a Dodgers fan found an unbelievable deal online. He found a pair of World Series tickets for $9 a ticket. The lucky fan couldn't believe the deal and quickly made the purchase. Jordan wasn't surprised to hear back from the online store that the low price was a big mistake. However, the company honored Jordan's purchase and found tickets for $9 per ticket. Can you imagine the conversation at the game with the people sitting around the person with the great deal? "How much did you pay?" "Oh, I got a great deal of $500 a ticket." The person responds, "I did better than that with $9 a ticket." Ouch! Have you ever been that fortunate with a good deal? I was reading from Psalm 103 today. It described an unbelievable deal with God. God "has not dealt with us according to our sins, nor punished us according to our iniquities. For as the heavens are high above the earth, so great is His mercy toward those who fear Him" (Psalm 103:10-11). What we deserve is death! What has been graciously given is forgiveness by God through a relationship with Jesus Christ. You will find no better deal.

DEAR LORD, HELP ME TO ALWAYS BE GRATEFUL FOR THE GREATEST GIFT ...

1. Pray for gratitude to God, who is responsible for the greatest gift.
2. Pray for the attitude to realize the value of salvation over any other gift.

> *"For the wages of sin is death, but the gift of God is eternal life in Christ Jesus our Lord."* **(Romans 6:23)**

Day 22

DEAR LORD, THANK YOU FOR FINISHING WHAT I CAN'T DO ...

What goes through your mind at a funeral? Do you think of your last moment with the deceased person? Do you have regrets? Do you think the deceased person had unfinished goals, jobs, or business? Much of our lives is about finishing. First of all, we have grade school to finish. All twelve years of it. Then, we go to college or right into the workplace. Whenever we finish one thing, we move to the other. We will not complete or finish everything in our lifetimes. Death is a reminder of that. God understands our failures. Jesus said on the cross, "It is finished." The Greek word is *tetelestai*. It means to bring to an end, complete, and fulfill. Another way of saying it is "mission accomplished." Jesus did that on the cross when He paid it all. There is no need to do what Christ has done. "It is finished" allows us to live complete lives because Jesus accomplished it for us.

DEAR LORD, YOU'VE COMPLETED SO WE DON'T HAVE TO ...

1. Pray with thanksgiving for Christ and His willingness to finish for you.
2. Pray for the peace you know you have because of what Christ has done for you.

"When Jesus had received the sour wine, He said, 'It is finished!' And bowing His head, He gave up His spirit." (John 19:30)

DEAR LORD, GIVE ME THE COURAGE TO KEEP FEAR AWAY ...

"Be strong and of good courage; do not be afraid, nor be dismayed, for the LORD your God is with you wherever you go" (Joshua 1:9). God repeatedly told His servant, Joshua, to take courage and be strong. Joshua had some big shoes to fill by following the steps of his leader, Moses. He would lead God's people into hostile, uncharted territory. God affirmed His presence. We must be the same in our world today. I never thought, as a preacher, that in my lifetime someone would come into our churches with the intention to kill. Yet we had someone do this in South Carolina, Tennessee, and Texas. I will not live in fear because of this. I will continue to stand up and proclaim God's Word. I take comfort that the church itself was formed under the threat of terror. Go back and read the assault on the early Christians. What did they do? They grew and multiplied. What will Christians do today? I cannot answer for you. I can answer for myself. I will work on being strong and courageous in the Lord. May God help us in difficult times.

DEAR LORD, MY STRENGTH IS IN YOU ALONE ...

1. Pray for courage in a trying world and difficult times.
2. Pray for understanding that difficult times are not new for God's people. You need to be strong and have courage.

> *"Finally, my brethren, be strong in the Lord and in the power of His might."* (Ephesians 6:10)

Day 24

DEAR LORD, HELP ME TO BE FLEXIBLE ...

What do you do when your plan doesn't work? There are times when we need to go to plan B, C, or D. Are you flexible enough to change and adjust to doing something different? Recently, I worked on some activities at night for the next day. I assumed the internet would be working with what I was planning. Well, we had some heavy rain, and internet was out in the area. The online activities and questions didn't happen. I made it through the day doing other things. I have learned the hard way the necessity of having a backup plan. The internet could go down, the copier could break, or something could interrupt the class like a tornado or fire drill. Do we have a backup plan outside our jobs? How have you responded to events that didn't go the way you thought? Life is filled with unplanned events. I believe our lives in Christ are examples of being flexible and going to plan B, C, or D. We tried to do things on our own and failed. We eventually learned that we needed help, so we turned to Christ. Life won't always happen the way you think. Be prepared for the unprepared things. Be flexible. Be willing to go about something in a different way.

DEAR LORD, HELP ME DRAW CLOSER TO YOUR CONSTANT PRESENCE ...

1. Pray for the willingness to adapt to life events.
2. Pray to see God as a constant in a changing world.

"Now when they had gone through Phrygia and the region of Galatia, they were forbidden by the Holy Spirit to preach the word in Asia." **(Acts 16:6)**

Day 25

DEAR LORD, HELP ME TO APPRECIATE YOU MORE ...

Does God owe us anything? Is there anything we can demand from God and be right? What would you say if your child came to you and said, "I want your stuff plus access to your accounts and my name on all titles"? What if their reasoning for such a great request was, "I'm your child, and I deserve it"? You deserve it! This is the root of every sale commercial. In years past, people used their hands and worked. Today, many go through life feeling entitled. I deserve it without putting in the work. Do we view God like this? Is He there to help us when we need Him? Do we demand the right answers to our prayers? Do we put conditions on Him to prove He really is God? God owes us nothing. Paul put it this way: "Will the thing formed say to him who formed it, 'Why have you made me like this?'" (Romans 9:20). God owes us nothing, but He did something for us. He demonstrated His righteousness by Jesus Christ. The work of Jesus Christ on the cross allows us to become the righteousness of God.

DEAR LORD, I PRAY FOR A BETTER APPRECIATION OF WHAT YOU HAVE DONE ...

1. Pray for humility to approach God with understanding of what He has done.
2. Pray to God with gratitude for the gift of eternal life that was given because of love.

"... His righteousness, that He might be just and the justifier of the one who has faith in Jesus." **(Romans 3:26)**

Day 26

DEAR LORD, I CANNOT FATHOM EVERYTHING, BUT I PRAISE ...

There are some events that words cannot describe. It is difficult to put into words what I was experiencing at the births of our three boys. The day my bride came down the aisle to join my side is hard to express accurately as well. The day I was saved by the blood of Jesus Christ leaves me speechless. What about God? How do we describe an infinite Being with our limited vocabulary? Try explaining God the Father, the Son, and the Holy Spirit to a five-year-old. I gave it a try over dinner one night, and I lost him about three seconds into my answer. Paul felt the best way to describe God was in an expression of praise. "Doxology" is the name given to brief forms of praise to God. One of the greatest doxologies comes at the end of Romans 11. Paul argued over Israel's rejection and how God used their disobedience to give Gentiles the opportunity to be saved. God used the Gentiles to motivate Jewish obedience. God's ultimate purpose began with Abraham and continued to Jesus for the righteousness to all who believe. This led to Paul's doxology.

DEAR LORD, I'M THANKFUL FOR YOUR AMAZING GLORY AND POWER ...

1. Pray for a disciplined heart to seek and know God better.
2. Pray to God, thanking Him for being the great, awesome God.

"Oh, the depth of the riches both of the wisdom and knowledge of God!" **(Romans 11:33)**

DEAR LORD, MAY I BE AN ENCOURAGER FOR OTHERS ...

My wife captured an awesome moment on camera. Our oldest son was running a cross-country race. The course was a two-mile run. On the last leg of the race, he was tired and worn down. He was hitting the runner's wall mentally. As he was pushing to finish, his brother ran alongside him as he finished the race. They crossed the finish line together. My wife took a picture of both of them running together. I believe encouragement is a powerful thing. It can help you finish a tough race. It can help you finish a day. It can help you finish a medical treatment. It can help you focus more on God. The Christian life has been called a race. It's not a race where we are trying to finish first, second, or third. It's a race for as many as are running to finish. Do you have people to encourage you each day? Are you someone who gives encouragement to others? We are called to encourage each other daily. Why would the Bible stress the frequency of our encouraging? I believe God knows in His wisdom how much a compliment or good word can do for us. What would an encouraging word every day for a week do for you? We all need encouragement. May we be on the receiving end as much as we need to hear encouragement from others.

DEAR LORD, HELP ME TO USE MY WORDS MORE ...

1. Pray for an attitude that seeks good rather than the bad.
2. Pray to God to give you the awareness to encourage someone today.

"But exhort one another daily, while it is called 'Today,' lest any of you be hardened through the deceitfulness of sin." **(Hebrews 3:13)**

Day 28 

DEAR LORD, MAY I NOT BE TOO BUSY IN THE HOME ...

My family took a vacation to the Ark Encounter in Kentucky. The story of Noah and the ark has always fascinated me. It leaves so many questions about the family of eight with all the animals on board. I wonder what it smelled like. The story of Noah and his faith caused my wife and me to name our firstborn son Noah. Our son bought a shirt at the exhibit that says, "God spoke to Noah." I hope he doesn't think about using that when it comes to getting out of chores and homework. One of the greatest things said of Noah was that he "saved his household." I know Noah was not perfect, and the Bible shows that. However, Noah and his wife raised three sons, and they believed and had faith. I believe that says a lot about Noah and his wife. All three sons and their wives were saved too. I cannot think of anything more rewarding than knowing my family is safe. We can get busy and try to save the world while our families suffer without us. Do we put in the time that is needed in the home? Do we see the importance of saving our families? Noah didn't save the world, but he did save his family.

DEAR LORD, HELP ME TO SET THE RIGHT PRIORITIES WHEN IT COMES TO FAMILY ...

1. Pray for the mission to save your family by being there.
2. Pray to God to help you keep your time in the more important things.

"By faith Noah, being divinely warned of things not yet seen, moved with godly fear, prepared an ark for the saving of his household." **(Hebrews 11:7)**

Day 29

DEAR LORD, HELP ME TO FIX MY EYES ON YOU ...

Do you think seeing is always believing? One Sunday morning, I was met by a local police officer. He wanted to speak to me. He escorted me through the auditorium within minutes of our time to start worship. Can you imagine what the people thought? What did the preacher do? We walked out of the side door, and the people coming in paused and looked in confusion. I don't blame them. I would have too. It's not every day that the preacher is followed by a police officer in a church building. What they saw was not what it looked like. I wasn't in trouble or being arrested. The emergency call center had received a phone call from our landline number. The funny thing was our landline was dead. What happened? I don't know. I believe seeing is not always believing. What we think we saw may not be. If we not careful, we can easily assume based on what we see only. I thanked the officer and let him know how much I appreciated him. When it comes to Christ, we don't need to see in order to believe. We don't need to assume He's something He's not. We have His words, life, and ministry. Believing is seeing!

DEAR LORD, THANK YOU FOR THE WORDS OF LIFE ...

1. Pray for strength not to assume based on what you see all the time.
2. Pray to the Lord who gave us His Word so we can believe even though we don't see.

"... whom having not seen you love. Though now you do not see Him, yet believing, you rejoice with joy inexpressible and full of glory." **(1 Peter 1:8)**

Day 30

DEAR LORD, HELP ME NOT TO RATIONALIZE SIN ...

I had a student who struggled with his quiz. Why? He failed to study. The next thing I knew, the unprepared student went from a blank test sheet to a sheet filled in with the right answer. I asked him how that could be. Was this a modern-day miracle that I needed to embrace or something else? He said that a student gave him the answer. I asked the other student who helped him, and he nonchalantly said, "I just helped him with one answer." He had rationalized in his mind that giving one answer was not bad. I asked him, "What's the difference between giving one answer and ten answers?" It was the principle of cheating regardless of whether it was one answer or all the answers. Do I rationalize things that are untrue in life? Do I tell myself that it's okay if it's not a big deal? Wrong is wrong, and right is right. A little wrong is still wrong.

DEAR LORD, GIVE ME THE STRENGTH TO CALL SIN FOR WHAT IT IS ...

1. Pray for strength to be a person of integrity.
2. Pray to the Lord for a heart committed to His Word when it comes to right and wrong.

"Woe to those who call evil good, and good evil." **(Isaiah 5:20)**

DEAR LORD, HELP ME NOT TO BE SO DISTRACTED ...

When I came home from work one day, my youngest son had a show on for his grandparents. The show was some animated, silly show. This particular episode, the father struggled with his kids using phones and other electronic devices. The daughter convinced her father to try "texting," and he started typing full sentences. As the episode went on, the father was obsessed with his phone, tablet, and computer. The kids became the parent and complained about how much their dad was on electronics. The episode ended with the internet getting unplugged, and everyone enjoyed face-to-face conversation. Wow! What a great message! Technology by definition is to make our lives easier. Has it? We seem to be more connected and distracted than ever. What if God dealt with us the same? Instead of Jesus coming, what if God just sent us a text with a heart emoji? God has every good reason to be distracted and not listen to us. God took the time to dwell among us. Maybe we need to put down our devices and spend time with others in conversation. It's good to communicate through technology. It's better in person.

DEAR LORD, HELP ME TO BE LESS DISTRACTED WITH TECHNOLOGY ...

1. Pray for strength when it comes to technology and the temptation to abuse it.
2. Pray to the Lord for help to take time away from your phone and spend time with people who matter to you.

"The Word became flesh and dwelt among us." (John 1:14)

Day 32

DEAR LORD, HELP ME TO BE AN ENCOURAGER TO OTHERS ...

One time I convinced my youngest son to ride a roller coaster with me. The ride was a steel coaster that went forward and backward. Before we got on the ride, I hugged my son. I could feel his little heart beating fast. To say he was nervous would be an understatement. We started off, and I thought we were okay. When we stopped on the ride to go backward, my son had this awful, frightful look. He was on the verge of tears. I tried to hug him as best as I could and encouraged him the rest of the way. "You are doing a great job." "We are almost at the end." "I'm so proud of you." When we made it to the end, I asked him if he liked it. My brave son informed me that it was fun, and he wanted to do it again. My presence and constant encouragement got him past his fear. It's amazing what our presence and words can do to others. You may know someone who is facing something scary. It may be that you are facing a scary situation. Is there a presence on earth that reminds you of God's presence and comforting words? Are you that person to others? I believe showing up and affirming someone can be all the difference.

DEAR LORD, ENCOURAGE ME SO I CAN ENCOURAGE OTHERS ...

1. Pray for an awareness toward those around you.
2. Pray for the opportunity to be present in the lives of others who are facing scary situations.

> *"Therefore comfort each other and edify one another, just as you also are doing."* **(1 Thessalonians 5:11)**

Day 33

DEAR LORD, FORGIVE ME FOR MAKING EXCUSES ...

I read a poll that released some memorable excuses for not coming into work. One excuse was "my mother poisoned the ham." Another was "I got stuck under the bed." What about this one: the doctor said I needed more vitamin D, so I went to the beach? For every responsibility in life, there is a limitless supply of bad excuses. The Bible gives its share of excuses from people who wanted to get out of spiritual responsibility. The Roman governor, Felix, told Paul it wasn't a convenient time for him to hear the Word. When God chose Moses, Moses gave the excuse that he was slow in speech. Jonah excused himself by running the opposite way from God's mission. I believe one of the biggest excuses today is the sense of entitlement. Instead of "I'm responsible," we hear "I deserve." This mentality takes us away from the potential God has in us. We have been made with a unique set of talents and abilities. We are not to bury it with excuses. We are to use them in the service of God. You have good works ahead of you in your marriage, parenting, career, and mission. All of it is according to God's plan. Remember "I'm responsible" and not "I deserve."

DEAR LORD, HELP ME TO BE APPRECIATIVE ...

1. Pray for a better appreciation of how God has blessed you every day.
2. Pray for the opportunity to serve and use your talents for the glory of God.

"For we are His workmanship, created in Christ Jesus for good works, which God prepared beforehand that we should walk in them." **(Ephesians 2:10)**

Day 34

DEAR LORD, I PRAY TO BE DEDICATED TO YOUR WORDS ...

If we have no memory, we are adrift because memory anchors us to the past, present, and future. In a book about a patient losing his memory, he had a rare neurological disorder called Korsakoff syndrome. He had stopped remembering after a certain year. He remembered his childhood and serving in the Navy. After that, he had no memory. He had to be introduced and reintroduced constantly to his doctor. He stayed the rest of his life in a convalescent home, where the staff referred to him as a "lost soul." Without memory, we are lost souls also. On the night of Jesus' betrayal, He said, "Do this in remembrance of Me" (Luke 22:19). One of the ways we remember Christ is speaking. We do this through prayer and music (Colossians 4:2; 3:16). Biblical memory connects us to the past and shows us where we are in the present and moves us to a promised future. Remember Christ today! What He did and what He promised to do!

DEAR LORD, HELP ME TO REMEMBER YOUR WORDS ...

1. Pray for the memory of what you know and have read about Christ.
2. Pray for the patience to await the revealing of knowing Christ more.

> *"And they remembered His words."* (Luke 24:8)

Day 35

DEAR LORD, HELP ME TO TRUST IN WHAT YOU HAVE SAID ...

A patient called his doctor and said, "It has been one month since my last visit, and I still feel miserable." The doctor asked him, "Did you follow all my instructions with the medicine I prescribed for you?" "I sure did," answered the patient. "The bottle said, 'Keep tightly closed,' so I did." I remember, as a student growing up, my teacher saying, "Before you start, make sure you read and follow all the instructions." One time I had a teacher who had hidden in the instructions to circle a certain number and underline another. He was testing on reading the instructions. I didn't do so well. We can easily rush through and take or assume what God has said. I can take any verse and pull it out of context to say what I want it to. However, we are to follow all of God's commands. In matters of salvation, we need to read all of the instructions in God's Word. Don't settle with a verse here and there. Be diligent to study it all.

DEAR LORD, HELP ME TO BE OBEDIENT TO YOUR WORDS ...

1. Pray to the Lord, thanking Him for a copy of His words so you can know for yourself.
2. Pray for the willingness to follow all of His commands.

> *"All Scripture is given by inspiration of God, and is profitable for doctrine, for reproof, for correction, for instruction in righteousness."* **(2 Timothy 3:16)**

Day 36

DEAR LORD, THANK YOU FOR BEING THE GIVER ...

What is your best gift? Would it be a piece of jewelry, a new vehicle, a home, a special vacation, or good health? I believe my beautiful wife and three boys are tremendous gifts from God. I love them very much. My love for them begs the question: Which do I love more? The gift(s) or the Giver? Abraham was put to the test between his love for God's gift and God. Isaac was a twenty-five-year-old promise to Abraham and Sarah. He finally came, and they enjoyed many years with him. One sudden day, God asked Abraham to give Isaac to Him. Wow! *Abraham, how much do you love God? Where are your priorities? In your gifts or the Giver?* I would like to say that I would do as Abraham had done. However, I don't know. The story of Abraham and Isaac in Genesis 22 is a hard lesson of letting go in order to mature. Don't misunderstand me. We should always be grateful and appreciative for every good gift from God. He loves to give to those who love Him. However, the gift should not replace the position of the One who gave the gift. Abraham never had to go through with the test of giving up his promised son. However, God did. He gave up Jesus to die for sins.

DEAR LORD, I THANK YOU FOR WHO YOU ARE ...

1. Pray to the Lord for help in putting your priorities in the right place.
2. Pray with thanksgiving for God rather than the gifts of God.

> *"Seek first the kingdom of God and His righteousness, and all these things shall be added to you."* **(Matthew 6:33)**

DEAR LORD, I THANK YOU FOR BIBLICAL HOPE ...

One of my favorite movie scenes is in *The Shawshank Redemption* with the two main characters, Andy Dufresne and Red Redding. The scene comes at the end when Red is breaking his parole in hopes to reunite with his friend. He uses the word "hope" to express his strong desire to find his friend. Red says, "I find I'm so excited that I can barely sit still or hold a thought in my head. I think it's the excitement only a free man can feel. ... I hope I can make it across the border. I hope to see my friend and shake his hand. I hope the Pacific is as blue as it has been in my dreams. I hope." I want to cry every time I watch that scene. I'm glad the character used the word "hope." We are waiting to see our loved ones who have gone on before us. We are waiting to see God as He is. The best word to describe our journey to see them is "hope." Biblical hope is not wishing. It's "expecting, assurance, confidence" in what we will experience some day. Hope is for us right now. We won't need to hope once we are there. Thank You, God, for the hope we can have in You and Your words.

DEAR LORD, HELP US TO HAVE BIBLICAL HOPE ...

1. Pray for thanksgiving for the hope you can have in this hopeless world.
2. Pray for a commitment in what God has said and trust enough in Him to follow Him through life.

> *"This hope we have as an anchor of the soul, both sure and steadfast, and which enters the Presence behind the veil."* **(Hebrews 6:19)**

DEAR LORD, NOTHING IS BETTER THAN LIVING BY FAITH ...

Would've. Should've. Could've. I think about this when it comes to watching sports or even in life. Will my team, who is expected to win, win? I know that games are not won on paper. A team can have the best talent on paper but fail to be successful on the field. It seems like every week we see or read about an upset. The lower-ranked team overcomes the higher-ranked team in an amazing upset. I imagine the team expected to win replays the loss over and over. No one can go back and redo something that happened in their past. We can learn and grow from it. I believe the same "would've, should've, could've" idea applies to everyday life. We have a translated copy of God's Word. We may know it and have it in our minds. If we don't apply it in our lives, what does it profit? We have been promised victory through Christ; however, we are left wondering "would've, should've, could've" if we fail to take the opportunities given to us each day. I believe the mother of Jesus said it best when Jesus performed His first miracle at a wedding feast. She told the servants of the feast to do what Jesus said. I believe the same advice applies to all of us. Stop playing "would've, should've, could've" with life. Just do it!

DEAR LORD, GIVE ME THE STRENGTH TO BE A DOER OF THE WORD ...

1. Pray for the willingness to do what the Bible says.
2. Pray for no more excuses when it comes to doing what Jesus says.

"Whatever He says to you, do it." (John 2:5)

Day 39

DEAR LORD, THANK YOU FOR THE GREATEST MEMORIAL IN THE CROSS ...

I remember. I have a picture that was taken at the 9/11 Memorial in New York City. It's about the Twin Towers and the engineering feat of designing and building them. I've been blessed to see the 9/11 Memorial several times. Each time, I have learned something different. One of the parts of the museum is a dark room with a television playing a video on a loop. It's the reading of each person who died that day. Some of the names have a picture of the deceased person and a family member talking about that person in the background. It's a sobering setting. There are no cameras or videos allowed. You go and sit and think about each person who died that day. I remember. I know each year is another year removed from the event. It's my job as an American to help students born after 9/11 know about it. I want them to see why it's important to remember. God gave several memorials to His people. Why? It was to help people remember God and what He had done for them. It helped to keep them from forgetting about it. The greatest memorial is in Jesus' name. He instituted it with His disciples in the upper room. The Lord's Supper is to be done in memory of Jesus. If not, we begin to forget. I remember. Do you?

DEAR LORD, THANK YOU FOR THE VISUAL AID TO REMIND ME ...

1. Pray to God, thanking Him for the memorial Jesus established that you can take part in.
2. Pray for your mind to focus on what the bread and fruit of the vine represent.

"This is My body which is given for you; do this in remembrance of Me." (Luke 22:19)

Day 40

DEAR LORD, I DISLIKE ADDICTIONS AND WHAT THEY DO ...

I hate addictions! They are destructive and deadly. Most families have been touched by addictions, such as drugs, alcohol, or pornography. I recently eulogized a mother who had overdosed. She leaves behind a five-year-old and eleven-year-old. It was a sad service and difficult to do. Like so many, I've personally worked with some dealing with the demon of addiction. One person dealing with addiction can pull down others around them. I've seen up front the effects of addictions. I have the ultimate respect for those in recovery and in the process of becoming sober. Any recovering addict knows that he or she has not fully recovered. They are in the process of recovering. This is a lifelong journey. Any recovering addict is one drink, drug, or internet page away from falling. I say shame on us if we think that we are better than them. Our society can easily dismiss it or hide it. We are all recovering from sin. I cannot truthfully say that I have mastered sin. I'm a work in progress, and it is a daily fight. What can we do? Be open to those hurting. We can be encouraging and supportive. We are called in Scripture to bear each other's burden. Not easy, but important.

DEAR LORD, HELP ME TO BE MORE SUPPORTIVE ...

1. Pray for the strength to deal with those tangled in the webs of addictions.
2. Pray to God to be supportive of others because you have been forgiven by God.

"Bear one another's burdens, and so fulfill the law of Christ." **(Galatians 6:2)**

DEAR LORD, LET ME NOT BELIEVE IN THE LIES ...

If I held a $50 bill, would you want it? What if I took the bill and threw it on the ground and rubbed the dirty sole of my shoe on it? What if I took the bill and crumbled it up and put it in the trash? Would you still want it? I believe you would. The crumpled $50 bill still has value. We are much more valuable than a bill of any denomination. Does our value with God change when we sin and mess up? We can relate to falling in this broken world and feeling crumpled by our emotions. Circumstances like these can make us feel worthless. We don't feel like anyone wants us, especially God. Some can feel like they have messed up to a point of not being forgiven or wanted by God. God has already demonstrated how much He loves us by sending His only begotten Son. God believes our souls are worth saving. He calls for us to cast our cares on Him because He cares for us. He has invited us to come to Him with the heavy burden, and He will give us rest. He does not want anyone to perish but for everyone to repent. No one is past the point of God's forgiveness unless their time is up.

DEAR LORD, HELP ME TO ACCEPT YOUR FORGIVENESS ...

1. Pray for help to forgive yourself and trust in God's forgiveness.
2. Pray to God, thanking Him for the value and worth He has placed in you.

"But God demonstrates His own love toward us, in that while we were still sinners, Christ died for us." **(Romans 5:8)**

Day 42

DEAR LORD, HELP ME TO ENDURE ...

I had the opportunity to go and serve at a place called "Hope Lodge." It's housing for those receiving treatment for cancer at the local hospital. It gives families a free place to sleep during their treatment. We serve by providing a meal to them. We get the food set up, offer prayer, and clean up. As people lined up for food, I had a conversation with a woman who was excited. She was about to finish one hundred days of treatment. She was going home. I gave her a high five and said, "That is amazing." She said something that made me think. She said, "I don't know what to do." She had been fighting cancer so long that it was the main focus of her life. I felt helpless when she said this. I wanted to say something profound. I just listened. Have you ever felt like that? Praise be to God that we know what to do at the beginning, the middle, and the end. We continue to trust, obey, and lean on the everlasting arms. Can you imagine enduring something like cancer without God? Can you bear the thought of losing someone without knowing Christ and the resurrection? We continue to trust in God. We do as those before us did. We finish what we have started.

DEAR LORD, I PRAY FOR THE STRENGTH AND WISDOM TO ENDURE THIS PAIN ...

1. Pray to God to be content in not knowing, because He is in control.
2. Pray to God for the wisdom to know Him when you are left not knowing in this life.

"Let us run with endurance the race that is set before us." (Hebrews 12:1)

Day 43

DEAR LORD, HELP ME TO BE A LIGHT FOR OTHERS REGARDLESS ...

We are familiar with major rivers like the Nile, Amazon, Yangtze, and Mississippi. These major rivers gain more attention than the smaller streams that help create them. Can we name the tributaries of these major rivers? Without the tributaries, there would be no mighty river flowing through states, countries, or provinces. I believe the metaphor can be made about people. Some lives are like rivers. Their lives are in recognizable positions. Others are like tributaries. They are lesser-known but just as important. They influence the athlete, public servant, military commander, CEO, or doctor. As parents, we influence our children to become productive citizens. As teachers, we influence students to do their best. As adults, we influence the younger generations by the way we talk and act. Influence is a powerful thing. It would be a shame to waste or abuse it. There is someone we can touch by what we do. Some of us have a greater audience than others. Everyone is needed to influence the lives of others.

DEAR LORD, REMIND ME THAT IT'S ALL ABOUT YOU AND NOT ME ...

1. Pray for ways you can let your light shine more with those around you.
2. Pray for contentment in who you are and how God can use you.

"Let your light so shine before men, that they may see your good works and glorify your Father in heaven." **(Matthew 5:16)**

Day 44

DEAR LORD, HELP ME IN MOMENTS WHERE I FEEL SO HELPLESS ...

I believe letting go can be the hardest thing we do. I was informed someone I knew was in critical condition at a local hospital. I went as soon as I could to be with the family. They were waiting as patiently as you can in the ICU waiting room. Their loved one was on a ventilator, and the family was pressed with a tough decision. The spouse was overwhelmed with the decision of pulling the plug and letting go of their loved one. Think about it. You've been married fifty-nine years, and now you are faced with the decision to let go. I cannot imagine that difficult decision. I take some comfort in knowing that family belongs to the Lord. This helps, but it doesn't make the situation easy. It's difficult to let go of someone we have known for most of our lives. I wish there was a formula or pill that would make it a little easier to let go. I do believe the best help for those having to let go is prayer and our presence. We can be there to support and love them. We can call on God in prayer to bless the decision and situation. We pray for comfort, and we become a source of comfort to them.

DEAR LORD, HELP ME SIMPLY TO BE THERE ...

1. Pray for those going through difficult decisions and circumstances.
2. Pray for God to comfort them with the same comfort He has offered you in tough times.

"Blessed be the God ... who comforts us in all our tribulation, that we may be able to comfort those who are in any trouble, with the comfort with which we ourselves are comforted by God." **(2 Corinthians 1:3-4)**

Day 45

DEAR LORD, IT'S YOU I LOOK TO ...

In the event of a house fire, the last thing you want to do is walk upright. The temperature at head level can reach 600 degrees. At that temperature, one blast can destroy your lungs. The way to survive is to get down on the floor and crawl out. This would accurately describe the Christian life in a broken world. We need to be on our hands and knees because of our great need for God. I cannot imagine a day, let alone a life, without God. I need Him more than every hour; I need Him every moment of my life. I believe one of the most important things we need to help us with prayer is humility. We need to clothe ourselves with humility. This means to have a healthy view of ourselves before God and others. It's difficult to do in our culture when so much emphasis is placed on human achievement and ingenuity. What do you expect from prayer? Is it to know more about you or God? I want to feel God's presence because of my prayer life. I want the love and power of God to surround my heart and humble me into the richness of His grace. God, may Your will be done through my life.

DEAR LORD, I PRAY TO KNOW YOU MORE ...

1. Pray for a better understanding of God's Word when it comes to prayer.
2. Pray with a purposed heart for God's will to be done.

"O my soul, you have said to the Lord, 'You are my Lord, my goodness is nothing apart from You.'" (Psalm 16:2)

Day 46

DEAR LORD, I HAVE SINNED AND FALLEN SHORT OF YOUR GLORY ...

I have wonderful memories as a child of going creek fishing with my father. We would wade upstream and downstream to catch crawdads and fish. We had a minnow bucket to put our crawdads in. We would get into the river and look for the bait first. We would spend maybe thirty minutes looking for and catching crawdads. When we had enough, we looked for the right fishing spot. I learned several lessons in those fishing experiences with my father. I learned the walk downstream was easier than upstream. In life, it's much easier to do the wrong thing than the right thing. I also learned the fish wouldn't get into trouble if it didn't open its mouth. How often do we get into trouble by our words! I learned from fishing that a hook is not enough. We must add the right bait for the fish to bite. We get attracted by sin and engage in it. A temptation is that right bait for us to bite and drag away. "But each one is tempted when he is drawn away by his own desires and enticed" (James 1:14). The word "enticed" refers to baiting a hook. We get distracted and hooked by sin, and then we engage. The only release from sin is Christ. I'm thankful for the release from sin we receive from Christ.

DEAR LORD, I'M THANKFUL FOR JESUS AND FORGIVENESS ...

1. Pray to God for strength to admit when you sin.
2. Pray to God for forgiveness with a repented heart willing to change from the sinful act.

> *"If we confess our sins, He is faithful and just to forgive us our sins and to cleanse us from all unrighteousness."* **(1 John 1:9)**

Day 47

DEAR LORD, HELP ME TO BE ME AND NOT SOMEONE ELSE ...

Most of us can experience putting on a mask. We become what the mask represents for a short period of time. It's fun to pretend to be something else for a time. Do we continue wearing a mask throughout the year? With our masks, we can have a smile on our faces and appear to have our lives together. However, we are falling apart on the inside and hurting from life. I think we struggle with masks as a culture. What we see advertised is not real. People try to become something they are not. Who are you? What does your heart reveal? Jesus condemned the practice of wearing a mask. He called it "hypocrisy": "Woe to you, scribes and Pharisees, hypocrites! For you cleanse the outside of the cup and dish, but inside they are full of extortion and self-indulgence" (Matthew 23:25). Jesus could see through their masks to the spiritual. On the inside, they were unclean. Jesus can see through us as well. We can put on a face and fool people but not God. He knows our hearts. We must be honest with Him and ourselves. God made us to serve Him and follow Him. We don't need to wear a mask or pretend.

DEAR LORD, HELP ME TO BE OPEN AND HONEST ...

1. Pray for strength to be honest with God when it comes to your heart.
2. Pray for a heart transparent with God with no barriers or fence with Him.

> *"Do not look at his appearance or at his physical stature, because I have refused him. For the Lord does not see as man sees; for man looks at the outward appearance, but the Lord looks at the heart."* **(1 Samuel 16:7)**

Day 48

DEAR LORD, HELP ME TO APPRECIATE THE GIFT ...

I read about some expensive gifts given on Valentine's Day. One celebrity gave his wife a $25,000 phone case. Another gave her husband a $340,000 Bentley car. The most expensive gift was a movie star giving his wife a $20 million Gulfstream jet for Valentine's Day. I wonder if that comes with a pilot. We may shake our heads at such lavish gifts; however, they don't compare to the greatest gift ever. The most well-known verse in the Bible describes the greatest gift, giver, and measure. The verse begins with "For God." There is no one living or who has lived who comes close to God when it comes to giving. He is the Giver of life and eternal life. The verse continues with "so loved the world." There is no greater measure of love than loving the entire world. It's natural to love family and friends, but strangers and enemies? God loved the world. The verse goes on to say, "He gave His only begotten Son." Jesus was God's unique, one-of-a-kind Son. He gave His only Son up to die for our salvation. No phone case, ring, car, or jet can come close to the gift of God's only begotten Son. Praise be to God for the glorious gift of Jesus Christ.

DEAR LORD, MY CONTENTMENT IS IN THE GIFT OF JESUS ...

1. Pray for gratitude for what God has done and continues to do.
2. Pray with thanksgiving to your God, who gives so graciously to you.

"For God so loved the world that He gave His only begotten Son, that whoever believes in Him should not perish but have everlasting life." **(John 3:16)**

Day 49

DEAR LORD, YOUR WORD LIVES AND ABIDES FOREVER ...

We have created some strange laws in our country. Some of them make sense while others leave us scratching our heads. Some state laws were once a good enough idea. It was illegal to cross state lines with a duck on your head in Minnesota. It was a law in Maine not to have your shoelaces untied. In Florida, an unmarried woman may not parachute on Sunday. You could, Monday through Saturday, but not Sunday if you were single. Finally, it was illegal to carry an ice-cream cone in your pocket in Kentucky. It amazes me to look at the Bible and consider its long history throughout the ages. Its words still make sense and apply today. Everything we need to know is right in our Bibles. It's been that way for a long time. In the beginning of creation, God placed Adam and Eve in the garden. His words provided guidance, boundaries, and dos and don'ts. How did they know what to eat and what was forbidden? God provided what they needed to know by His words. He continues to provide what we need by His words, which live and abide forever.

DEAR LORD, THANK YOU FOR YOUR INSPIRED WORDS ...

1. Pray for thanksgiving for having a copy of the written Word.
2. Pray to God, asking for what you need to know in it.

"... having been born again, not of corruptible seed but incorruptible, through the word of God which lives and abides forever." (1 Peter 1:23)

Day 50

DEAR LORD, GIVE ME PATIENCE TO WAIT ON YOU ...

I've read, "Everyone spends at least an hour waiting every single day. We will spend five years of our lives doing nothing but waiting." I don't know if that is true; however, we do wait a lot in this life. We are put on hold, sit in a waiting room at a medical office, stare at the red light, or impatiently wait our turn to check out at the store. Most of us find it frustrating, aggravating, and irritating. Ask anyone, "What do you like to do for rest and relaxation?" More than likely, that person will never tell you, "I just like to wait." Remember the ketchup commercial of an eager eater waiting for the thick, rich ketchup to drip out of the bottle. He waited and waited. Does this spill over into our relationship with God? We beg Him to show up and intervene, but our biological clocks keep ticking. We grow impatient and sometimes go our own way because we grew tired of waiting. Why did Jesus sometimes wait? In John 11, Jesus waited until Lazarus was dead. His purpose was to glorify us and not to satisfy us. The glory of God surpasses our desires, wants, and preferences. Remember, Jesus is never late, and He is always worth the wait.

DEAR LORD, THANK YOU FOR KNOWING WHAT IS BEST FOR ME ...

1. Pray for patience to wait on God's answer and timing.
2. Pray for your faith to strengthen in the time of waiting.

"When Jesus heard that, He said, 'This sickness is not unto death, but for the glory of God, that the Son of God may be glorified through it.'" **(John 11:4)**

Day 51

DEAR LORD, FORGIVE ME FOR BEING DISTRACTED BY OTHER THINGS ...

You come home to notice that your neighbor is hysterical. You get out of your car and walk over to see what is going on. Your neighbor tells you that their child is missing. You say, "I'm sorry—I hope you find the child," and calmly walk back home. Would that be you? Jesus passed through Jericho on His way to Jerusalem. An unexpected opportunity was open to Jesus. He saw a man in a tree trying to see Him. Jesus could have walked on to Jerusalem. He could have said, "I'm too busy, and I need to stick to my schedule." The Lord saw an opportunity to help someone lost, and He changed His schedule for him. "As we have opportunity, let us do good to all" (Galatians 6:10). Are we open to more opportunities? Are our lives too busy to adjust to an open opportunity? Jesus showed us the importance of being flexible when it comes to helping others. Opportunities will not always be convenient. They will not always happen on your day off. We need to be open and ready to serve whenever the moment comes. Will you help?

DEAR LORD, GIVE ME FAITH TO BE OPEN TO THE SURPRISES OF LIFE ...

1. Pray to God to become more like Jesus and not a slave to your time and schedule but open to help.
2. Pray for the heart to help when the need arises and not after the fact.

"God is not unjust to forget your work and labor of love which you have shown toward His name, in that you have ministered to the saints, and do minister." **(Hebrews 6:10)**

Day 52

DEAR LORD, THERE IS NO GREATER GOOD THAN YOU …

What is your *summum bonum*? This is a Latin phrase that was introduced by the Roman philosopher Cicero. According to *Webster's Dictionary*, it means "the highest good; the absolute good that towers above any other good." American consumerism has hijacked *summum bonum* and put in the idea of sitting on a beach and watching the world go by. Another advertised idea is driving down an open road in a luxurious vehicle and having no place to go or be. Be the master of your own schedule and life. What is the highest good? The psalmist proclaimed, "My goodness is nothing apart from You" (Psalm 16:2). This literally means "my goodness is not above You." God is greater than anything and everything of true worth in this life. Jesus saw God as the supreme good. He viewed life in God as the highest good because of the blessing of being in Him. Do we possess the same attitude and feeling toward God? Is knowing and serving Him satisfying your heart? There is no other good place, person, or thing that towers over the supreme goodness of God. Maybe we should count our blessings and see how involved God is in our lives.

DEAR LORD, HELP ME TO APPRECIATE …

1. Pray for a deep desire to follow God.
2. Pray for strength to block out the noises in this world and focus more on God's Word.

> *"So Jesus said to him, 'Why do you call Me good? No one is good but One, that is, God.'"* (Luke 18:19)

DEAR LORD, I CANNOT IMAGINE THE PAIN YOU ENDURED ...

What's the worst pain you've experienced? What would it be on the pain scale from one to ten? Pain comes in different forms. There is physical, emotional, and spiritual pain. I was a strong nine on the physical pain scale with complications from a brain surgery. I had spinal headaches from brain fluid leaking out. It was almost more than I could take. I can only imagine what our Lord suffered on the cross. "To this you were called, because Christ suffered for us" (1 Peter 2:21). Jesus briefly summarized His physical pain by saying, "I thirst." The pain was so extreme that they had to invent a new word. "Excruciating" means "out of the cross." What does it mean that Jesus suffered and experienced pain? Do His pain and suffering make it more appealing to follow Him? The days we are hurting, we can look to Jesus to empathize with our pain. He understands. This helps me when I am hurting because I serve a Savior who understands physical pain.

DEAR LORD, HELP ME BEAR THIS PAINFUL MOMENT ...

1. Pray for Christ to strengthen you.
2. Pray for comfort and understanding by looking to Jesus on the cross.

"When Jesus had received the sour wine, He said, 'It is finished!' And bowing His head, He gave up His spirit." (John 19:30)

Day 54

DEAR LORD, I'M MOVED BY MARY'S ACT OF GIVING ...

A gift is defined as something freely given from one person to another without any agreement or contract. We take great pleasure in giving to the people we love. I enjoy giving to my wife and three boys. I love to surprise them with that special gift. Many people had the opportunity to give to Jesus. Some gave Him food by inviting Him to dinner. Some allowed Jesus to use their boat so He could preach from it because of the crowds. One permitted Jesus to use his colt in His arrival. Joseph gave an empty tomb to the body of Jesus. Mary gave Jesus something so great that she is remembered for it. Mary didn't waste this fragrant oil when she used it on Jesus. She took advantage of a great opportunity. Jesus' time on earth was limited, and she seized the moment. She wanted to give her best to the One she loved with her whole heart. What about us? What have you given to Jesus? Do we love Him enough to give to Him? I believe the greatest gift we can give is our time. Time is something we can easily covet. What if we spent more time with God than what we do? Let us be Mary-like when it comes to taking advantage of the opportunities we have with God on earth.

DEAR LORD, I PRAY TO BE MORE GIVING TO OTHERS ...

1. Pray to God for help in giving up some time to serve Him.
2. Pray to God for strength to follow through with what your heart desires.

"You shall love the LORD your God with all your heart." (Matthew 22:37)

Day 55

DEAR LORD, THANK YOU FOR ALLOWING ME TO COME BACK TO YOU ...

Our second son loved to run away from us when he was little. He could run away from our sight quickly. One early evening, I took my eyes off him while grilling, and he was gone. It wasn't long when I realized that he wasn't near me. I immediately left the grill and began to holler and scream out his name. I ran around to the front, and he had made it to the road. I was so scared and hollered his name. I've never been so scared as a parent. My heart felt like it was beating out of my chest. I'm thankful that he heard me and stopped. He was a few feet from running in front of a car. I cannot be too hard on him because I'm guilty of running away from my heavenly Father. There is no good reason as to why I did. I wanted to do things my way. I looked to myself rather than God with the things in life. Each time, God called me back through His Word and people. What a gracious, loving, and forgiving God! Can you hear Him? God still calls out to those who have left Him. We need to stop and listen before we decide to run away.

DEAR LORD, I PRAY FOR FORGIVENESS IF I FIND MYSELF AWAY ...

1. Pray to God with humility for His constant, gracious hand that lovingly receives you when you fall.
2. Pray to God with humility for the heart to go to Him while you still can.

> *"Come to Me, all you who labor and are heavy laden, and I will give you rest."* **(Matthew 11:28)**

Day 56

DEAR LORD, I LOOK TO YOU AS THE REASON ...

I've felt the "hand of God." I was rushed to the emergency room on Thanksgiving night. I was admitted because of low sodium and pain in my head. The next day, Black Friday, was a tough day. The strong medication didn't knock out my pain. The doctors sent me down to get an MRI while my head was hurting. I overheard that one of my doctors was coming the next day to perform a lumbar treatment in my spine. That next day, I woke up with no headache, and I felt stronger. The doctor came in ready to do the spinal treatment but saw a significant change in me. He canceled the order for the spinal treatment. I was so moved by the difference in twelve hours that I got on my knees over my hospital bed, wept, and thanked God. I was so overwhelmed by emotion that it felt as if God's hand was on me. His strong presence in that moment felt like Him saying, "Fear not, I will help you." Have you been overwhelmed by a moment that seemed as if God's mighty hand was on you? A moment when you knew that the reason was God and nothing else? I believe we will be pleasantly surprised just how involved God is in our lives on earth. Thank You, Lord.

DEAR LORD, I'M HUMBLED BY YOUR AWESOME POWER ...

1. Pray to God with thanksgiving for His care and consideration of your life.
2. Pray to God by recognizing how God has been with you and guided you to this point.

> *"Humble yourselves under the mighty hand of God, that He may exalt you in due time."* (1 Peter 5:6)

Day 57

DEAR GOD, YOU ARE THE ONLY AWESOME GOD ...

We are blessed to live in a country where we can appoint leaders. I cannot imagine what it is like to live under a totalitarian government. I cannot imagine living under a Communist government. Has God left us in moments of wars and fighting? Is He no longer in control like He once was? God continues to remain on His throne regardless of governments and leaders. No matter what happens to people on earth, the throne of heaven is safe and secure. Sometimes it can seem turbulent with the rise and fall of nations. No matter how stormy the nations become, God is still in charge. The foolish words and deeds done are by people only. We are the clay, and He is the Potter. Do not focus on the threats around you; focus on the throne above you. Remember to look up, knowing there is a supreme Ruler of us all. He has seen every fight, war, and conflict. We only study what we know and experience the ones we presently go through. When we start to doubt and fear what is happening around us, we need to open our Bible, read it, and pray from it. We need a good dose of the good news in a world that loves bad news.

DEAR LORD, YOU REIGN SUPREME OVER ALL THE EARTH ...

1. Pray for God's will to be done regardless of opposing governments and leaders.
2. Pray for God's will to be done, not yours, and not to question His plan or authority due to the current political change.

> *"He who dwells in the secret place of the Most High shall abide under the shadow of the Almighty."* **(Psalm 91:1)**

Day 58

DEAR GOD, I PRAY TO TAKE A DAY AT A TIME ...

Doesn't every day deserve a chance? The psalmist proclaimed, "This is the day the Lord has made; we will rejoice and be glad in it" (Psalm 118:24). This is the day. That would include days we have surgery, pay our taxes, watch our children move off to college. It's every day. We sometimes think "this is the day" when it comes to birthdays, anniversaries, days off, vacation days, holidays. The psalmist only specified the present day and not special days in your life. What should be our response with each day? We will rejoice and be glad in it. Sometimes I would like to swap "in" with "after." *I'll be glad after the day is up. I just wish this day would end so I can see if tomorrow fares better.* You know the drill. If the day is bad, we immediately look for any other day but the one we are currently in. The verse challenges us to "rejoice in it." David rejoiced in the wilderness. Paul rejoiced while shackled in prison. Jesus prayed in the garden. We should try to be grateful for every day. Gratitude is an extension of the grace of God. Gratitude is the appropriate response for the blessed. How does today look?

DEAR LORD, EVERY DAY IS A GIFT FROM YOU ...

1. Pray for patience to endure the days that are difficult and tough.
2. Pray for an attitude of gratitude when it comes to every day you have.

"They are new every morning; great is your faithfulness." (Lamentations 3:23)

Day 59

DEAR GOD, HELP ME TO BE OPEN TO THE HURTING ...

Have you ever gotten close to someone famous? Did you have a strong desire to reach out and touch them? People line up and pay out to get a picture with a celebrity. What about the non-famous people we encounter every day? How many times have you been surrounded by people who needed to know you were aware that they were there? They wanted to know that someone cared about them. We fail to see it because we are so focused on ourselves that we aren't paying attention to their needs. On one occasion, Jesus was traveling with His disciples. They were in the midst of a bustling crowd. I imagine people were pushing and shoving to get a look at Jesus. In the crowd, there was a woman with a terrible disease. A continuous flow of blood was slowly killing her. This unnoticed woman pressed her way through the crowd with desperate determination. When she reached out in faith to touch the hem of Jesus' garment, her bleeding instantaneously stopped. The woman needed what all hurting people need. They need to know that someone loves and cares for them. Jesus had been both available and accessible to her. Have I positioned myself to be both available and accessible to those who are hurting?

DEAR LORD, I PRAY TO MAKE MYSELF AVAILABLE TO THE HURTING ...

1. Pray for an openness toward those who need to know someone loves them.
2. Pray for a heart willing to be a hand of Jesus to them.

"Let each of you look out not only for his own interests, but also for the interests of others." **(Philippians 2:4)**

Day 60

DEAR LORD, HELP ME TO BE THANKFUL ...

I had some complications after my second brain surgery. I was leaking brain fluid. The doctor's orders were for me to lie down flat for seven days. I spent those seven days reflecting a lot on my life. I felt so helpless in the moment. It's in these moments that the mind can start to wander off. I tried to keep focusing on God and the next step. When the seven days were done, the physician assistant did a procedure to check if any fluid was leaking. I slowly got up, hoping it was fixed. Before I knew it, I started to leak more brain fluid. I was told to lie back down for another seven days. I was so disappointed. I had to wait another week on my back. During that time, I thought about Job and what he endured. I thought more on his response after everything was taken from him. He said, "The LORD gave, and the LORD has taken away; blessed be the name of the LORD" (Job 1:21). I worked really hard to focus more on the "blessed be the name of the Lord" for that week. I spoke it, thought about it, and prayed it. I wanted to learn from others to be content in His name.

DEAR LORD, I BLESS YOUR NAME IN ALL ...

1. Pray for strength during a difficult moment.
2. Pray for the attitude to look beyond the circumstance and to trust more in God.

> *"Trust in the LORD with all your heart, and lean not on your own understanding."* **(Proverbs 3:5)**

DEAR GOD, YOUR GLORY SURROUNDS ME ...

Have you ever marveled at the balance in God's creation? We know that rabbits are on the food chain for a lot of predators. Rabbits are able to reproduce quickly. A female rabbit can give birth to nine kits with a gestation period of thirty days. After six months, the new rabbits are ready to have their own families. On the other end of nature, the elephant has very few enemies. A female elephant gives birth to one elephant with a gestation period of two years. What if the reproduction of rabbits and elephants were reversed? Could you imagine elephants springing up every thirty days? What if rabbits reproduced every two years? We would have a world consumed by elephants, and many predators would be extinct with the lack of rabbits. The glorious design of nature continues to show the display of a designer and creator. There is too much evidence to demand it all happened by chance. We have enough evidence that we are without excuse. The One who balanced nature can balance our lives. We need to marvel at the One behind it all.

DEAR LORD, THANK YOU FOR THE EVIDENCE WE CAN SEE IN NATURE ...

1. Pray for thanksgiving for the wonders of creation and how they show design.
2. Pray for a love for God, who cared enough to create and share in you some of His glory.

"For since the creation of the world His invisible attributes are clearly seen, being understood by the things that are made." **(Romans 1:20)**

Day 62

DEAR LORD, THANK YOU FOR SERVING US ...

How would you respond if Jesus took off your shoes and began to wash your dirty feet? I would pull a Peter and ask, "Why are You washing my feet? You don't have to do this. Let me serve You, please." I would feel so unworthy and uncomfortable. I imagine I would not feel worthy enough to be in the same room, let alone let Him wash my feet. At the root of faith is the truth that God humbled Himself to serve and die for us. God wants us to resemble His Son. Do we gather together, looking for ways to serve? We live busy lives, and many times we are running on fumes. We want to do our own thing and not bother anyone else. I can easily go into a store with my mind on what I need, and that is it. I may have passed opportunities to serve someone. This happens more in the unplanned moments of our lives. You know, those moments where we turn serving God off and turn on time for ourselves. We need to be open to the possibilities to help serve in the name of Christ. This may happen on our days at work and days off. It may take place when we are looking and when we are on vacation.

DEAR LORD, YOU HAVE LEFT AN EXAMPLE OF SERVICE ...

1. Pray for an open heart like Christ to follow in His steps of service.
2. Pray for an open mind to ways you can serve those around you.

"I have shown you in every way, by laboring like this, that you must support the weak. And remember the words of the Lord Jesus, that He said, 'It is more blessed to give than to receive.'" **(Acts 20:35)**

Day 63

DEAR LORD, THANK YOU FOR THE FORGIVING ACT OF DEATH ON THE CROSS ...

We are given moments of light in a dark world that remind us God is with us. One of those moments is radical forgiveness. I sometimes come across amazing stories of people forgiving others of horrible things. One remarkable story was a woman who forgave the one who killed her sister. This didn't come at once. She was upset that he showed no remorse at the trial. She did not wait for him to repent while he served his sentence. She wrote a letter, forgiving him. The inmate wrote back to her apologizing and admitting his guilt. It was forgiveness that freed the prisoner to be honest and remorseful. If anyone had the right not to forgive, it was Jesus. If anyone had the right to lash out in anger, it was Jesus. The Roman soldiers didn't express remorse for what they did to Jesus. Jesus not only forgave them, but He prayed for them. The soldiers weren't thinking about the need to be prayed for and forgiven. They were doing what they had done before to those sentenced to be crucified. They were acting out of command and order. Jesus offered a prayer of forgiveness for those not asking for it. He did this while on the cross.

DEAR LORD, YOU HAVE SHOWN US THE EXAMPLE OF FORGIVENESS ...

1. Pray for a heart willing to forgive regardless of remorse or repentance.
2. Pray for your reason to forgive to be because of how God has forgiven you.

"'Father, forgive them, for they do not know what they do.' And they divided His garments and cast lots." (Luke 23:34)

Day 64

DEAR LORD, THANK YOU FOR TELLING US ABOUT LIFE AFTER DEATH ...

Have you ever questioned life after death? Have you ever wondered what awaits us after death? Is all of this faith in vain? Will I really be rewarded or punished? What has happened to the people I love? Jesus understands our doubt about the afterlife. While on earth, He talked to His troubled disciples about a prepared place. On the cross, Jesus told the repentant thief about life after death. My father-in-law spoke at our youngest son's preschool program. He talked about a member who had passed away. He visited the person at his home three days before his death. They had a good visit, and the dying man's last words to him were "I'll see you in heaven." How could someone say that at the end? It's the words and action of Jesus. He came to remove all doubt in Him and the end. He informed us about the afterlife. He spoke of life after death to a grieving sister.

DEAR LORD, YOU HAVE GIVEN US WORDS TO LIVE BY ...

1. Pray for peace in knowing that what Jesus said still applies to you today.
2. Pray for comfort in knowing that your death is not an end but the beginning of a life in Him.

"Jesus said to him, 'Assuredly, I say to you, today you will be with Me in Paradise.'" **(Luke 23:43)**

Day 65

DEAR LORD, THANK YOU FOR THE GIFT OF FAMILY ...

Many years ago, the British Council surveyed seven thousand people in forty-six countries to find the most beautiful words in the English language. The number one word is "mother." I've been blessed to be in the homes of many members. I've noticed a common theme. Each person is more likely to talk about something that happened to them when they were young at home rather than something that happened last week. Some of them recalled events that happened over sixty years ago but remember it as if it just happened. Why? I believe we are greatly impacted, whether good or bad, by the home. Parents are a huge influence on us. Occasionally, I hear people say that they would love to talk to their deceased mother and/or father again. Jesus understands the value of a parent's love. While on the cross, He spoke to His mother. Jesus died so that His mother could live as a child of the heavenly Father. Yes, a parent's love is strong, but it could only watch as divine love took action. This is the depth of God's love for us. God's love is greater than a parent's love and even a spouse's love. "Greater love has no one than this, than to lay down one's life for his friends" (John 15:13).

DEAR LORD, YOU HAVE DEMONSTRATED BETTER LOVE ...

1. Pray for the gift of family and how it helped shape you in the image of the Son.
2. Pray with thanksgiving for the matchless love that was shown for you.

"Then He said to the disciple, 'Behold your mother!' And from that hour that disciple took her to his own home." (John 19:27)

Day 66

DEAR LORD, HELP ME TO BE COMMITTED MORE ...

Imagine two people in love. The young man decides she is the one for him. The one he'd like to spend the rest of his life with. He creates that special moment to propose to her. The time arrives, and the moment to ask happens. She says yes, and they embrace each other in happiness. The young man thinks, "I am the most fortunate guy alive." Everything is great until she says, "Of course, there are other guys I still like, so I may date them occasionally." Stunned, the young man says, "That's not going to work." She responds, "Why not? I love you more than any other man. But I have this need. I simply can't be committed to one person. My desire is to be with you." What would you do? No healthy relationship can withstand that. Why would we expect God to be any different? The greatest command is to love God with all our being. We cannot do that if we have another love just as great or equal to God. What God wants is to be on top and for nothing else to be there. He is either God of your life or not. This is a choice we all must make. Am I going to love God or love someone else more?

DEAR LORD, YOUR LOVE DEMANDS AND DESERVES ...

1. Pray for forgiveness if your time or interest shows a love equal to or stronger than your relationship with God.
2. Pray for strength to stay faithful to God and His Word and to continue to keep Him in the proper place in your spiritual heart.

> *"Jesus said to him, 'You shall love the LORD your God with all your heart, with all your soul, and with all your mind.' This is the first and great commandment."* **(Matthew 22:37-38)**

Day 67

DEAR LORD, THANK YOU FOR LISTENING TO ME ...

"For your Father knows the things you have need of before you ask Him" (Matthew 6:8). If God knows our needs prior to prayer, why pray? Have you ever asked that question? My children have asked that question. "Dad, why do you pray?" Do you pray because it's a tradition for you? Do you pray because you have been forgiven? Do you pray to get what you want from God? Our desire to communicate runs deep. Most parents will tell you that babies seem to have an innate drive to talk. They don't need vocabulary drills or other formal training in order to learn. They begin to pick up words without prodding and pushing because the urge to talk is strong. There is no greater blessing than to know that when we pray, God listens to us. Can you think of anyone more important to listen to you talk? The One who listens is the one who spoke a universe into existence. He did this with power far beyond our comprehension. God is listening, and that is why we pray.

DEAR LORD, IT'S AN AWESOME THOUGHT TO KNOW HOW YOU CARE ...

1. Pray for a heart dedicated to talking to God more on a daily basis.
2. Pray for humility in knowing just how big of a deal it is to know that God listens to us.

"Do not be like them. For your Father knows the things you have need of before you ask Him. In this manner, therefore, pray: Our Father in heaven, hallowed be Your name." **(Matthew 6:8-9)**

DEAR LORD, THANK YOU FOR SHOWING US THE IMPORTANCE OF PRAYER ...

"For your Father knows the things you have need of before you ask Him" (Matthew 6:8). Why do you pray if God knows what you need beforehand? One of the things Jesus did on earth was pray. He not only taught on prayer, but He demonstrated it in His life. He prayed at specific times in His life. He prayed at His baptism, before selecting His disciples, in the garden of Gethsemane, and on the cross. Jesus is also known for His prayers. He modeled prayer in His Sermon on the Mount. He also prayed for unity among all believers. Why do we pray? Jesus prayed while on earth. It wasn't because He had sinned. It wasn't only because He had a pressing need. He prayed because of His relationship with the Father. He prayed to show us the importance of prayer in all areas of life. We are called to walk in His steps. One of the ways we do that is to go to God in prayer. I'm of the opinion that if Jesus prayed, how much more should we?

DEAR LORD, THANK YOU FOR THE EXAMPLE OF PRAYING IN ALL SITUATIONS ...

1. Pray to God for the awesome example of prayer in Jesus Christ.
2. Pray to have a life dedicated to prayer just as Jesus had.

"Jesus spoke these words, lifted up His eyes to heaven, and said: 'Father, the hour has come. Glorify Your Son, that Your Son may glorify You.'" **(John 17:1)**

Day 69

DEAR LORD, THERE ARE SO MANY TIMES I DON'T KNOW ...

What do you do when you don't know what to do? Have you ever found yourself in a situation where you felt stuck? I'll never forget that first night alone as new parents without our moms. We had spent eight months reading and rereading *What to Expect When You're Expecting.* I had the plan and was ready to carry it out. Then, our firstborn came, and I was lost in what to do. I had that blank, scared look. My mother-in-law stayed when we came home from the hospital, but it was time for her to go home. My mother wasn't coming until a few days after that. That meant it was up to us to care for our baby. My wife was a pro. She held him in love and cared for him. I was a nervous wreck. I thought, "How are we going to do this?" He didn't even come with a manual! We made it. I don't know about you, but when I get into situations where I don't know what to do, I feel lost and desperate. Every time, I get through with the Lord's help. We are just a prayer away from telling God our concerns, worries, and cares. If God has seen you through to this point, why would He abandon you now? We may not have all the answers when it comes to moments in life; however, we do have the promise of God that He is with us and we are not alone.

DEAR LORD, I LEAN ON YOU WHEN I DON'T UNDERSTAND ...

1. Pray to God for reassurance of Him being there with you.
2. Pray for the strength to endure the moment you find yourself in.

"Let your conduct be without covetousness; be content with such things as you have. For He Himself has said, 'I will never leave you nor forsake you.'" **(Hebrews 13:5)**

Day 70

DEAR LORD, HELP ME TO RESPOND BY FAITH …

The world is a stressful place, and we can easily react in a stressful way. How? We can react by addictive habits we have created because of the stress. The percentage of people addicted to something is high. We hear "addiction" and immediately think the major ones like substance abuse, internet abuse, relational abuse, but addictions can be just about anything. We can get addicted or attached to something that helps us numb the pain or lessen the boredom of our lives. Sometimes we can be addicted to things that aren't necessarily bad, but they become obsessive by the amount of time we put into them. One of the ways we entrust our lives to the care of God and have true freedom from whatever we are over-attached to is improving our mental contact with God through prayer and meditation. Prayer is not just asking for something. It's also a process where we grow our connection with God. We read in Scripture that there are times to fight with the whole armor of God, but other times to be still and wait on the Lord. In both situations, prayer is needed for us to make the best decision. We respond in prayer rather than react through some sort of addiction.

DEAR LORD, I LOOK TO YOU IN ALL SITUATIONS AND CIRCUMSTANCES …

1. Pray for a heart dedicated to God, not the things in this world.
2. Pray for the patience to endure the moments you face by trusting in God's guidance and direction.

"Be still, and know that I am God; I will be exalted among the nations, I will be exalted in the earth!" **(Psalm 46:10)**

Day 71

DEAR LORD, HELP ME TO BE THANKFUL …

What is your greatest advantage, talent, or gift? Is it possible that your greatest gift is what you perceive as a disadvantage? I read about a woman who was born in an abortion clinic in 1976. She survived a saline abortion in her mother's womb. Her birth certificate reads "born during a saline abortion." Shouldn't this person feel anger because of her health complications because of a decision made? Shouldn't she blame God for allowing this to have happened? She looks at what happened as an advantage to glorifying God. She is able to speak about Jesus in places where God is not permitted because of what she has been through. The story makes me wonder if my greatest advantage is a disadvantage. When was the last time you thanked God for what you cannot do? "God, I thank You that I'm not an eloquent speaker. I praise You that I'm not a person of means. I'm grateful for the challenges in my life." I've never heard a prayer like that. Have you? Without struggles, we wouldn't learn the lessons we gain from such events. Paul understood the value of a disadvantage. He saw Christ's power being perfected in His weakness. In return, he boasted about his infirmities. We can learn a lot from a disadvantage.

DEAR LORD, I PRAY TO YOU FOR HELP …

1. Pray for God to open your mind to the possibility of good in your situation or circumstance.
2. Pray for a better understanding of God in the difficult moment.

"And He said to me, 'My grace is sufficient for you, for My strength is made perfect in weakness.' Therefore most gladly I will rather boast in my infirmities, that the power of Christ may rest upon me." **(2 Corinthians 12:9)**

Day 72

DEAR LORD, HELP ME TO RELEASE MY GRIP ON …

It takes a brave or crazy rider to get on a roller coaster that is over sixty-five hundred feet of steel track at the top speed of ninety-three miles per hour. The first hill is a three-hundred-foot vertical fall from the sky. The only safety device is a lap bar and belt. The first time I rode it (yes, this was not my best move), I held on tight to that lap bar. The idea of letting go and putting my hands up was out of the question. The words "tightly, closely, firmly, and holding on" would describe my hands moving ninety-three miles per hour. The same words can be said of not wanting to let go of the people, possessions, and positions we have. Sometimes our grip on these things is so tight that it ends up having us. We are told to trust God in such a way that we are not to hold on to what we understand. We want to have God and be in control of our things as well. When something happens, we feel that we have lost control. The only control we have is with ourselves. We can control ourselves to let go of the hold we have on things and turn more to God. Life is filled with changes, but God can be the constant in your life.

DEAR LORD, GIVE ME THE STRENGTH TO …

1. Pray to release your grip on things.
2. Pray for more trust in God and the ability to give Him control.

"In whose hand is the life of every living thing, and the breath of all mankind?" (Job 12:10)

DEAR GOD, HELP ME TO BE A STUDENT OF YOUR WORD ...

A student won first prize at a science fair by attempting to urge people to petition to control or eliminate the chemical "dihydrogen monoxide." The student gave many reasons why this chemical needs to be controlled, including it is a major component to acid rain, it contributes to erosion, it decreases the effectiveness of automobile brakes, and it has been found in tumors of terminal cancer patients. The student presented the negative things to adults. Out of fifty people, forty-three said, "Yes, to controlling and eliminating dihydrogen monoxide." Six people were undecided. Only one person knew that dihydrogen monoxide was water. The title of the project was "How gullible are we?" How gullible are we when it comes to the faith? How many of us take what someone says and verify it with the Word of God? I believe our souls are too important for us to believe just anybody. The Bible says, "Beloved, do not believe every spirit, but test the spirits, whether they are of God; because many false prophets have gone out into the world" (1 John 4:1). We need to see for ourselves in our Bibles what God is saying to us. We need to be proactive when it comes to the growth and development of our faith.

DEAR LORD, I NEED TO SEE FOR MYSELF ...

1. Pray to God for wisdom to understand what He has said to you.
2. Pray to God to be more Berean-like when it comes to matters of faith and not to take things for granted.

> *"These were more fair-minded than those in Thessalonica, in that they received the word with all readiness, and searched the Scriptures daily to find out whether these things were so."* **(Acts 17:11)**

Day 74

DEAR LORD, HELP ME TO REMEMBER THAT SOMEONE ...

My heart was overwhelmed by the love and support of my students when I was in the hospital. When I came back to school, I had some homemade cookies and nice cards from students. One student wrote, "I also hope that you will be as fun when you recover." What? I just had low sodium, not a personality change! The most touching was a letter from a student who was new to the school. He wrote, "Dear Mr. B. I hope you get better soon. You have impacted my life immensely in the few short months I've known you. You have helped and guided me through 6th grade. Middle School has been tough for me but you've made it 10 times better. I thank you and wish you a speedy recovery. Thank you so much for being impactful in my life. Before I came here, I knew nothing about the Bible. You showed me that God is the Lord and Savior and that alone is the best thing anyone could have done for me. Mr. B, you are the best teacher I've ever had. I appreciate how hard you work for your students." It's notes like this that make it all worthwhile. I can live off an encouraging word. This card makes my heart smile for a long time. You never know who is watching and listening to you.

DEAR LORD, I PRAY TO BE MORE CAREFUL BECAUSE SOMEONE IS WATCHING ...

1. Pray to God to be more mindful of what you do.
2. Pray to God to be more mindful of what you say.

"Let no one despise your youth, but be an example to the believers in word, in conduct, in love, in spirit, in faith, in purity." **(1 Timothy 4:12)**

Day 75

DEAR GOD, I'M AMAZED THAT IN THE BILLIONS OF PEOPLE, NONE ...

I continue to be amazed at the differences with our three boys. All three have the same mother and father, but their personalities, interests, and gifts are so different. I noticed one afternoon what each one was doing. Our oldest son was reading two different books. One book was for fun, and the other was for school. Our youngest son had written his first chapter book titled "The Trip." It started on chapter zero. Our middle son and his beautiful mother sang the songs for an upcoming audition for a school play. I have a writer, a reader, and an actor. Welcome to the home of differences! God gave us three boys, and none of them are exactly the same. Why should they be? We are all different in identity, interests, and talents. It would be great if everyone were a *Star Wars* fan, but I'm fine if not. Our differences shouldn't divide us. It should unite us even more that we serve a God who made such differences. Like with my boys, there is no group of people on earth better than another. As Christians, we are not better than others. We are different. Our differences show the unity of God. "There are diversities of gifts, but the same Spirit. There are differences of ministries, but the same Lord. And there are diversities of activities, but it is the same God who works all in all" (1 Corinthians 12:4-6).

DEAR LORD, I'M GRATEFUL FOR THE DIFFERENCES IN THIS WORLD ...

1. Pray to God, thankful that our differences don't take away the oneness in Him.
2. Pray to God to learn the something you can do when it comes to serving Him.

> *"For as the body is one and has many members, but all the members of that one body, being many, are one body, so also is Christ."* **(1 Corinthians 12:12)**

Day 76

DEAR LORD, I'M FEARFULLY AND WONDERFULLY MADE ...

My youngest son asked me if I wanted to see a picture of God. Sure, I'll bite. He brought a picture he had taken with a camera that prints pictures. It reminds me of the old Polaroid camera. I looked at the picture carefully and saw what he didn't see. He took a picture facing a mirror. The picture was dark with a flash and a tiny dark dot in the middle of the flash. He thought of the flash and dot as being God. He really wants to see God. I said, "Oh, I see." He doesn't realize the real picture of God is himself. He has been "fearfully and wonderfully made." He is created in the image of God. When God created the world, sky, sun, seas, plants, and animals, He said, "It is good." When He created mankind in His image, He looked at everything and said, "It is very good." My son's ability to love, laugh, and think creatively are all evidence of God's wondrous plan. My son is not the only one to whom this applies. We are all evidence of the image and creativity of God.

DEAR LORD, I MARVEL AT YOUR CREATIVE WORKS ...

1. Praise God in prayer of His marvelous works and being made in His image.
2. Praise God for the ability to use your creativity to express your devotion to Him.

> *"I will praise You, for I am fearfully and wonderfully made; marvelous are Your works, and that my soul knows very well."* **(Psalm 139:14)**

Day 77

DEAR LORD, I'M NOT PERFECT, SO I NEED A SAVIOR ...

I enjoy the college brackets in the month of March. I always print one and fill it out before the first game. I'm not the only one. Many people fill out basketball brackets for bragging rights or to win a prize for the most perfect bracket. I read that an employer offered his employees one million dollars a year if they were able to have a perfect bracket. The odds are in the employer's favor. The odds of picking a perfect bracket are extremely low. Some believe they are as low as 1 in 9,233,372,036,854,775,808. This is 1 and 9.2 quintillion. In other words, it's a really big number. The odds are better to find a four-leaf clover, bowl a perfect game, and make an albatross in golf. If you fill out a bracket, the odds are against you. Yet the odds would be even worse if it weren't for Christ. Life before Christ demanded perfection. The only problem is no one is perfect except Christ. Christ came and broke up the disadvantage we had because of our sins. He became sin for us so that we might become righteous. I will continue to fill in my brackets and lose multiple times, but I am living a victorious life because of Christ.

DEAR LORD, THE ODDS ARE AGAINST US ALL WHEN IT COMES TO SIN ...

1. Pray to God, thanking Him for the blessing of being forgiven because of Jesus.
2. Pray to God for strength to live not a perfect life but a better life in Christ.

"Yet in all these things we are more than conquerors through Him who loved us." **(Romans 8:37)**

Day 78

DEAR LORD, HELP ME TO REALIZE THE POWER IN WORDS ...

"A good man out of the good treasure of his heart brings forth good; and an evil man out of the evil treasure of his heart brings forth evil. For out of the abundance of the heart his mouth speaks" (Luke 6:45). I was blessed to have a high school group come and teach a lesson to my sixth-grade students about the power of words. They demonstrated the use of words with special jelly beans. Some of the jelly beans were good flavors like strawberry, banana, and chocolate. Others were disgusting flavors like booger and vomit. I often wonder who decides what that tastes like and how do they know. The younger students didn't know from the bowl which jelly bean was good or bad. It was fun to watch those who selected a disgusting flavor because they would immediately spit it out. What a great exercise to taste the differences between fruitful and unfruitful and how that relates to our words. I love when older kids spend time with younger ones. The power of influence is great, and they are watching and hearing them. We are all role models to people around us. It's important to watch what we say and do. Are we fruitful or unfruitful by our words and choices? Tremendous power and weight are in what we say. We are either building up or tearing down.

DEAR LORD, STRENGTHEN ME WHEN IT COMES TO CONTROLLING MY WORDS ...

1. Pray to God for a mindfulness of who is watching and listening to you each day.
2. Pray to God to be a fruit-bearer by the words and actions you choose today.

"A wholesome tongue is a tree of life, but perverseness in it breaks the spirit." **(Proverbs 15:4)**

Day 79

DEAR LORD, HELP ME TO OVERCOME THE BELIEF THAT I DON'T MATTER…

Can one person make a difference? What can one single life do for the many problems of this world? There is a veteran who served in the infantry in the Iraq War who is troubled by the problems of our veterans. During his service, he received several distressing emails about war veterans struggling financially. The situation was so great that he felt powerless. He decided to hike for our veterans. He started a seven-thousand-mile hike with a drum and a faithful dog companion. He started in Louisville, Kentucky, and traveled thousands of miles and through thirty-seven cities. He collected donations through his website and delivered checks to the doorsteps of needy military families. He averaged twenty miles a day. He slept in donated hotel rooms, host homes, and his tent. His journey took him sixteen months. In the end, he raised enough awareness to collect over five million dollars for veteran families. He said, "Every step is worth it because when I arrive to help another family, it is the best feeling." One life can make a difference to someone. Think of all the good you could accomplish today by choosing to do good.

DEAR LORD, GIVE ME THE DETERMINATION TO DO WHAT I CAN FOR THOSE IN NEED …

1. Pray to God for the blessing of helping someone and not everyone.
2. Pray to God for the opportunity to be the difference in a person's life rather than the whole world.

> *"… that you may walk worthy of the Lord, fully pleasing Him, being fruitful in every good work."* **(Colossians 1:10)**

Day 80

DEAR LORD, GIVE ME A WILLINGNESS TO LET YOU BE GOD ...

A father was watching his son play in the backyard. His son was moving several rocks. There was one large rock that the son was unwilling to move. He tried, but he ended up getting hurt from trying to move it. The father came to his crying son and asked, "Why didn't you use all your strength?" The boy said, "I did!" "No, son, you didn't ask me for help." I believe we can be like the son and try to do too much on our own without asking our heavenly Father to help. Why would we do that? He is willing to do more than what we can think or ask. What would keep us from asking the One who can? Is it pride? Have you grown up learning to do things on your own so that needing God is foreign? Can you imagine living a whole life without God? I can't. God is a prayer away. Our prayers show the need for Him and to depend on Him. There is no day where this would not apply. We need to ask God to help us every day. We cannot make it without Him. I don't believe people are making it without Him. "If we ask anything according to His will, He hears us" (1 John 5:14). We need God's help!

DEAR LORD, HELP ME TO DEPEND ON YOU ...

1. Pray to God for a life that needs Him every day, not just on emergency days.
2. Pray to God for humility when it comes to pride and learning to abide in His will.

> *"This is the confidence that we have in Him, that if we ask anything according to His will, He hears us."* **(1 John 5:14)**

Day 81

DEAR LORD, HELP ME TO ABIDE BY YOUR WORDS ...

When all else fails, read the instructions. I find it sad when people make absurd claims about the future. I read where a man in Wyoming claimed to be from the year 2048. He had traveled back in time to Earth to warn us about an impending invasion of extraterrestrials. I felt like the man had just binge-watched too many science fiction shows. He told the police that the "aliens were coming next year, and we needed to make sure to leave as fast as possible." Why was he talking about this to the police? He had been arrested for public intoxication. It amazes me the number of people who make claims about the future. When it comes to the "day or hour," God knows and will make it happen. It won't happen because of anything or anyone else. When we start to get alarmed about such stories, remember to read the instructions. God means what He said. The instructions say, "But of that day and hour no one knows, not even the angels of heaven, but My Father only" (Matthew 24:36). We would be wise to go by them.

DEAR LORD, YOU ALONE KNOW THE FUTURE ...

1. Pray to God for help to trust His words and be committed to them.
2. Pray to God to be a true disciple by being dedicated to His words.

"Then Jesus said to those Jews who believed Him, 'If you abide in My word, you are My disciples.'" (John 8:31)

DEAR LORD, HELP ME TO BE PATIENT WITH OTHERS ...

We were excited to receive the packages of our wonderful gift. It was an electric fireplace and entertainment set. My wife was envisioning a fire happening that day. We could pretend to roast marshmallows. I took the multiple pieces out of the box and started to scratch my head. I looked and relooked. Where were all the screws, bolts, and nails? I realized that everything was delivered except for those things. The company forgot to send the whole order. I felt like a sequel to *Christmas Vacation*. I was just looking for Cousin Eddie to come down the road. Instead of having what we saw online, we were stuck with unboxed pieces of what could be a fireplace. People are people. We are flawed, imperfect, and full of mistakes. We are going to run into problems because of human error. It's foolish to expect perfection all the time from people. This is another reason why I'm thankful for God. God doesn't disappoint. He is trustworthy, faithful, and dependable. He has proven these since the first people. This is why our trust, faith, and foundation must be with God and not man. In the middle section of our Bibles, it says, "It is better to trust in the Lord than to put confidence in man" (Psalm 118:8).

DEAR LORD, THANK YOU FOR YOUR PERFECTION, AND LET ME ...

1. Pray to God with a better understanding when it comes to your imperfections.
2. Pray to God with a better appreciation for Him.

> *"But the Lord is faithful, who will establish you and guard you from the evil one."* **(2 Thessalonians 3:3)**

Day 83

DEAR LORD, HELP ME TO HAVE MORE PATIENCE ...

I felt like running out of my classroom screaming my head off in frustration. That was a big temptation for me. I had reached my patience level with my class. I was running on empty. Why? I gave an assignment about what they had learned. This assignment was simple. It would show me what they had learned and how it could apply in their lives. The one problem was many students didn't get the assignment. They felt like it was too many steps. I thought, "I did a terrible job explaining it." The rain clouds had clouded their minds. After I reached my limit of explaining, I decided to move the assignment to file 243 and move on to something else. Have you ever felt like that? You wanted to run out and scream because your patience had left the building. Do you get away from the situation or person? If not, what brings you back in? What helps me is knowing how God is patient with me. I feel like I have exhausted my limit on saying "sorry" to God. I expect God to say no more. He doesn't. If God can be this patient with me, I can try to be a little more patient with others.

DEAR LORD, LET ME BE REMINDED OF YOUR PATIENCE WITH ME ...

1. Pray to God that in the moments when your patience is spent, you will think of Him.
2. Pray to God for the strength to remove yourself from a situation that makes you impatient.

"The Lord is not slack concerning His promise, as some count slackness, but is longsuffering toward us, not willing that any should perish but that all should come to repentance." (2 Peter 3:9)

Day 84

DEAR LORD, HELP ME TO KEEP THE OVERALL PICTURE IN MIND ...

We often read of gifted athletes who declare to go to a major school to play their sport. Many younger athletes aspire for the same opportunities as those before them. The window to the next level is much smaller because of the competition. Those given the chance declare to a collegiate school known for being on top for that particular sport. They want the opportunity to play at the professional level. I believe it's extraordinary to read of someone with that ability and work ethic to choose for a different reason. I read of a young man who chose a college known more for academics. He was a five-star basketball player in the state. He said in an interview, "Someday the ball will stop bouncing, and I want to prepare myself for that situation." Wow! He had wisdom beyond his years. Do we ever think about the overall picture? One day we will stop doing what we do, and then what? Do we have enough wisdom to live with a perspective toward heaven and not so much for the day? We can easily get caught up in the muck of the day. We concentrate more on the moment than the purpose of life. Someday, what we do well will be no more. Have we prepared for that?

DEAR LORD, HELP ME TO PREPARE NOW FOR WHAT WILL BE SOON ...

1. Pray to God for the wisdom to see the overall picture and what really matters.
2. Pray to God for the strength to commit to doing what it takes to prepare for what will be.

"I press toward the goal for the prize of the upward call of God in Christ Jesus." **(Philippians 3:14)**

Day 85

DEAR LORD, HELP ME TO BE THANKFUL BEYOND THE HOLIDAY ...

I love celebrating the Thanksgiving holiday! I enjoy the celebration of putting up the inflatable turkey and pilgrim set. The Hallmark Channel plays its many Thanksgiving movies on loop. I can't wait to see the thankful story line. The family gets back together and sits down to eat the meal, and it starts to snow outside. Then, there is the local radio station playing all of our favorite Thanksgiving songs. Obviously, I'm going over the top with a holiday that seems to get the short end of the deal. Halloween has its costumes, movies, music, and trick-or-treat (or trunk-or-treat). After that, we get a quick glimpse of Thanksgiving. In total domination, Christmas comes with its movies, songs, decorations, and commercials for spending money. Don't get me wrong. I enjoy the holidays. However, I believe we all have something to be thankful for always. Our thanksgiving doesn't need to be led by a holiday or meal. The holiday of Thanksgiving should remind us all of the importance of being more thankful for what we have. We should be thankful for our freedom. We are thankful for family. We are thankful for the ability to work and make a living. We are thankful for an awesome God. Be thankful always. We are blessed.

DEAR LORD, I'M THANKFUL FOR WHAT I HAVE AND WHAT HAS BEEN DONE FOR ME ...

1. Pray for a contented heart that is full of gratitude for God.
2. Pray to God to be more grateful in every day and every circumstance.

"In everything give thanks; for this is the will of God in Christ Jesus for you." **(1 Thessalonians 5:18)**

Day 86

DEAR LORD, LET ME MAKE NO MORE EXCUSES ...

What can I possibly do? I'm just one person with faults and limitations. Can I really make a difference? We are not called to save the world because that has been done. We are called to make a difference with people we can reach. There was an eight-year-old girl whose family adopted a dog. The young girl was recuperating from a fourteen-month chemo treatment for her brain tumor. The young girl loved her dog so much that she wanted other sick patients to feel what she felt. She started a small lemonade stand and raised $1,000. Now, her nonprofit organization has raised $33,000 to adopt dogs for children fighting cancer. She was interviewed about her amazing mission, and she said, "I wanted to do a million adoptions, but my mom made me lower it." I believe one life can be the difference in the lives of others. I believe your life can be that difference in someone's life. Each of us can reach and connect to some people better than someone else. Why? We have established relationships with them. You can be the difference by the way you live your life. We are not called to save the world. We are called to be an example. This starts with one person at a time.

DEAR LORD, INSTILL IN ME THE CONFIDENCE TO HELP ONE ...

1. Pray to God for the awareness of those around you.
2. Pray to God to realize that your one life is enough to make a difference.

"Only let your conduct be worthy of the gospel of Christ." **(Philippians 1:27)**

Day 87

DEAR LORD, I PRAY THAT MY LIFE CAN SHOW YOU …

I was humbled by an experience. I was observed in my first block class by one of my former students. This college student was in my first-year teaching class. He was an education major and wanted to be a teacher. He needed to observe a class for one of his assignments. He chose me. I was so honored to have a previous student think of me as a mentor. This experience reminded me of the power of influence. Each of us possesses the ability to influence others. Our influence is either good or bad. We can say and do something in their lives that forever changes their direction. We can break them down or build them up. We can help them become the people that God planned for them to be or try to be a stumbling block. I try to be as cautious and careful as I can when it comes to my words and actions. I know that someone is watching. The apostle Paul realized that he was an influential person to others. However, he put his influence in the right perspective. You can follow me as long as I follow Christ. People are going to be influenced by what we say and do. I hope that we can show them Christ. Jesus is the only one worth following!

DEAR LORD, I HAVE THE POWER OF INFLUENCE WITH OTHERS …

1. Pray to God to use your influence to promote good by the way you follow Jesus.
2. Pray to God to be an example in all things so others can see Christ.

"Imitate me, just as I also imitate Christ." **(1 Corinthians 11:1)**

DEAR LORD, I PRAY TO HAVE THE FAITH TO SEE BEYOND THE MOMENT ...

What do you do when a good friend has been shot after worshipping God in a church building? You come together in prayer. Yes, things happen that leave us wondering why. Bad things happen to good people. Situations can cause us to question our safety. However, the first and most important step when things of this nature happen is to pray. Prayer is the practice of placing our trust in God. We offer our requests from a limited perspective compared to His. This is exactly what Jesus did in His trying situation. Jesus knew firsthand bad things happen to good people. He innocently suffered the worst kind of death. In the garden of Gethsemane, Jesus was overwhelmed by the events that would soon happen. What did He do? He prayed. His prayer helped equip Him for what He was about to endure on the cross. Jesus did what we can do today. I take a few things from the Lord's troubled prayer in the garden. (1) Be specific about your fears as Jesus was. (2) Make it known to people you trust. (3) Don't forget God's promises. Thank You, Lord, for showing us the good from something horrible.

DEAR LORD, THANK YOU FOR YOUR MIGHTY EXAMPLE IN TIMES WHEN THINGS ARE BAD ...

1. Pray to God to lean on Jesus, who empathizes with what you go through.
2. Pray to God to take a bad situation and work it toward the good.

> *"And we know that all things work together for good to those who love God, to those who are the called according to His purpose."* **(Romans 8:28)**

DEAR LORD, I HAVE FAILED MANY TIMES IN MY LIFE ...

I had a student give me a T-shirt from a comic convention. The shirt was a picture of the original characters from *Star Wars* when it came out in 1977. The T-shirt was set up like a yearbook of senior superlatives. My favorite was the Stormtrooper's: "Worst Aim." The Stormtroopers constantly missed their targets. The heroes run away without a single injury. It's almost humorous to see how bad of an aim they have. I think we can relate to bad aim when it comes to life goals, expectations, and responsibility. We choose to give up or give in rather than endure. Jesus spoke of the way of life as being narrow because it's difficult. The difficulty is not with understanding. It's with doing. Why can't we just do what God expects of us? Why does it take more effort to live right than to live wrong? Why does the dark side have a stronger attraction than the good side? There are a lot of answers to these questions. God would not expect us to do something if we were unable to do it. He does expect us to do what we are capable of doing. Stop aiming at the wrong things. Start focusing on the target that God has set for you today.

DEAR LORD, HELP ME TO HIT THE TARGET ...

1. Pray to God to be more mindful of His Word and focused on what you can do.
2. Pray to God to have the strength to recognize when you fail and to get back up.

"For this is the love of God, that we keep His commandments. And His commandments are not burdensome." (1 John 5:3)

Day 90

DEAR LORD, HELP ME TO KEEP ALL OF THE ADVICE GIVEN ...

I spent time with my boys while my wife was enjoying time with her mother. We did some chores around the house, and I treated them with lunch. We went to a place where there were fortune cookies. I like the cookie better than the fortune. I know the fortune is just printed words. My middle son quickly opened his fortune cookie to see what it had to say. He didn't like it and said, "I can't use this one," and tossed it away. In all my years of eating and reading fortune cookies, I never thought of it that way. The fortune words don't work for me, so out it goes! I love it. I took from his reaction to the fortune that I don't need to take everyone's words. If there is one thing people are full of, it's advice. They think they know more about something than we do on the subject. Who is the authority of life to give us the right advice? What person has lived it enough to know what is best for you? The only one I know is Jesus Christ. I'm like my son with the advice of people. If I can't use it or don't need it, I dismiss it. I know my greatest source of advice is Jesus.

DEAR LORD, THANK YOU FOR THE WORDS OF LIFE FROM JESUS ...

1. Pray to God, thanking Him for the wisdom of Jesus and how there is no better source on life.
2. Pray to God to dismiss any advice that doesn't follow the words of Christ.

"Simon Peter answered Him, 'Lord, to whom shall we go? You have the words of eternal life.'" (John 6:68)

DEAR LORD, HELP ME TO CONFIDE MY FEAR AND WORRIES TO OTHERS …

Does anyone like to wait? We may want to wait when it comes to taxes and death. But we struggle to wait for most other things. In fact, waiting can be the worst part. I can relate to anyone who has had a surgery scheduled. My first brain surgery wasn't successful, and it happened so quickly. My second surgery was rescheduled with a month of waiting. I did my best to keep busy with my family and job. However, the thought of having to go through the same surgery again was always in my mind. The surgery was on a Monday, and I was thankful for that. The reason was what I did on Sunday. I worshipped and felt encouragement from God's people. I left that evening after being prayed for with an indescribable peace. My worries and anxious heart were still there, but they weren't as strong as the presence of peace. If you find yourself in a moment of waiting, let me encourage you to share with others. Ask them to pray for you. I believe with all my heart that there is nothing greater than praying for someone. It's a peaceful thought to know someone is mentioning my name to the Creator. The great thing about that is God listens.

DEAR LORD, THANK YOU FOR THE RELATIONSHIPS THAT LOVINGLY PRAY FOR MY NEEDS …

1. Pray to God for the peace that surpasses understanding to guard your heart and mind in Christ.
2. Pray to God, thanking Him for friends who also believe in the power of prayer.

"Be anxious for nothing, but in everything by prayer and supplication, with thanksgiving, let your requests be made known to God." **(Philippians 4:6)**

Day 92

DEAR LORD, I PRAY TO LIVE ACCORDING TO YOUR WORD ...

Poor Fred! His epitaph reads:

> Here lies good old Fred
> A great big rock fell on his head.

No "rest in peace" for him. By the way, this is one of the props for the Haunted Mansion ride at Magical Kingdom. It's my favorite ride there. Many epitaphs read, "Rest in Peace." This is written regardless of someone's character and actions on earth. Have you ever wondered what people might think of you when you are gone? I sometimes think about that when I'm at a funeral home. Does the character of my life match what is placed on that stone monument? Am I really "resting in peace" by the way I have chosen to live my life? Our words on stone bear no weight with God. I can take the most horrible person who has ever lived and put on their gravestone "Rest in Peace." My words don't change how that person lived. Our lives matter now and not when we are gone. It's what we do in the body that matters. We will give account to God alone, and He will judge us regardless of what our epitaphs read or what others think. Live today, and don't wait for tomorrow!

DEAR LORD, HELP ME TO LIVE BY YOUR WORDS ...

1. Pray to God, thanking Him that it's Him you give an account to.
2. Pray to God, mindful that our actions are judged by Him and not people.

> *"For we must all appear before the judgment seat of Christ, that each one may receive the things done in the body, according to what he has done, whether good or bad."* **(2 Corinthians 5:10)**

Day 93

DEAR LORD, I PRAY FOR STRENGTH TO ENDURE TODAY ...

Wouldn't it be great if we could order what's next in life like our favorite cup of coffee? We could mix and match the ingredients of our future. *I would like a large cup of fun and excitement, no shots of danger, with double good health.* What about a decaf brew of longevity, heavy on agility and cut the disability? Life comes with a bundle of ingredients and surprises. Some are welcome; others are not. It can create fear of what's next in this life. The disciples didn't like the surprise Jesus put on them. He told them that He was leaving them after three extensive years. Thomas said, "Lord, we do not know where You are going" (John 14:5). Christ handed them a large cup of major transition, and they tried to hand it back. What person passes through life unscathed? Jesus gave the promise to them that the Comforter would come to them and bring to remembrance the words of Christ. We have the same promise of eternal glory. No, it will not erase the cares and concerns of this life, but I will guarantee based on the words of God that whatever you are going through is worth heaven. There is no better place like the home of God.

DEAR LORD, HELP ME TO SEE MY PAINFUL SITUATION IS WORTH HEAVEN ...

1. Pray to God for the promise of eternal life with Him.
2. Pray to God for the strength to endure the day as you wait for tomorrow.

"For our light affliction, which is but for a moment, is working for us a far more exceeding and eternal weight of glory." **(2 Corinthians 4:17)**

Day 94

DEAR LORD, I'M CONTENT WITH MY LIFE AND WILL DO MY BEST ...

"Therefore we also, since we are surrounded by so great a cloud of witnesses, let us lay aside every weight, and the sin which so easily ensnares us, and let us run with endurance the race that is set before us" (Hebrews 12:1). The key to this statement is the verb tense. The verb tense suggests that we keep on running. In other words, it's a marathon and not a sprint. We must never think we have reached the goal or made it by not having to do anything else. There is no retirement in Christianity. Paul's mentality was not being content with his current life. He kept pressing on ahead, forgetting those things behind him. It's important to run the race that is set before us. Each of us has a race to run. We cannot compare our situations with someone else's. This race suggests conflict, struggle, or fight. We are to run the race set before each of us. This is what we are accountable to God for. We can easily get busy comparing our lives with someone else's. We can compare our situations to someone else's. We are to run the race set before us! Happy running!

DEAR LORD, I WILL RUN BY LIVING EACH DAY TO THE BEST OF MY ABILITY ...

1. Pray to God for the spiritual stamina to live a life, not a moment, in Him.
2. Pray to God for the peace to accept what you are going through and not to compare it to others.

"I will run the course of Your commandments, for You shall enlarge my heart." **(Psalm 119:32)**

Day 95

DEAR LORD, HELP ME TO STOP MAKING EXCUSES ...

Imagine walking out of your local grocery store and hearing the sound of metal scraping metal. You go to your car and notice that a teenage driver is responsible for your fender. He quickly apologizes and tells you that he cannot let this go on his driving record. He has only been driving for a couple of months, and he is on probation with his car insurance. "How much will it take to make this go away?", he asks you. Would you make an offer and take it? The nation of Israel had a terrible record with God. They ran into ditches and damaged their identity. They had rejected God too many times. They asked God, "How much?" Israel pulled out their spiritual checkbook and tried to negotiate with God because of their record. What if that teenage driver, or any driver, sideswiped your child (or grandchild) instead of your car? This is similar to what we do when we try to negotiate with God about our sins. There is nothing God will take because of what He gave up for our sins. The one thing God wants is the one thing He has always asked for—our spiritual hearts. It's by His grace and mercy that an offer has been made.

DEAR LORD, I LOVINGLY AND FREELY GIVE OVER MY HEART FOR YOU TO RULE ...

1. Pray to God for wisdom to set your heart in order.
2. Pray to God about being open and honest and making no excuses.

"He has shown you, O man, what is good; and what does the LORD require of you but to do justly, to love mercy, and to walk humbly with your God?" **(Micah 6:8)**

Day 96

DEAR LORD, HELP ME TO REMEMBER WHO I AM AS A CHRISTIAN ...

I'll never forget that Sunday night after church service. I was a sixteen-year-old kid, and I volunteered to use my car to drive some of the youth group to an event. On our way, we stopped at a local fast-food restaurant. When I walked in, it was immediate to us that something was off. The workers were moving slowly and avoiding eye contact. It didn't take long to see why they were acting this way. Someone was robbing the place through the drive-through window. We slowly backed out of the store and into my car. I foolishly drove around the store and passed the person robbing the place. I suddenly noticed that a police car was chasing me down. I pulled over, and the officer asked me to get out. He then told me to put my hands on the car. I looked up and noticed my youth minister in the church van was passing by as I stood with my hands up with an officer. Thankfully, my identity wasn't tarnished by the mix-up. However, it made me think about how easily we can misuse the identity we have in Christ. Peter openly denied his identity with Christ on the night of His arrest. Peter was not the only one to deny the faith or misuse the name of Christ. We must realize the name we bear.

DEAR LORD, FORGIVE ME FOR WHEN I DIDN'T REPRESENT YOU AS I SHOULD HAVE ...

1. Pray to God to be more careful about the name you bear in Him.
2. Pray to God to know Him more through His Word and to live it out more.

"Yet if anyone suffers as a Christian, let him not be ashamed, but let him glorify God in this matter." (1 Peter 4:16)

Day 97

DEAR LORD, LET ME REMEMBER THE AWESOME RESPONSIBILITY OF PARENTING …

I called it "Organized Chaos." At the time, my seven-year-old took my iPad and made his own video about what a seven-year-old thinks. He walked around in the church building, talking about everything from Tootsie Roll suckers to dancing like a clown. He wore my hat and pretended to be me. I don't dance like a clown. Maybe he was giving me his interpretation of my lesson. It could have been his critique of the sermon that day. Children sure do watch their parents. They listen to what we say and do what we do. Our boys are always watching my wife and me. I feel like everywhere I go in my home, there are three sets of eyes recording all of our moments. I know that I will not always be the best example. However, I hope their overall takeaway from us is our love for Christ and His church. I realize the awesome responsibility that we have as parents. Their ideas of a Christian, father, mother, husband, and wife come from us. A parent's influence is monumental in a child's life. Whether good or bad, it will remain with that child throughout their lives. How to be in the home and with the church comes from the home. What kind of message are we giving them?

DEAR LORD, I PRAY THEY ARE GETTING YOUR MESSAGE FROM MY LIFE …

1. Pray to God to be on guard with your tongue and actions, especially at home.
2. Pray to God to use your time wisely with your children.

"My son, keep your father's command, and do not forsake the law of your mother." **(Proverbs 6:20)**

Day 98

DEAR LORD, I PRAY THAT YOU BLESS ME ...

When was the last time you prayed for God to bless you? Is it possible that God wants you to trust Him enough to ask? There is a prayer buried in the Old Testament by an unfamiliar person. He is not familiar to us, but his prayer is. His name is Jabez, and he asked God, "Oh, that You would bless me indeed" (1 Chronicles 4:10). The word "bless" has been watered down over time. The word is overused. We bless people and ask God to bless the food. In the South, we say, "Oh, bless your heart," when we feel sorry for someone. The biblical word for "bless" means to ask for divine favor. Jabez asked for only what God was able to give. He didn't tell God how to bless him. He left it with God. His needs were secondary to what God wanted for him. It takes tremendous faith only to ask and let God decide what we need. The example is clear. We need to ask. It's hard to receive if we don't ask. "You do not have because you do not ask" (James 4:2). Do you trust God enough to ask Him to bless you?

DEAR LORD, I TRUST IN YOUR ANSWER TO MY PRAYER ...

1. Pray to God to trust Him to give you what you need.
2. Pray to God, asking in faith for His blessing in your life.

"Ask, and it will be given to you; seek, and you will find; knock, and it will be opened to you." **(Matthew 7:7)**

Day 99

DEAR LORD, I PRAY FOR THOSE AFFLICTED WITH SICKNESS ...

I had a professor who brought out the prayer of Hezekiah. He told us about his wife having cancer in their first years of marriage. When this happened, he was also a new Christian. He prayed fervently for his wife to be healed. He read and prayed prayers from the Bible. One particular day, he discovered the prayer of Hezekiah in the room of a hospital. He asked God to give his wife ten years, and they have been married over forty-five years. Of all the times to pray, sickness can bring us to our knees quicker than anything else. When we are sick or a loved one is sick, our whole world comes to a complete stop. I realize this prayer hasn't healed everyone like we want. I've been in some tough moments where I wished the sick person would be healed for the family's sake. The prayer of Hezekiah is not a magical set of words to recite when you want someone to be healed. The prayer of Hezekiah is a reminder for us to be prayerful when it comes to sickness. I'm thankful that we can go to God in prayer and give our burdens to Him. There is no greater burden than in sickness.

DEAR LORD, I TAKE COMFORT IN KNOWING THAT YOU HEAR MY CONCERN ...

1. Pray to God to trust in His will and for it to be done in this time of sickness.
2. Pray to God for healing if it be His mighty will.

"Is anyone among you sick? Let him call for the elders of the church, and let them pray over him, anointing him with oil in the name of the Lord." **(James 5:14)**

Day 100

DEAR LORD, I THANK YOU FOR SEEING ME THROUGH EACH DAY ...

The one-hundredth day of school is a big deal where I work. The early grades dress up like they're old and feeble. They march around the school, showing off their old-looking costumes. Some of the kids use walkers and canes. Some of the older elementary grades do one-hundred-day projects. One year, my son had to make a T-shirt. I helped him write various operations in math that equaled one hundred. For example: ninety-nine plus one, fifty times two, one hundred fifty minus fifty. It's great to be in the practice of celebrating accomplishments. I want to congratulate you in making it to one hundred days of devotional thoughts and purposeful prayers. It's easy to start something. Many do this at the first of every year. They have these promising resolutions to do better and be better. However, the day-to-day grind can cause many to drop off. It becomes more difficult as we start to go further into a new habit or routine. I believe starting something is good, but finishing it is better. One thing needed to finish what we start is commitment. It takes commitment for students and teachers to finish the school year. It takes commitment to finish a 365-day prayer book. It takes commitment to follow and serve God. Let me encourage you to keep reading, thinking, reflecting, meditating, and praying.

DEAR LORD, I PRAY FOR A HEART COMMITTED TO FINISHING WHAT I START ...

1. Pray to God for accomplishments and success, but not to stop there.
2. Pray to God for the strength to keep on and not listen to the temptation to stop.

"Commit your works to the Lord, and your thoughts will be established." (Proverb 16:3)

Day 101

DEAR LORD, I RECOGNIZE THAT I DON'T CHOOSE WHAT IS BETTER ...

"Hello there." You can imagine my surprise as I was opening the door to leave the men's restroom of a restaurant. A cute, curly-haired girl was standing right in my way. It startled me. Her little fingers were right inside the door. Two of my boys were waiting outside and saw her as well. She had no shoes, no socks, and no problem. I was expecting her mother to come rushing in, but no mother. She wanted to go in, but I got her attention toward my boys. I kept asking her, "Where is your mommy?" I kept looking around the restaurant, and no one came. Finally, her mother stood up, and I heard her say, "Where have you been?" I was thinking, *Where have you been?* Am I so distracted with my life that I lose track of my children? We know that it can only take a moment for things to change. We can get so distracted in the non-essential things of life that we neglect the most important ones. We can be distracted on our phones, in adult conversations, and in our work. The text message, email, and missed call can sometimes wait when it comes to things that are better.

DEAR LORD, I NEED TO BE REMINDED MORE EACH DAY OF THE IMPORTANT THINGS ...

1. Pray to God for the willingness to take advantage of the time you have with those you love.
2. Pray to God for faithfulness in the moments you have with those you love.

"[Love] bears all things, believes all things, hopes all things, endures all things." **(1 Corinthians 13:7)**

Day 102 

DEAR LORD, HELP ME TO SEE HOW THE YOUNG CAN HELP ...

It was horrible. One of our faculty members was involved in a church shooting. He was in critical condition in the local hospital. Our school gathered together to get the latest update on his condition, hear the reading of God's Word, and pray. We broke into smaller groups to talk more about it with our own classes. My group of students asked a tough question: Why do bad things happen to good people? I struggle with that question at my age We closed the session with them looking up verses that can help when feeling mad, sad, or confused. The verses found are great, inspiring, and comforting. When you struggle with events and try to figure out why they happened, you should have some verses to think on. I'm constantly amazed by what kids can do when you give them a chance. The disciples came to Jesus, asking Him, "Who will be the greatest in the kingdom of heaven?" Jesus called a little child to Him and said, "I say to you, unless you are converted and become as little children, you will by no means enter the kingdom of heaven" (Matthew 18:3). Jesus placed value and glory in a child rather than His handpicked disciples.

DEAR LORD, COMFORT MY HEART FROM TRYING TO FIND AN ANSWER ...

1. Pray to God for the wisdom that can be found in someone younger.
2. Pray to God for the comfort of His words and people in tough situations.

"Let no one despise your youth, but be an example to the believers in word, in conduct, in love, in spirit, in faith, in purity." (1 Timothy 4:12)

Day 103

DEAR LORD, THIS IS THE DAY YOU HAVE MADE ...

I've been impressed with the 9/11 Memorial in New York City. It reminds me of where I was when I witnessed that horrible event played out on television. It's a sobering experience to read and see actual artifacts from the once Twin Towers. The exhibit does a great job of showing not just the bad but the good things that came from that day. One of the great acts of kindness came through a quilt. Four women in Pennsylvania started a grassroots effort to create a quilt that would honor the victims. They were called the "Steel Quilters" because of being employed by a steel corporation. By 2002, the Steel Quilters had stitched nearly 3,500 fabric squares from people in all fifty states and five countries. What a tremendous act of kindness from an act of evil. This project required getting others involved. What about today? There is still hurt, pain, sin, and violence in this world. The world today is no different than the world Jesus came into. What did He do about it? He went around doing good (Acts 10:38). God doesn't expect us to help everyone, but He does desire us to do something. I'm willing to say that there is someone we can do good for today. Instead of using this day to complain, pray about it, and do something.

DEAR LORD, HELP ME TO ENCOURAGE OR HELP SOMEONE TODAY ...

1. Pray to God to use your body to glorify God through service.
2. Pray to God for the gift of the day to do good in the name of Christ.

"Therefore, as we have opportunity, let us do good to all, especially to those who are of the household of faith." **(Galatians 6:10)**

Day 104

DEAR LORD, I KNOW THAT I SOMETIMES WANT A QUICK ANSWER …

Imagine getting ready for an important event only to find out it's not happening. You travel to the hospital for your scheduled procedure only to be sent home. You go in for a scheduled interview only to be told "not today." Imagine doing this over and over without making any sound from your mouth. No complaining, whining, or questioning. No "hurry up and get this done." Would you have the patience to turn around and do it again six times? This was the situation of Israel when it came to Jericho. The men of war, seven priests, and ark of God were to march around the city once a day for six consecutive days. Israel was to do this until the day Joshua said "Shout!" Think about it. The people prepared for the battle only to march around the city and return home. Those six days of marching only to return home required patience. It was impatience that kept Israel in the wilderness, and patience was what gave Israel victory. We want quick answers to complex questions. We eat fast food, use self-checkout, pay for overnight shipping, and honk at the car in front of us when the light turns green. What's the solution? We need a little more patience.

DEAR LORD, HELP ME TO PATIENTLY WAIT ON YOU …

1. Pray to God for the patience to endure what you are going through.
2. Pray to God, thanking Him for the knowledge that this impatient world is not all there is.

"You also be patient. Establish your hearts, for the coming of the Lord is at hand." (James 5:8)

Day 105

DEAR LORD, I KNOW THAT OUR BOYS SEE US AS EXAMPLES OF A CHRISTIAN ...

I had a teachable moment with my oldest son. We were running errands in town. We passed a family of three needing help with food and gas. We went inside the store, and I talked to God about wanting to show my son the importance of helping others. We left the store, and they were still there. We stopped, and they were so appreciative. They gave me their only gas can to fill up. They trusted me to come back. We came back and filled it up a little. I told him to follow me to the gas station, and we would fill it up. While filling the car, I listened to the father the best I could. I told him the reason I was helping him was because of Christ. He was excited and got out his wallet and had a picture of a Renaissance-looking Jesus. I asked to pray when the van was filled up. My son was there, taking it all in. I explained to him afterward the importance of doing good. We need to help them as Jesus did. We gave them food, clothing, prayers, gas, and a listening ear. We do good to others because God has been good to us. Dear God, thank You for the opportunity to show my son the importance of helping others.

DEAR LORD, HELP ME TEACH MY SONS HOW TO HELP IN THE NAME OF CHRIST ...

1. Pray to God, thanking Him for the daily teachable moments that you have with your family.
2. Pray to use your time wisely if you still have children at home.

> *"Teach them to your children, speaking of them when you sit in your house, when you walk by the way, when you lie down, and when you rise up."* **(Deuteronomy 11:19)**

Day 106

DEAR LORD, THE LIVES OF OTHERS CAN INSPIRE US TO ...

"Just one more, Lord." These are the words of Private Doss. Over sixteen million people fought in World War II, and only 431 received the Congressional Medal of Honor. President Truman gave Doss the award and said, "You really deserve this. I consider this a greater honor than being president." Private Doss objected to carrying a gun and killing a person because of his beliefs. He joined the army because he wanted to save as many lives as possible. He served as an army combat medic, and he was assigned an infantry. On May 5, 1945, the unit was under a heavy surprise attack, and the officers ordered an immediate retreat. Less than one-third of the men made it to safety. The rest of the infantry laid wounded and abandoned. Only one soldier disobeyed orders and stayed. Doss rescued seventy-five wounded soldiers in enemy territory. He carried each person to a place of safety. His courage and strong conviction saved seventy-five lives. What about our conviction? Are we willing to make a stand when it comes to the faith? The cross of Christ demands that we are convicted in Him. May we live out our daily lives like Private Doss. "Just one more, Lord."

DEAR LORD, I PRAY FOR THE COURAGE TO LIVE OUT THE DAY FOR YOU ...

1. Pray to God for the courage to demonstrate Christ's love.
2. Pray to God, thanking Him for the men and women who have shown tremendous faith in their time and way.

"We have become partakers of Christ if we hold the beginning of our confidence steadfast to the end." (Hebrews 3:14)

DEAR LORD, THANK YOU FOR BEING AVAILABLE WHEN I PRAY ...

I decided to change the batteries in the smoke detectors after moving into our new home. We had just moved from West Tennessee to Middle Tennessee. The first smoke detector gave a continuous, high-pitched beep after replacing the battery and testing it. I thought nothing about it and went on changing the other smoke detector. When I finished, I went downstairs to our basement and began tinkering with another project. A few minutes went by before my wife quickly informed me that someone was knocking at our front door. She wanted me to open it. I got to the door expecting a church member only to find the fire chief and two fully dressed firefighters. I looked past them to see a huge fire engine parked in our front yard. When the smoke of confusion was cleared, they happily left. I was so embarrassed by what had happened but thankful to know how quickly they had responded to our door. In the case of a real fire, I would want the same response. Those firemen were standing behind my door, ready to serve. Jesus is standing by our doors, ready to do the same. He wants the doors to our hearts open so He can save us from spiritual death. Is Jesus knocking at your door? Open it, and let Him in.

DEAR LORD, I PRAY TO RESPOND TO YOU MORE EACH DAY ...

1. Pray to God, thanking Him for His continuous invitation.
2. Pray to God for the strength to allow Christ to meet your daily need.

> *"I am the door. If anyone enters by Me, he will be saved, and will go in and out and find pasture."* **(John 10:9)**

Day 108

DEAR LORD, I HUMBLY SUBMIT TO YOUR WILL AND WAY ...

Our son was not too keen on sharing with his younger brother. Whether it was food, toys, clothing, or space, he made his point with "MINE!" My wife and I quickly corrected him for hurting his little brother's feelings. He would say sorry, and then the cycle started all over again. Whether we are three years old, thirty years old, or sixty-three years old, the selfish behavior of "mine" can be a temptation. My way appears to be the best way. My feelings are superior to your feelings. It is my life, and no one can tell me how to live it. However, time will eventually expose the fallacy of selfishness. It did for Israel. God's people faced the repercussions of neglecting God's advice to follow their own. Their joy ceased. A time of celebration turned into mourning. Why? "Woe to us, for we have sinned!" (Lamentations 5:16). If there is anyone who knows best, it is God. His way is not to irritate us or make us feel overburdened. God wants us to have a better life, but it must be done His way. Before you think "mine," remember it is God's way that makes life divine.

DEAR LORD, HELP ME TO SQUASH MY DESIRES TO PROMOTE MYSELF MORE ...

1. Pray to God for the humility to see yourself through the lens of Christ.
2. Pray to God for strength in the war within yourself between what your flesh desires and what your spirit needs.

"Let nothing be done through selfish ambition or conceit, but in lowliness of mind let each esteem others better than himself." **(Philippians 2:3)**

Day 109

DEAR LORD, I PRAY TO HAVE COMPASSION FOR THOSE HURTING AT THIS TIME ...

Is crying a sign of weakness? Is there no crying in life? Rejoicing comes easily over someone's achievement. We honor graduates, glow over newborn babies, and cheer aloud at various events. Do we gather together to cry? Jesus showed us the importance of weeping in John 11. He was moved to tears by the sorrow of Lazarus' two sisters. His weeping was because of their pain from losing their brother. He joined them in their sorrow. We can easily neglect the living because our attention is on what was lost. Do we weep more for the dead rather than the living? Jesus came and wept after the funeral of Lazarus. He openly expressed His emotion. Job's three friends came after the funeral of Job's ten children. They came to Job with good intentions. They cared enough to come without being asked. When they saw Job, they were overwhelmed with emotion. They openly expressed deep sorrow by weeping aloud and throwing dust in the air. Instead of bottling up their emotions, they expressed sorrow over their hurt friend. It can be lonely to be the only one weeping, but it helps if others are there to support us in our sorrows.

DEAR LORD, I PRAY TO SHARE IN OTHERS' JOY AS WELL AS MOURN IN THEIR SORROW ...

1. Pray to God to provide comfort for those hurting.
2. Pray to God that you will take the time to be present in both the good and bad of people's lives.

"Rejoice with those who rejoice, and weep with those who weep." **(Romans 12:15)**

Day 110

DEAR LORD, I PRAY FOR CONSTANT FORGIVENESS FOR MISSING THE MARK ...

I'm no Robin of the Hood! A good friend showed me his medieval crossbow after morning worship. He and his wife perform in medieval reenactments. He set up the target right below a rural road. He showed me how to hold and shoot the crossbow. He warned me to put pressure on the handle and fire the bow. Well, I held it like he said. I was trying to push up on the lever; however, it didn't shoot. I naturally applied more pressure while pointing the bow upward. The lever released the arrow. Oops! The arrow shot over the target and went through some trees into someone's backyard. I was so nervous. I was thinking of the next day's headline: "Local preacher went medieval and killed a neighbor's cat." I didn't come close to the target. I do that so well in life. The word "sin" means "miss the target." I have sinned numerous times in my life. I must let you know that I desperately need Christ every day. I'm a forgiven servant of Christ. I'm nothing more and nothing less. It's a lie to believe that churches are full of perfect people. We are a group of forgiven sinners. We have missed the mark many times in our lives.

DEAR LORD, HELP ME TO LIVE MY FORGIVEN LIFE WITH GRATITUDE AND PATIENCE ...

1. Pray to God for Him to have mercy on you, a sinner.
2. Pray to God that you can be willing to accept His forgiveness.

"For all have sinned and fall short of the glory of God." **(Romans 3:23)**

Day 111

DEAR LORD, HELP ME NOT TO STAY DISCOURAGED ...

The disappointments in this life can be difficult. I cannot forget my neurosurgeon's words to me at my follow-up visit. Six weeks earlier, I had semi-emergency brain surgery to remove a tumor crushing my optic chiasm. Six weeks later, I had nothing but positive feelings with my follow-up appointment. I expected to hear good news. I was shocked when my doctor informed me that the tumor was still there, and they had to do the same surgery again. I left the visit feeling dazed. I was in a state of confusion and disgust. I had to endure the surgery and recovery again. I sat down on a bench near the hospital facility. My disappointment was so heavy that I had to sit. My experience reminds me of the disappointment I have for offending God with my poor choice in words or actions. Imagine the depth of God's love when He helped to save us from ourselves. He gave His only begotten Son. His Son endured to the point of death on the cross. I take the gift of His Son, and in time, do something I know is wrong. I cannot imagine the disappointment God feels on a daily basis. I'm thankful for new days and opportunities to seek God's forgiveness. The disappointment we feel with God should move us to confession.

DEAR LORD, HELP ME TO LIVE MY FORGIVEN LIFE WITH GRATITUDE AND PATIENCE ...

1. Praise God for the blessing of forgiveness through the blood of Jesus Christ.
2. Pray to God for help to display forgiveness to those around you, not condemnation.

> *"The Lord is near to those who have a broken heart, and saves such as have a contrite spirit."* **(Psalm 34:18)**

Day 112

DEAR LORD, THANK YOU FOR YOUR WORTHY EXAMPLE ...

It amazes me the number of times Jesus prayed in Scripture. When we consider the number of times Jesus prayed, how much more should we pray? Jesus prayed often and in all moments. We need to be more constant and consistent with our prayers. We need to pray before making decisions as Jesus did prior to choosing His disciples. We need to pray in those moments when we are struggling as Jesus did in the garden. We need to pray for forgiveness for others as Jesus did on the cross. We need to be persistent as that widow was before the unjust judge because of her adversary. We have an adversary, and he would want nothing more than for us to disconnect all communication to the Father. Jesus demonstrated that prayer is not a ritual or done to get what we want. It's about connecting to the Father and learning to trust Him more through the moments and days of our lives. There is no better teacher on the subject of prayer than Jesus. He shows us in everything that we should pray.

DEAR LORD, THANK YOU FOR SHOWING US TO PRAY REGARDLESS OF THE ANSWER ...

1. Pray to God to resemble Jesus by your prayer life.
2. Pray to God to see prayer not just as asking for what you want but as connecting more to Him.

"Continue earnestly in prayer, being vigilant in it with thanksgiving." (Colossians 4:2)

Day 113

DEAR LORD, I PRAY NOT JUST TO LOOK AROUND ME BUT ALSO TO LOOK WITHIN ME ...

When our boys volunteer to pray, they generally pray for the poor, people in the hospital, and family. I love to hear their prayers because they come from innocent hearts. They haven't reached a point in life where prayer will also be for them because of their sin. They will soon reach an age of knowing what sin is and its separation from God. They will understand that their parents cannot fix the problem. We cannot forgive the sins committed against God. We cannot save them from God. When they realize that, prayer will be much more than a routine or formality. It will have a deeper importance because prayer involves them as well. They are also in the list of those in need of help. We need to be reminded of that as adults. It's one thing to pray for the sick and poor, but it not affect us directly. It's another thing to pray for the sick while going through sickness. It's more personal to pray for the poor when we experience spiritual poverty before God. Prayer is not about looking around at others. It's also a deep examination inside of us.

DEAR LORD, MAY I REALIZE MORE OF MY NEED FOR YOU BECAUSE OF SIN ...

1. Pray to God for forgiveness for your sins and those who have sinned against you.
2. Pray to God to always express the need for Him every day.

"If we confess our sins, He is faithful and just to forgive us our sins and to cleanse us from all unrighteousness." **(1 John 1:9)**

Day 114

DEAR LORD, I PRAY TO BE OPEN TO MORE TIMES ...

What does it mean to "pray without ceasing"? We need to live each day with a conscious reference to God. We must be disciplined in heart and mind to be regular in our prayers. Daily prayers have been a practice since the Old Testament. Daniel was disciplined in praying daily. He prayed three times a day (Daniel 6:10). If we look forward to the Middle Ages, monastic communities developed a practice of daily prayers. This came to be seven fixed times to pray each day. The seven prayers and times were Matins (midnight), Lauds (3:00 a.m.), Prime (6:00 a.m.), Terce (9:00 a.m.), Sext (noon), None (3:00 p.m.), Vespers (6:00 p.m.), and Compline (9:00 p.m.). Each time included psalms, Scripture reading, and set prayers. When the Protestant Reformation came to Great Britain, the Reformer Thomas Cranmer was faced with the question of how to help ordinary people with a full day of work do daily prayer. His solution was to reduce the numerous prayer times throughout the day except Morning Prayer and Evensong. If only life was disciplined enough to be structured with our prayers. There are times to fit in those specific times to pray like in the morning and evening. However, much of life is sporadic and everywhere.

DEAR LORD, I WILL LOOK TO YOU MORE THAN AT THE BEGINNING AND END OF THE DAY ...

1. Pray to God to be more mindful of Him in the middle of your day when a lot happens.
2. Pray to God to have a prayer habit that demonstrates your need for Him.

> *"... praying always with all prayer and supplication in the Spirit, being watchful to this end with all perseverance and supplication for all the saints."* **(Ephesians 6:18)**

DEAR LORD, I THANK YOU FOR NOT BEING FAIR ...

I said to the family in the eulogy that "life's not fair." Nowhere in the Bible can you find that phrase or anything like it. God doesn't promise us that if we love Him and obey Him, life will be fair. It's a myth to think that following Jesus will give us immunity from this world. There are too many factors that don't involve God. We are sinners who live in a fallen, broken world. The funeral service was for a man who had recently buried his wife and only child. It was his turn. He worked at the post office, and several employees came and helped as pallbearers. They were impressed with how he kept going after losing so much. Could you keep on going if everyone near you passed away? Would you ever question God? Would the thought that "life is not fair" dominate your thoughts? What is fair in God sending His only begotten Son? What is fair in God providing mercy, grace, and forgiveness? What is fair if we are the ones who fail Him? I propose, based on the choices we have made, that we don't want life to be fair. We want life to be filled with His grace and mercy. I'm thankful for the unfairness of God.

DEAR LORD, I'M GRATEFUL FOR YOUR LOVE, MERCY, AND GRACIOUS ACTS ...

1. Pray to God to be more appreciative of what God has done for you.
2. Pray to God not to fall into the temptation that you deserve fairness from Him.

"Let us therefore come boldly to the throne of grace, that we may obtain mercy and find grace to help in time of need." **(Hebrews 4:16)**

Day 116

DEAR LORD, GIVE ME THE STRENGTH TODAY TO RUN MY RACE ...

I enjoy watching my older son run at cross-country meets. I remember one particular race that was difficult because of the course and how humid it was that day. Many of the runners crossed the finish line with tears. They were exhausted physically, mentally, and emotionally. They had poured so much into the race that it left them empty. I stood near the finish line, waiting for my son. I witnessed many runners shedding painful tears as they crossed. I was so moved by their effort. Each of them was fighting the battle of finishing what they started. The more I watch two-mile races, the more I appreciate the sport. It's both a mental and physical sport. The runners are constantly faced with the thought of giving up and quitting. The spiritual race is not a smooth and pleasant trip. Paul said, "Therefore I run thus: not with uncertainty. Thus I fight: not as one who beats the air. But I discipline my body and bring it into subjection" (1 Corinthians 9:26-27). Did you catch that phrase? "I discipline my body." This doesn't come naturally. It requires work and sacrifice. We must be disciplined and pour our hearts and souls into it. It's not about first, second, or third place. It's about finishing what we have started. Let me cheer you on as you continue to run the race for Christ.

DEAR LORD, THANK YOU FOR THE EXAMPLE OF OTHERS WHO HAVE FINISHED ...

1. Pray to God for mental strength not to fall into the temptation to stop what you started.
2. Pray to God to be supportive of others and encourage them to finish as well.

"Let us lay aside every weight, and the sin which so easily ensnares us, and let us run with endurance the race that is set before us." **(Hebrews 12:1)**

Day 117

DEAR LORD, HELP ME TO SEE THAT A HERO DOESN'T HAVE TO BE EXTRAORDINARY ...

Would you recognize Batman's symbol, Superman's logo, or Wonder Woman's shield? How do you picture a hero? Is it someone with special powers or someone who does a tremendous act like carrying people from a burning building, disarming a dangerous criminal, or pulling a survivor from a wrecked vehicle? Could a hero be an everyday, ordinary person? Would someone committed to God and His Word be worthy of being called heroic? What about keeping ourselves from being polluted by the world? I believe everyday people show heroic characteristics by bearing other people's burdens, fighting daily battles, and continuing to shine God's light in this world. People like this may not make headline news, but God sees their lives and honors them. The eleventh chapter of Hebrews is a great passage of heroic people. It's a list of both men and women who displayed tremendous faith in their times and situations. At the end of the chapter, more people are mentioned; however, no names are given. These nameless heroes are so great in the eyes of God that the world isn't worthy of such faith. The world needs more heroes. We need people to step up and live faithfully no matter what. That person needs to be you.

DEAR LORD, BLESSED ARE THE HEROES WHO LIVE OUT THEIR FAITH DAILY ...

1. Pray to God to live a life worthy of the calling.
2. Pray to God to demonstrate constancy and faithfulness in the lives of others.

"But without faith it is impossible to please Him, for he who comes to God must believe that He is, and that He is a rewarder of those who diligently seek Him." **(Hebrews 11:6)**

Day 118

DEAR LORD, ONE OF THE GREATEST THINGS I CAN SHOW IS CONSISTENCY ...

My mother did it. After the sixtieth mile, she crossed the finish line. It took her three days to accomplish this goal. She had dedicated a whole year to training for the "3-Day for the Cure Walk." Her determination and focus impressed me because she had never done anything like this. Regardless of the weather, she got up each morning and walked. She was disciplined to get out of bed and walk her distance for the day. I would think, "Oh, it's Saturday, so I'll skip today and sleep in." She didn't do that. She was determined to walk for a worthy cause of breast cancer awareness. Her shining example reminded me of another worthy walk. The apostle Paul described the Christian faith as a race that requires strict training for a crown that will last forever (1 Corinthians 9:24-25). The crown that doesn't fade is what makes living out our faith day-to-day worthwhile. What can be a better reward than heaven? What lasts longer than eternal life? Whatever rewards or goals we have achieved in this life don't compare to the reward that awaits those who finish the race. This requires daily commitment and self-control to live a life worthy of the calling. This is to be done every day. There are no breaks, shortcuts, or time-outs. We must demonstrate to God, ourselves, and others our consistency in the faith. An everyday Christian!

DEAR LORD, HELP ME TO LIVE WITH THE PURPOSE TO FINISH ...

1. Pray to God to be reminded that you finish this race by taking it a day at a time.
2. Pray to God to live step-by-step in line with His will for your life.

"Only let your conduct be worthy of the gospel of Christ, so that ... you stand fast in one spirit, with one mind striving together for the faith of the gospel." **(Philippians 1:27)**

Day 119

DEAR LORD, I'M HUMBLED BY THIS VETERAN'S LIFE AND EXAMPLE ...

I came across a gentleman sitting and waiting for his name to be called at the waiting room of a local hospital. There was nothing extraordinary about the man except for the writing on his hat. His hat said "USS *Indianapolis*." I stopped and asked about the hat. I found out this man had survived one of the worst-known shipwrecks. On a July night in 1945, two torpedoes hit the USS *Indianapolis* in the Philippine Sea. Those who survived the sinking of the ship were 900 of a 1,196-man crew. The survivors jumped into the cold, oil-soaked water as the ship sank. The men unknowingly spent five days in the open sea. They were faced with shark attacks, salt-water poisoning, hypothermia, and dehydration. Those who survived when the rescue came were 317. How did this veteran survive the sinking of the ship and days stranded at sea? His answer is powerful and inspiring. He said, "No one offered to help me because no one else could help me. I was there alone—or so it seemed. But as I reached out in desperation to the Savior of my soul, He suddenly made it clear to me that He was also going to be the Savior of my life." In a horrific event in our country's history, this veteran looked to God alone for help. The other sailors may have done the same. However, he survived and continues to remember by sharing his faith and salvation in God.

DEAR LORD, HELP ME TO APPRECIATE MY RELATIONSHIP WITH YOU LIKE THIS VETERAN ...

1. Pray to God for His saving grace and redemption.
2. Pray to God that He alone can work a tragedy to the good.

"For whatever is born of God overcomes the world. And this is the victory that has overcome the world—our faith." (1 John 5:4)

Day 120

DEAR LORD, I'M THANKFUL FOR THE HOLY SPIRIT HELPING ME ...

Have you ever felt so overwhelmed that you didn't know how to pray to God? The event was so great that you were at a loss for words. When I woke up from the anesthesia after my surgery, my head was throbbing in tremendous pain and pressure. I felt like a truck had hit me at full speed. My pain was so intense that I was at a loss for words. I wanted relief, but there was none. I struggled with what was going on. The apostle Paul understood moments of weakness. He understood there are times when we don't know what to pray for. He struggled with his "thorn in the flesh." He had been beaten, flogged, and shipwrecked. What did Paul do? He spoke of the blessing of the Holy Spirit helping us in our prayers. The Holy Spirit intercedes for us. I don't know how He does it. I like to think he acts as an interpreter. He does this with groaning or words that cannot be heard. When we struggle to know what to say in prayer, the Holy Spirit helps us. We don't need to know all the details as to how this is done. The Holy Spirit helps us in our weakness when it comes to what we need to say in prayer. We need to take comfort that God is there when we are at our worst.

DEAR LORD, I PRAY FOR THE HOLY SPIRIT TO HELP ME SAY WHAT I NEED TO ...

1. Pray to God, thanking Him for His overwhelming help in your life.
2. Pray to God, telling Him you love how He is there when you need Him the most.

"For we do not know what we should pray for as we ought, but the Spirit Himself makes intercession for us with groanings which cannot be uttered." **(Romans 8:26)**

Day 121

DEAR LORD, HELP ME WITH MY MOUTH ...

If there is one thing people are full of, it's advice. We hear advice from family, friends, coworkers, neighbors, and even random people we encounter in town. I've been given wrong advice from people who meant for it to be right. I remember when someone advised me to pursue a relationship after going out on one date with someone. If I had followed their advice, I wouldn't have met the person who became my wife. I've been given right advice when I thought it was wrong for me at that time. I had someone tell me what I should do about my health. I didn't listen, and it has cost me, in my opinion, complications with my health. We can agree that not all advice is good even if the person giving it believes it to be right. Job's three friends piled on him their advice about why he had lost so much in his life. We know as the reader that the cause of Job's problems was Satan. He believed that no person followed God for nothing. God disagreed and proved it with his servant Job. Job didn't know about Satan testing him. He didn't know why he had lost so much. His friends took the position of knowing what had happened, but they were wrong. We can easily give our two cents about something. Are we hurting or helping the person with our words? Sometimes the best thing to do is not give advice but listen.

DEAR LORD, I NEED STRENGTH TO GUARD MY WORDS MORE CAREFULLY ...

1. Pray to God to apply your listening skills more than your speaking ones.
2. Pray to God to be a help to someone and not say something that will hurt them.

"The way of a fool is right in his own eyes, but he who heeds counsel is wise." **(Proverbs 12:15)**

Day 122

DEAR LORD, GIVE ME STRENGTH TO CARRY MY OWN LOAD ...

"Why do I have to pay taxes? I didn't ask to be born." "It's not my fault that the job didn't get done. I was too busy." "It's not my problem that I couldn't pay the bill. I spent my money on other things." Do you think we have a problem with accepting responsibility? What would it be like if we all accepted our responsibility? Instead of an alien or dog eating my homework, I didn't do it. "I was wrong when I didn't do my job and got fired." "I was wrong when I thought I could live like a nineteen-year-old when I'm forty." The easy way is to shift blame and responsibility on someone else. It's my parents' fault, teacher's fault, church's fault—and it goes on and on with everyone but the one who is responsible for their own choices. Sometimes it is the fault of someone else, but our choices and expectations fall on us. We must be responsible people. The Bible says, "For each one shall bear his own load" (Galatians 6:5). My load looks different than your load. The load we have is what we can bear. Like Jesus, sometimes we need someone to help us carry our load. We serve a Lord who carried our load to the cross. Can we not do the same for Him? Don't make excuses for something you can do today.

DEAR LORD, FORGIVE ME WHEN I MAKE EXCUSES FOR MY LIFE ...

1. Pray to God to look to Jesus when your load seems unbearable.
2. Pray to God to make wiser choices because of the consequences they bear.

"So then each of us shall give account of himself to God." **(Romans 14:12)**

Day 123

DEAR LORD, FORGIVE ME FOR TAKING FOR GRANTED MY SALVATION ...

I have an Amazon app on my phone, and it's so easy to scroll to see a deal or create a wish list. Our quick-click culture can easily create dissatisfied people. This can spill over into everything we do. I can feel discontent with the people in my life. I can have discontent when it comes to my work. I spent twenty-two days in the beautiful country of Tanzania. I was there to teach in the college and talk to people in the rural areas. I learned more from them. I remember going into the country and coming across this small village. I saw this boy using a simple stick and rolling a bicycle wheel. There was no frame, pedals, chain, or brakes. It was just the tire of one bicycle wheel. He was having the best time spinning the wheel with the stick and running behind it. He was poor by our definition. He had very little, but he was smiling and enjoying himself. He was content. He comes to mind when I feel unsatisfied with all the stuff I have. I learned something from observing that boy. Contentment is not what we have on the outside. It's inside our spiritual hearts. We are content because of Christ. We are the recipients of His mercy, grace, and forgiveness. I deserved death because of what I have done and said. However, I received mercy. How can I not be content knowing and receiving that?

DEAR LORD, HELP ME TO APPRECIATE THE MERCY AND GRACE YOU HAVE SHOWN ...

1. Pray to God for a stronger desire for Him rather than things.
2. Pray to God to be satisfied with what you have because you deserve less because of sin.

> *"Now godliness with contentment is great gain. For we brought nothing into this world, and it is certain we can carry nothing out."* **(1 Timothy 6:6-7)**

Day 124

DEAR LORD, I PRAY FOR GEORGE AND THE RECOVERY MINISTRY ...

I've been blessed with the opportunity to go to New York City. It wasn't as a tourist to explore and have fun. It was to serve and spend time with the people of that city. One of the nonprofit ministries that we helped serve was a recovery place in Brooklyn. We entered the place and were pleasantly greeted by the one who runs the ministry. His name is George, and he is a retired police officer. I cannot imagine what his eyes have seen, ears have heard, and heart has felt. He is spending his retirement doing something about addiction. He has provided a safe space for recovering addicts to come and get a hot meal and a message from the Word of God. Our mission for that day was to cook breakfast, serve, and talk to the people. As we were serving breakfast, people were coming in and out. An older gentleman came in with an adorable baby girl. He told me that the girl's father is not in her life. The grandfather is helping to take care of her. He honestly told me that he wasn't around for his own children because he was locked up for twenty-seven years. I wondered where he and the others would be if it weren't for the recovery center. I know that we are not called to save the world because Jesus came to do that. We are called to help those who are hurting. Those battling addictions would be included in the list of the ones to help.

DEAR LORD, THANK YOU FOR SUCH GREAT HEARTS FOR PEOPLE STRUGGLING AND LOST ...

1. Pray to God to be a help to someone who is suffering from addiction.
2. Pray to God to remember that you are called to save one person at a time.

"But do not forget to do good and to share, for with such sacrifices God is well pleased." **(Hebrews 13:16)**

Day 125

DEAR LORD, THANK YOU FOR LOVING US ENOUGH TO ADOPT US ...

Our family ran into one of our friends we hadn't seen in a while. Our friend had his cute girl with him. She had beautiful blonde hair, and she had on her cowgirl boots. We found out in catching up with him that they had adopted the girl. I know several adoptive parents and see no differences between any parent of a biological child and a parent of an adopted child. The young girl's biological mother had passed away. I believe it's a wonderful blessing when parents have a place in their hearts to provide a godly home for a child. I believe every child should have a stable environment and loving home. I realize what is ideal is not always the case. My point is that every child should have someone who loves them and provides what is best for them. I commend all parents trying to provide that whether biological, adoptive, or fostering. The apostle Paul mentioned that we are children of God in Romans 8. Our relationship to God as His children is not by birthright but by adoption. "We cry out, 'Abba, Father'" (Romans 8:15). *Abba* is an Aramaic word a child would use for "father." Be thankful that through Jesus we can all be adopted children of God.

DEAR LORD, I'M HUMBLED BY YOUR LOVE FOR US ...

1. Pray to God, thanking Him for the close relationship you have because of Christ.
2. Pray to God for all parents trying to provide a stable, godly home for children whether biological, adopted, or fostered.

"Behold what manner of love the Father has bestowed on us, that we should be called children of God! Therefore the world does not know us, because it did not know Him." **(1 John 3:1)**

Day 126

DEAR LORD, I PRAY TO YOU TO HELP TAKE AWAY MY ANGER ...

I was so upset when I heard about a friend and coworker getting carjacked in the parking lot of a grocery store. The victim was someone I loved and respected. The idea of her being a target for a criminal to beat up was almost unbearable to think about. I went to the hospital to pray and kiss her sweet, bruised forehead. My first emotion was anger. My flesh wanted to inflict the same hurt as was done to her. On the same day of her attack, she had her family send a message via text. She said, "I personally ask that you pray both for those who helped her and those who attacked her." What? I can easily pray for the first responders who helped call an ambulance. I can pray for the medical staff who treated her as she entered the emergency room. She asked me to pray for the offender. I was humbled by such a request. Jesus taught on a mountainside to love your enemies and bless those who persecute you. *Jesus, You want me to pray for those who have hurt someone I loved?* The victim's attitude and response helped me in my moment of anger to pray for everyone, including the attacker. I must remember that I was once an enemy of the cross because of the sin in my life.

DEAR LORD, THANK YOU FOR THE FORGIVENESS SHOWN ...

1. Pray to God for help to be obedient to love and bless those who hurt you or someone you love.
2. Pray to God for strength to do the right thing even if it seems impossible to do.

"But I say to you, love your enemies, bless those who curse you, do good to those who hate you, and pray for those who spitefully use you and persecute you." **(Matthew 5:44)**

Day 127

DEAR LORD, I ASK FOR ENCOURAGEMENT …

Imagine waking up to your spouse's first words: "I love you so much. Thank you for being you. I hope you have a great day, and I look forward to seeing you after work." You smile and get out of bed to get ready for work. Your teenage child says, "You are the best. I'm so appreciative for everything you do for me." You leave the house and head off to work. You notice people are letting you in the lane without waiting so long. You enter your workplace to hear from your boss, "I wanted to tell you yesterday, but I forgot. I have noticed your hard work for the past several months. The company appreciates your work, so we want to give you a raise." At what point would you say, "Time-out. Something is wrong"? We are not used to encouragement from the people we love and encounter on a daily basis. We know that we are called to encourage one another; however, some days are better than others. We are human, and we struggle to be encouraging every day. However, we can ask God to give us the same encouragement and endurance as He gave His Son, Jesus Christ. This is the difference maker. We can ask God in prayer for His help to give us what we need to maintain the same attitude that Christ had. It may not be perfect all the time. But it will be better because our source is God and not us.

DEAR LORD, I ASK TO HAVE THE SAME ATTITUDE AS JESUS …

1. Pray to God for His help in becoming more like Jesus.
2. Pray to God for patience in the times and days when you don't represent Jesus.

"May the God of patience and comfort grant you to be like-minded toward one another, according to Christ Jesus." **(Romans 15:5)**

Day 128

DEAR LORD, MAY MY TRUST REMAIN IN YOU THROUGH ...

Someone took the liberty of putting together a list of things you don't want to hear during surgery. "Everybody, stand back! I lost my contact lens!" "Could you stop that thing from beating? It's throwing my concentration off." "Well, this is a first for me." If you think about it, we put a great deal of trust in a doctor, whom we hardly know, to cut into us. We also place trust in the driver ahead of us and behind us. We expect to get to our destinations without any accidents. We put trust in that tomorrow will happen. How much more should we trust God? He has made Himself known through His Word and creation. God is not unknown to us. We can know more about Him than the surgeon, time, and those driving around us. If we demonstrate trust in what is lesser, why not trust in God, who is greater? I can easily say "I trust in God" when my life is good. It becomes a challenge to trust when we endure hardship. It's hard to tell someone who has received setback after setback simply to trust in God. I believe it helps when we realize how much trust we put into people we don't know. I also believe that being there to help can help them trust in God in time. It's like the older hymn that says, "Trust and obey, for there's no other way."[1]

DEAR LORD, HELP ME NOT TO LEAN ON MY OWN UNDERSTANDING ...

1. Pray to God for the willingness to lean on Him during the ups and downs of life.
2. Pray to God to be an example for others who find it difficult to trust in God.

"Trust in the Lord with all your heart, and lean not on your own understanding." (Proverbs 3:5)

DEAR LORD, YOUR LOVE IS BETTER THAN MY LIFE ...

You have a choice. It's up to you to decide what to do. You can choose to go through life complaining and grumbling about every little thing. You can choose to be grateful for the blessings in Christ Jesus. I can choose to be surrounded by what's wrong with our country and blame everyone on both sides for it. I can go to work and complain about my job and that people don't do their jobs. I can be selfish and choose what I want to do regardless of the people in my life. I can refuse to be positive and remain negative and pessimistic about everything and everyone. If I choose to live my life like that, where would it leave me? Will it lead to a life of joy and happiness? I believe you know the answer. I can do that. However, I choose Jesus. I choose to praise and glorify Him in all I do. His love brings meaning and purpose in my life. Why? His love is better. It's better than my best day. It's better than any personal accomplishment or accolade. "Because Your lovingkindness is better than life, my lips shall praise You" (Psalm 63:3). Our love for God transcends this earthly life. It's better because it's the one thing that we carry with us after death. You can choose to complain every day for the rest of your life. What will that bring you in the end? You can choose to love God with all your heart, and it will see you through the end.

DEAR LORD, I CHOOSE TO PRAISE YOU AND STAY AWAY FROM NEGATIVES ...

1. Pray to God for the right perspective for every day.
2. Pray to God for the peace to live each day satisfied because of His love.

"I will bless You while I live;
I will lift up my hands in
Your name." **(Psalm 63:4)**

DEAR LORD, HELP ME IN MY STRUGGLES WITH SUFFERING ...

I'm praying for one of my students, who is eleven and a half. She has a genetic disorder called Marfan syndrome. This is a tissue disorder that affects the heart and spine. Her scoliosis is so bad that her spine is in an S shape. She has worn a back brace for twenty hours a day for most of her life. The curvature of her spine has progressed so that it has taken the quality of her life. She wants to come to school and have normal problems like any other kid her age. We have lifted her up in prayer often. She has been to specialist after specialist. I want God to heal her so that everyone who knows her will know that it's because of the power of God. He would be glorified by the healing of her spine. As one of her teachers, I struggle with watching her suffer in pain and have bad days in class. She doesn't complain about it. In fact, she displays a beautiful faith for such a young age. This is a tough moment for me. I don't blame God or question Him. I know He knows what is best for her. I selfishly want my own answer, and I want it fast. Do you find yourself wanting more of your own will than God's? I sometimes struggle like anyone when it comes to the brokenness of this life. I must remember that I don't serve God and pray to Him because He answers it my way. I serve and pray to God because He is God. I trust in Him even when I don't understand.

DEAR LORD, GIVE ME CLARITY WHEN THE TEMPTATION IS STRONG FOR MY WILL ...

1. Pray to God for strength when you struggle with what to pray when someone is hurting.
2. Pray to God for the patience to trust Him.

"May the God of all grace, who called us to His eternal glory by Christ Jesus, after you have suffered a while, perfect, establish, strengthen, and settle you." **(1 Peter 5:10)**

DEAR LORD, I CAN'T FLY, BUT I CAN LIVE FAITHFULLY FOR YOU ...

My wonderful wife surprised me one birthday with tickets to the Heroes and Villains convention in Nashville. She knows I'm a big fan of comic book characters, especially heroes. As a child, I remember wanting to fly like Superman. I wanted to have all the gadgets and special suits like Batman. I dreamed of being Clark Kent or Bruce Wayne. I'm sorry to disappoint, but I cannot fly like Superman. I don't live in a mansion and run a billion-dollar company like Batman. I cannot even run like the Flash. This doesn't mean I cannot be a hero. I can be a positive role model and example to those around me. I can live in such a way that people recognize in me the greatest hero, Jesus Christ. We can all be hero-like by going the extra mile for someone. You don't have to be fast or acrobatic. It takes a heart dedicated to serving and loving others. We don't have to be perfect, but we do need to be consistent in what we do. We need heroic mothers and fathers who are available to their children and model a worthy example. We need heroic church members who demonstrate the love of Christ to their community. We need heroic husbands and wives who withstand temptations in this life to ruin a marriage. The world needs heroes.

DEAR GOD, YOU CALLED US TO LET OUR LIGHTS SHINE ...

1. Pray to God to bear the fruit of the Holy Spirit to those connected to you.
2. Pray to God to be available and consistent with the people you love in your life.

"You are the light of the world. A city that is set on a hill cannot be hidden." **(Matthew 5:14)**

Day 132

DEAR LORD, I THANK YOU FOR THE TIME ...

The Code of Hammurabi is an ancient Babylonian code of law of ancient Mesopotamia, and it was anything but merciful and forgiving. These are some of the laws in the code: "If a builder builds a house and the house collapses and kills the owner of the house, the builder shall be put to death." "If a son hits his father, his hands shall be cut off." "If a man's wife becomes sick, the husband may take a second wife, but must continue to care for the sick wife as long as she lives." Can you imagine if the laws of our land were like this? What if we lived in an "eye for an eye and tooth for tooth" society? When I teach this section in my ancient world history class, the students are amazed at the ancient Babylonian code. One of the assignments is to agree or disagree with one of the 282 codes and explain why. Most of them are strongly against and cannot imagine living under such a law. Afterward, I believe they have a better appreciation for the laws of our land. The laws of this land cannot provide the way to heaven. They cannot tell us about salvation. They cannot demonstrate the love and forgiveness we read about at the cross. I look at the wisdom of the law of God after studying ancient laws. I reach the conclusion that His laws are not burdensome for us to abide by. Sometimes it's good to see how others lived to appreciate what we already have.

DEAR GOD, I'M GRATEFUL FOR THE WISDOM AND LOVE OF YOUR LAW ...

1. Pray to God in humility as you submit to His will and command.
2. Pray to God with joy in your heart, knowing the love and mercy given to you through Jesus.

"For this is the love of God, that we keep His commandments. And His commandments are not burdensome." (1 John 5:3)

Day 133

DEAR LORD, THANK YOU FOR THE COURAGE OF OTHERS ...

Many families have a certain interest when it comes to vacation. Some like to go to the mountains to hike and camp. Others enjoy anywhere with sand, sun, and the sound of waves crashing. My family went to amusement parks. We took our summer vacations riding the tallest, fastest, and craziest roller coasters. My thrill from coasters led me to try other things like bungee jumping and white-water rafting down class-5 rapids in West Virginia. My level of thrill seeking is moderate compared to others. However, there is no greater challenge than our final act in this life: death. Death is something we are guaranteed, but still, it leaves us afraid. I read, "It's not that I'm afraid to die, I just don't want to be there when it happens." I think that speaks for most of us. Moses lived an interesting life. In his last years, he climbed mountains. He climbed in his hundreds mountain peaks over 4,500 and 8,000 feet. His last climb was to his death. He climbed Mount Nebo to see a panoramic view of the Promised Land, and then he died "according to the word of the Lord." Isn't that a beautiful way to end? He was in God's care. His death was in God. This story helps me to have courage to live for the Lord and to one day die according to the word of the Lord.

DEAR GOD, I DON'T HAVE TO LIVE AFRAID OF DEATH ...

1. Pray to God that you don't have to be afraid of the unknown because of Jesus.
2. Pray to the Lord for the strength and courage to be like Moses and serve Him faithfully no matter what.

"So Moses the servant of the Lord died there in the land of Moab, according to the word of the Lord." (Deuteronomy 34:5)

Day 134

DEAR LORD, I CAN ONLY CHANGE ONE PERSON ...

Have you ever questioned your questions? Sometimes we find ourselves going round and round because we are asking the wrong questions. Let's consider questions normally asked when it comes to parenting. "When is my child going to listen to me?" "Why does she hang out with those kids?" What are better questions to ask? "How can I get to know my child better?" "What can I do to improve my parenting?" Instead of looking at your child, look at yourself. What about in marriage? "Why doesn't he let go of the past?" "When will she listen to me?" A better question to ask is, "What can I do to help out?" The better questions address personal accountability. The only person I can change is myself. We can influence and encourage others, but we cannot change them. Have you ever read a book, heard a lesson, or gone to a seminar and thought about how you wished someone you knew could have heard this because they need it? A more accountable approach is to pray, "God, grant me the serenity to accept the people I cannot change, the courage to change the one I can, and the wisdom to know it's me." Do you have personal accountability?

DEAR GOD, HELP ME TO HOLD MYSELF MORE ACCOUNTABLE ...

1. Pray to God to have the wisdom to start now in holding yourself accountable and not blaming someone else.
2. Pray to God to be more responsible with your words and actions.

"For we must all appear before the judgment seat of Christ, that each one may receive the things done in the body, according to what he has done, whether good or bad." **(2 Corinthians 5:10)**

Day 135

DEAR LORD, THANK YOU FOR THE EXAMPLE OF FAITHFULNESS ...

I had the honor on Christmas Day to renew the vows of a precious couple. The couple got married on Christmas Day. This particular anniversary fell on a Sunday. When the worship service ended, we invited everyone who had attended to stay for the vow renewal service. We had two members to take the runner down the center aisle. Our song leader and his daughter brought out their violin and played beautiful wedding music for the bride to walk down to. We even had a room decorated for a vow renewal reception. We had a cake, punch, and a beautiful floral arrangement. The church went all out for this couple. I forgot to mention that the couple renewed their vows on their seventieth wedding anniversary. They got married at a courthouse, so there was no wedding or reception. I believe after seventy years of marriage, we can provide that to the beautiful bride. I won't forget doing that for them. It was a wonderful experience on Christmas Day. What a great example for the rest of us who are not even close to year seventy! They show what it means to be faithful. We can all appreciate that whether married or not. We need to be faithful to the Lord and the people we love.

DEAR GOD, THANK YOU FOR THIS COUPLE AND THEIR EXAMPLE ...

1. Pray to God to be faithful to Him till death as you have been called to be.
2. Pray to God to forgive you when you are unfaithful to Him because of selfish desire and do what you want instead of following Him.

"Let us hold fast the confession of our hope without wavering, for He who promised is faithful." **(Hebrews 10:23)**

Day 136

DEAR LORD, THANK YOU FOR THE SPIRITUAL GIFTS WE RECEIVE ...

"And now abide faith, hope, love, these three; but the greatest of these is love" (1 Corinthians 13:13). Why is love greater? We must have faith to please God. We are told it's impossible to please Him without faith (Hebrews 11:6). What are the chances of God being blessed by our lives without faith? It's 0 percent. We are to walk by faith and trust in God even when we don't understand. What about hope? Can you imagine living life without hope? I cannot. We need biblical hope to anchor us in this crazy world. The hope we have is expecting to obtain what God has promised. We hope in eternal life, heaven, and being with God. Have you ever noticed that faith and hope are in the unseen? Faith is the "substance of things hoped for, the evidence of things not seen" (Hebrews 11:1). Do we need faith when we see God? Is faith required when we are surrounding the throne of the King? Faith will not exist then. Hope "that is seen is no hope" (Romans 8:24). We don't hope in the things we see. It's in the things that we don't see. Will there be a need to hope when we are in the presence of our Lord? There will be no need to hope anymore. What will remain throughout eternity is love. The greatest is love because we need it here, and it will be there. There is no time with God where love is not needed. Love is the greatest.

DEAR GOD, I CANNOT IMAGINE A LIFE WITHOUT HOPE, FAITH, AND LOVE ...

1. Pray to God, humbled by the greatness of His love being stronger than life and death.
2. Pray to God, grateful in knowing that the love you have for Him will not end in death but continue.

"He who does not love does not know God, for God is love." **(1 John 4:8)**

Day 137

DEAR LORD, SOME OF THE MEMORIES WE HAVE CAN BE PAINFUL ...

Do you have a picture that plucks on your heartstrings? I have several like that, but one really hurts me. I'm sitting in a chair with our second son on my lap. He is leaning on me as to make sure I don't leave him. I'm weak and trying to recover from my first major surgery. I'm wearing a baseball hat that I got during that time. They don't want me to wear that hat today because it reminds them of when I was sick. It was a tough recovery for the first few weeks. It was the first time my boys saw their dad struggling and hurting in front of them. I couldn't mask the pain because it was obvious to them. Our second son has a big heart. It bothers him when someone he loves is sick or hurting. His precious little heart was hurting for me. His sadness hurt me more than my pain. I cannot look at the picture too long because it hurts to think about it. My son will occasionally ask if I'm hurting or need to rest. We want to protect our kids the best we can. There are times we can't, and they see some of the harshness of this life. One of those lessons is suffering. It's tough to see the people we love suffer. Whether a picture captures it or not, we hold those in our hearts. They are strong memories. I pray that through those painful memories, you can see how they eventually led to the good.

DEAR GOD, IN OUR DEEPEST PAIN, WE ARE NOT ALONE ...

1. Pray to God for His comfort and ability to work all things together for the good.
2. Pray to God to trust and lean on Him even when you don't understand why.

"Seek the LORD and His strength; seek His face evermore!" (1 Chronicles 16:11)

Day 138

DEAR LORD, I PRAY TO LOOK AT MYSELF ...

"Two men went up to the temple to pray, one a Pharisee and the other a tax collector" (Luke 18:10). The Pharisee's prayer showed no dependency on God. He did not ask for forgiveness, daily bread, or any of the things Jesus instructed us to pray. He informed God of his goodness, and God to him was someone to address rather than need. Am I guilty of saying or thinking, "I am glad that I'm not like that person"? It's easy for us to point out the mistakes of others rather than the plank in our own eyes. The tax collector prayed, "God, be merciful to me a sinner!" (Luke 18:13). He made no excuses with God. He mentioned no one else. He could barely raise his eyes toward God. He beat on his chest and begged God for mercy. His concern was with his relationship with God. He came from the streets into the temple as he was. The tax collector's presence was noticed. The Pharisee prayed not to be like him. I'll never forget the look early in my ministry when a young lady came forward to be baptized. It was known that she had HIV. I held her hand and let her know comfort. I was there for her as she made the hard step to God. It was between her and God regardless of what other people may have thought. I found out later that the baptistery was drained because she had been in it. Every baptistery, creek, pool, lake, or ocean needs to be drained and cleaned out because of the deadliest disease: sin.

DEAR GOD, HELP ME TO FOCUS ON MY STANDING BEFORE YOU ...

1. Pray to God for mercy as you show mercy to those hurting.
2. Pray to God to be comforting to those sick with sin because you have the same problem.

> *"David said to Gad, 'I am in great distress. Please let us fall into the hand of the Lord, for His mercies are great; but do not let me fall into the hand of man.'"* **(2 Samuel 24:14)**

Day 139

DEAR LORD, HELP ME TO ALWAYS BE KIND TO OTHERS ...

"All men are created equal" is a well-known phrase, but it's not always practiced. The expression was constituted in 1776 when slavery still existed. "All men are created equal" unless you were a slave. "All men are created equal" unless you were a woman. The expression to love your neighbor is a recognizable command. What about in practice? Do we have the courage to be a neighbor to someone unlike us? Rahab was first introduced in the Bible as "a harlot" (Joshua 2:1). She was an immoral woman living in a world totally devoted to everything that God hates. She was a neighbor to someone unlike her. Rahab risked her own life by showing kindness to spies. She went against her own people and past. Rahab asked the same neighborly kindness to be shown to her family. The spies could have said no. We would expect them to have said, "You are not one of us!" They showed the same kindness that was given to them. A little neighborly kindness can accomplish great things. I was invited into the home of a family that was very different from me. The mother had come to the United States from Southeast Asia. She was despised in her country. She struggled in our country and learned the hard way. I listened to her story and embraced her as she cried about all the things she had endured. We all came together in a huddle and prayed. Yes, we are different, but that doesn't keep us from being neighborly.

DEAR GOD, HELP ME TO BE KIND DESPITE DIFFERENCES ...

1. Pray to God to be a doer of the second commandment.
2. Pray for strength to do the right thing always.

> *"And the second is like it: 'You shall love your neighbor as yourself.'"* **(Matthew 22:39)**

Day 140

DEAR LORD, FORGIVE ME FOR MAKING EXCUSES ...

I came across a website that provided excuses for all kinds of situations. It had a list of excuses for work, school, and jury duty. We are good at excusing ourselves from what we need to do. Jesus asked a person who seemed willing to follow Him. The person seemed ready and able because the first word out of his mouth was "Lord." However, he was not ready, because he said, "Lord, let me first go and bury my father" (Luke 9:59). He wanted to follow Jesus, but it wasn't a good time for him. When is it a convenient time to follow Jesus, change your lifestyle, and be transformed? It's not like running an errand, making a resolution, or setting a small goal when it comes to following Jesus. He didn't tell Jesus "no," but "not right now." We can treat a relationship with Jesus like a workout plan. We have every intention to start walking, running, or working out. We go to bed telling ourselves, "Tomorrow I'm going to wake up early and start changing my life for the better." The morning comes, and we push the snooze button so many times that it's too late. That night we find ourselves getting into bed, promising again: "Tomorrow for sure." The more we put Jesus off, the less likely He is to be our Lord. You want to love God with all your heart? You want to show kindness to someone? You want to be forgiving so God can forgive? What about now?

DEAR LORD, GIVE ME THE COURAGE TO DO WHAT I NEED TO TODAY ...

1. Pray to God to be a doer and not a thinker when it comes to doing something good.
2. Pray to God to set in your mind that there is no better time than now.

"For He says: 'In an acceptable time I have heard you, and in the day of salvation I have helped you.' Behold, now is the accepted time; behold, now is the day of salvation." **(2 Corinthians 6:2)**

Day 141

DEAR LORD, I NEED TO TAKE ONE DAY AT A TIME ...

I have a friend who has disciplined his body to get in better shape and prepare for Spartan runs. Some of his training in a day consists of 5x5 heavy bench, 3x8 squats, 3x8 lateral raises, 3x8 barbell curls, 50 burpees, 500 flutter kicks, 30 pull-ups, and running 5 miles. The amazing thing about him is not too long ago, he was flat on his back after major back surgery. He willed himself slowly to change his habits. He amazes me because he does this every day no matter what. I've seen him train in the rain and cold weather. He doesn't make excuses for himself. He has inspired others to get active and become healthier. I'm thankful for his daily example to do the things that make you feel better. The metaphor for the Christian life is running. It's not compared to throwing a disc, swimming a long race, or riding a bike up a mountain. I believe the example of running accurately describes the Christian life. There are many times in our lives when our day is not a big event or flashy moment. It's not a "burning bush" experience. No, it's the daily grind of dropping kids off at school, going to work, eating lunch, going back to work, picking up the kids, going to practice, fixing or eating dinner, doing homework, finally having alone time, and falling asleep on the couch to wake up and do it all over again. In our daily routines, there needs to be the spiritual discipline of endurance, faith, perseverance, and self-control. Finish the race!

DEAR LORD, MAY I RUN WITH ENDURANCE ...

1. Pray to God to be dedicated to the life of following Christ every day.
2. Pray to God to know the reason and reward for living are worth it.

> *"But I discipline my body and bring it into subjection, lest, when I have preached to others, I myself should become disqualified."* **(1 Corinthians 9:27)**

Day 142

DEAR LORD, HELP ME TO BE PATIENT WITH YOU ...

Have you ever had a "God moment"? It's an experience that strongly reminds you God is involved. If so, you know it's not an everyday thing. I remember a moment like that. My endocrinologist came to me after a morning worship service. I was blessed to have weekly checkups with my doctor on Sundays. She asked me if I was taking a certain medicine. I told her no. In fact, I had never heard of it. She went on to tell me that she had a dream about drawing my blood at the church building. In the dream, I needed to take a certain medicine to help with the problem with my sodium. She had this dream after we called her to tell her that I was feeling bad. The way she looked in my eyes and talked to me felt like a "God moment." It was like God had used her to speak to me and tell me what I needed. She called in the medicine from her dream, and I'm still taking the medicine years later. This moment was more than coincidental. The right doctor and the right time in my life led to the medicine I needed. What are the chances of that happening? I was strongly moved through her that God was letting me know that my health was in His hands. I was moved by the answer of prayers through this great "God moment." I was reminded again that I serve a God who can do more than I can ask or even imagine. What an awesome God!

DEAR LORD, HELP ME TO BE OPEN TO THE WAYS YOU ANSWER MY PRAYERS ...

1. Pray to God, thankful for the reminders through the Word and people of how He cares for you.
2. Pray to God, humbled by His provisional care in your life.

> *"Now to Him who is able to do exceedingly abundantly above all that we ask or think, according to the power that works in us."* **(Ephesians 3:20)**

DEAR LORD, FORGIVE ME FOR THINKING ONLY ABOUT ME ...

Have you ever done a prayer walk? What is it? You walk around a specific place with the purpose of praying for issues that pertain to where you are. It takes time and effort to research and invest in an area or place. I've done this in New York City. It was in Queensborough. The day we walked and prayed was a cool, wet day. We walked several miles to certain parts of Queens. We heard someone read statistics about certain problems in that part of the city. We could smell and see the area where some of the problems took place. The problems in New York are not just in New York. They can happen anywhere. Some of the problems we talked about and prayed for were human trafficking, homelessness, and poverty. We are aware that things like that exist and happen. It's another thing to hear about them more and see the locations and take the time to pray about them specifically. That walk with our school group really helped me and opened my eyes more. It opened the things I pray for by giving a visual of places where these problems happen. I also realized that morning that I'm guilty of being too busy. I'm so fixed on what I have to do that I feel like I bypass the daily opportunities. We must be purposeful about the needs in our neighborhoods. It means being more aware and prayerful about them.

DEAR LORD, OPEN MY EYES AND HEART TO THE THINGS AROUND ME ...

1. Pray to God, realizing that the answer to some prayers is getting up and doing something about the problems.
2. Pray to God to be more aware and, therefore, specific in praying for the needs of those in difficult situations.

"And he said, 'He who showed mercy on him.' Then Jesus said to him, 'Go and do likewise.'" (Luke 10:37)

Day 144

DEAR LORD, HELP ME TO GIVE MORE THOUGHT TO MY IDEAS …

Have you done something stupid? I believe I could write a book on dumb decisions I've made. One of those decisions was when I rode a boat with some friends down the Cumberland River. It was a really nice boat ride. We stopped to get out and play in the water. I stood knee-deep in the river looking over to the other side. I kept thinking, "Can you swim over to the other side?" I told everyone I was going to swim to the other side. They didn't think I would do it. Well, I did it. I dove into the water and started swimming. I swam about halfway when the current was pulling me down the river more. It was stronger than it appeared on the dry bank. The current of the river made me work harder to swim across. I realized as I kept swimming that I was moving farther down the river. It was in that moment that I realized this was a dumb idea. I finally made it to the other side without floating too far from the boat. My friend came and picked me up. He couldn't believe it. I slowly got onto the boat and collapsed on the seat. I was so exhausted and tired. He measured it, and the distance was over two hundred yards. My wife reminded me on our way home the reality of me being older, a husband, and a father of three boys. I deserved that lecture. I'm thankful for the people in my life who help counsel me.

DEAR LORD, SOMETIMES I REACT WHEN I NEED TO RESPOND MORE …

1. Pray to God to be attentive to the people in your life whose counsel you should consider.
2. Pray to God, thankful for the people He has placed in your life who want the best for you.

"The way of a fool is right in his own eyes, but he who heeds counsel is wise." **(Proverbs 12:15)**

Day 145

DEAR LORD, TEACH ME TO WAIT ON YOU ...

I remember the old ketchup commercial of an eager eater waiting on the thick red ketchup to drip out of the bottle. He waited and waited. I don't know of anyone who enjoys waiting. Does our frustration of waiting on people spill into our relationship with God? We pray for God to show up and intervene, but time keeps ticking with no change. We can grow impatient and try to do what only God can do because we are tired of waiting. We feel that God owes us a quick response. We follow Him and do the best we can at obeying His word. If we need Him, He should answer immediately. What we need to be reminded of is that God is never late. His answer is on time. We can wait a day, week, month, or years. God's answer will be right and timely because He answered us. If we feel like God has put us on hold, why does He make us wait? One answer is given in the raising of Lazarus. Jesus waited to go see him. He received word that the one He loved was sick. Jesus stayed two more days at the place where he was. He didn't stop everything and go to the family immediately. He waited. By the time Jesus came to see Lazarus, He had been dead for four days. Martha said, "If You had been here, my brother would not have died" (John 11:21). Jesus waited for the "glory of God" that He "may be glorified through it" (v. 4). Whatever the Lord is doing in our lives, it's not to satisfy us. It's for His glory. The glory of God surpasses our needs, wants, and waiting.

DEAR LORD, HELP ME REMEMBER THAT IT'S NOT ABOUT ME ...

1. Pray to God that He may be glorified through your life.
2. Pray to God with the attitude not that your will but His will be done.

> *"Therefore, whether you eat or drink, or whatever you do, do all to the glory of God."* **(1 Corinthians 10:31)**

Day 146

DEAR LORD, FORGIVE ME WHEN I REACT TO LIFE ...

"Teacher, do You not care that we are perishing?" (Mark 4:38). These are not the words of a class. These come from the mouths of grown men. Some of them had faced a storm on the Sea of Galilee. However, these disciples felt the pressure of the furious storm. They lost their focus. Before the storm, Jesus had told them that they were going to the other side. If Jesus says you are going from one side to another, no storm, typhoon, or hurricane can stop you from getting there. If Jesus says it, it will happen. Jesus was with them asleep at the stern of the boat. It was not enough for the disciples to be told where they were going and for Jesus to be with them. They were still afraid. How easy it is to take our focus off Him because of unexpected problems. What did Jesus do with the fearful disciples? He simply said, "Peace, be still!" (Mark 4:39). I believe He says that to us as well in our own storms. We need both "peace" and to "be still." We need to stop and think clearly about what God has said. We need to be reminded of His constant presence. We need to be anchored in His promises. If Jesus is Lord over your storm, no matter what shape the world is in, you will find peace. When the next storm comes, don't panic or freeze in fear. Remember that Jesus is with you. Pray for peace, but be still enough to receive it.

DEAR LORD, I PRAY FOR THE PEACE THAT SURPASSES ALL UNDERSTANDING ...

1. Pray to God for His help to guard your thoughts and ask for peace.
2. Pray to God to be still long enough to know that He is God and in control.

"Peace I leave with you, My peace I give to you; not as the world gives do I give to you. Let not your heart be troubled, neither let it be afraid." **(John 14:27)**

DEAR LORD, THERE IS NOTHING GREATER THAN YOUR GRACE ...

What is your worst sin? The one you keep hidden even though you asked God to forgive you. What about the one that is safely locked in your mental closet? You still feel like it's so bad that even God couldn't erase it. I believe most of us feel that way about something we have done. We feel so guilty, and the thought of it shames us. If you struggle with forgiving yourself, consider the following:

> The grace of Jesus > (greater than) my worst sin
> The grace of Jesus < (less than) my worst sin

Which equation is correct? Is Jesus greater than the sin you keep hidden from everybody? Is that hidden sin so great in your mind that you feel the grace of Jesus is less than it? God's grace is greater. I take comfort in knowing others with sins that I would consider hiding in my mental closet. Paul is one example. He considered himself the number one sinner. He referred to himself as the "chief" of all sinners. He was a religious terrorist before his encounter with Christ. He dragged men and women into prison because of their faith. He was guilty by association at the stoning of Stephen. Paul felt that if the mercy of Christ could reach him, it will reach everyone. If the grace of God is greater than a religious terrorist, it's greater than my sin.

DEAR LORD, FORGIVE MY SINS BY THE ABUNDANT GRACE AND MERCY FROM THE CROSS ...

1. Pray to God to have the courage to confess and repent from all sin.
2. Pray to God to believe in the truth that the grace of Jesus is greater.

"For if by the one man's offense death reigned through the one, much more those who receive abundance of grace and of the gift of righteousness will reign in life through the One, Jesus Christ." **(Romans 5:17)**

Day 148

DEAR LORD, THANK YOU FOR THE PROMISE OF LIFE AFTER DEATH ...

The words "when our loved ones we meet" can be found in the hymn "In the Morning of Joy."[2] This beautiful hymn speaks to meeting our loved ones in heaven. What an awesome thought! I have several people whom I have loved that I look forward to seeing again. Two of those loved ones are Adele and James. I know them as Granddaddy and Grandmother. I loved them very much in this life. I was known as their grandson. Will I still be that to them? Did death change them? Will you be you in heaven? What makes you *you*? It's your memories, personality, passion, gifts, abilities, traits, and interests. Will the same person on earth be the same person in heaven? I don't mean the same in the flesh. I mean our spiritual minds, hearts, or souls. If Josh on earth is not Josh in heaven, did Josh go to heaven? When we die, our identities don't stop or disappear. We continue without the flesh to be who we are. We will give an account of the things we have done in the body, good or bad, and this requires memory. Imagine, one day, we will continue our relationships with the ones we have already entrusted into Jesus' care. We will soon be laughing with old friends whose voices have been silent for too long. The greatest relationship that began on earth will live on throughout eternity. That relationship is with Jesus.

DEAR LORD, DEATH IS BUT A DOOR TO REAL LIVING IN YOU ...

1. Pray to God to live obediently so that one day you can continue the relationships that death has stopped.
2. Pray to God for the hope that one day you will be with Him and those who loved Him.

> *"And this is the promise that He has promised us—eternal life."* (1 John 2:25)

Day 149

DEAR LORD, THANK YOU FOR THE ABUNDANCE OF DAILY BREAD ...

What do you pray for each day when it comes to daily provisions from God? Jesus prayed, "Give us this day our daily bread" (Matthew 6:11). He prayed for only what he needed and not wanted. We can easily go over the side of praying more about what we want. We want our daily provisions to include a better paying job, a relationship, a more reliable car, and the list goes on. What Jesus prayed for humbles me. If daily bread is what Jesus prayed for, why do we have more? Why has God given us more than enough? I'm willing to say that each of us has more than a loaf of bread in our homes. We have a pantry of food. We have refrigerators, freezers, and cabinets full of daily provisions. We have closets and drawers full of daily provisions when it comes to clothes. We have comfortable beds that remind us we have more when it comes to daily provisions. Have you ever wondered why? We easily could have been born in a poor country. Instead, we were born here with more than enough. What does this mean for us? I'm not trying to make you feel guilty. I am making you think more on what you have rather than what you think you need. I also believe where much is given much will be required. With what we have, we need to help others.

DEAR LORD, HELP ME TO LOOK BEYOND MYSELF ...

1. Pray to God, thanking Him for having more than enough and for a willingness to share with those in need.
2. Pray to God for help to focus more on what you need rather than what you want.

"For everyone to whom much is given, from him much will be required; and to whom much has been committed, of him they will ask the more." **(Luke 12:48)**

Day 150

DEAR LORD, HELP ME WITH MY ANGER IN TIMES OF DIFFICULTY ...

I cannot forget when one of my students lost her mother. It was toward the end of the school year. Her mother was only forty-four years young. When it happened, I kept thinking about my student. I thought about all the things she would miss with her mother. I thought about her mother not being there to see her graduate from high school and college. I was hurting for her and the father. The mother passed away on a Thursday. The very next day, the father and the student came to school to say goodbye for the school year. They were in shock, but they were coming to thank us for the year. The father told me that his wife's death was not in vain. She lived a great life, prayers were answered, and these things gave him peace. There was no anger in his voice or words. He didn't reject God or blame Him. I was thinking that it was right to feel angry or be upset. *You have the right.* That was my attitude at that time. That father reminded me of Job. The godly man of Job lost all ten children at once. Wouldn't he have cursed God and blamed Him? Job "arose, tore his robe, and shaved his head; and he fell to the ground and worshiped" (Job 1:20). He would in time curse the time he was born but never God. It's natural to be angry when life hits us hard. It's important to channel that anger in a way that doesn't hurt us or others.

DEAR LORD, FORGIVE ME WHEN I BLAME YOU ...

1. Pray to God for the faith to endure the temptation of blaming Him in hardship.
2. Pray to God to learn from those in the Bible and in your life who demonstrate faithfulness in difficult times.

> *"'Be angry, and do not sin': do not let the sun go down on your wrath."* **(Ephesians 4:26)**

Day 151

DEAR LORD, FORGIVE ME FOR THINKING I CAN HIDE ...

Joe Louis was a heavyweight boxing champ. In 1946, he prepared to defend his title against the boxer Billy Conn. Louis was warned by the press and skeptics about Conn's speed and moves. Louis's famous response to those warning him was "He can run, but he can't hide." Why is hiding from God entertaining? Why do we think we can do it? It has been proven that we can't. The first people disobeyed God by eating the fruit of the forbidden tree. They realized what they had done and attempted to hide from God. They quickly found out that no one can hide from God. Jonah was told by God to go to Nineveh because of their wickedness. Jonah bought a boat fare to Tarshish, which was the opposite direction of Nineveh. If God told us to go east, we turn around and head west. This was what Jonah did. The Lord sent a great storm and fish to redirect Jonah back to following God's command. I don't know why running away from God or attempting to hide from Him is so appealing. There is no running, escaping, or hiding from God and His message. If we try to run or hide, there will be a "ship" carrying us away from our responsibilities to God. We may run, but we can't hide from God. There is no creature hidden from His sight. It's far better to approach Him than to try to run away.

DEAR LORD, I NEED TO BE REMINDED THAT YOU WANT WHAT'S BEST FOR ME ...

1. Pray to God for the commitment to go to Him always.
2. Pray to God to know that you can put off sin for a little bit, but eventually it catches up with you.

"And there is no creature hidden from His sight, but all things are naked and open to the eyes of Him to whom we must give account." **(Hebrews 4:13)**

Day 152

DEAR LORD, LET ME PAUSE TO SAY ...

I was in the neuro ICU recovering from brain surgery. My doctor was in my room reading the operation notes from my first surgery. She studied the notes for several minutes. She looked up at me and thought carefully about what she was about to say. She said, "God saved you." What? She explained that my blood pressure had bottomed out during surgery. It appeared to her that they were trying to revive me back. I broke down and cried. It was the first time I had cried since knowing I had a tumor. I was humbled to hear from a doctor that "God saved me." Those words have stayed with me since. If that was the case, God has saved me twice. He saved me through the sending of His Son. He saved me in the operating room. After processing it for some days, I felt guilty. Why me and not someone else? I humbly prayed a prayer of thankfulness. I thanked God for what He had done for me. I still had years to climb, but I was overall thankful because of that moment. I was so thankful for His answer. I prayed that I could always live in gratitude for the cross and that operating table. We are to be thankful in all things. Our gratitude is best expressed in our prayers to God. Have you thanked God lately? We don't need dramatic events like the one I described. Every day is reason enough to humble ourselves in thanksgiving for God. It might surprise you if you focus a prayer on doing nothing but thanking God.

DEAR LORD, I'M GRATEFUL FOR YOUR AWARENESS OF ALL LIFE ...

1. Pray to God, thanking Him for the blessings in your life.
2. Pray to God, thanking Him for the bad days and setbacks because they make you appreciate Him even more.

"In everything give thanks; for this is the will of God in Christ Jesus for you." **(1 Thessalonians 5:18)**

DEAR LORD, THANK YOU FOR THE FAITH OF A CHILD ...

Children have a way of doing things that we adults cannot do. We were visiting a shut-in from our church family. My oldest son and I ran some errands for her. My youngest son stayed with her to keep her company. When we came back from the store, my son had this elderly woman in her eighties outside on a hot, humid day in July. What were they doing? She was digging up the grave of her dead pet fish. My son had talked about pets dying, and he wanted to see her dead pet fish. I told the woman we visited that she can say no. She ignored me. She also allowed my youngest son to serve her tea in this expensive teacup. She pretended to drink tea with him. How did my six-year-old son get her to dig up a dead fish and use her expensive china cup? A child can bring joy in people in ways others cannot. The widow had forgotten her pain because of the attention she had with my son. I'm constantly reminded by my three boys the wisdom of Jesus when it comes to children. He took a child and showed the disciples the greatest in the kingdom of heaven. Children have a great perspective of God and the world. They possess this innocence of not knowing the cruel, evil side of life. My son didn't see an older woman who couldn't do much. He saw someone to play with and to get down in the dirt with him. I'm thankful for our children and how they teach us in ways that no other person can.

DEAR LORD, I'M AMAZED AT CHILDREN ...

1. Pray to God to see the wisdom of those who are younger and how they see things.
2. Pray to God for opportunities for children to learn and grow in Him.

"Assuredly, I say to you, unless you are converted and become as little children, you will by no means enter the kingdom of heaven." **(Matthew 18:3)**

Day 154

DEAR LORD, I NO LONGER WANT TO WORRY ...

Worry! Anxiety! We are familiar with these words. We know the feeling all too well because of what we have experienced. If you experience worry and anxiety often, let's look at the benefits. The first benefit of worrying and having an anxious heart is our health. We struggle to sleep because of them, so they will help us to live longer and be more productive in the day. Who needs rest? It's overrated. Another benefit of worry and anxiety is what they bring us. They give us so much joy. A heavy dose of worry with a mixture of anxiety makes our day great. It's the secret to longevity. Obviously, I don't believe in this, and neither do you. There are no advantages to worry and anxiety. They ruin health, rob joy, and leave us with no peace. They poison the Holy Spirit's fruit. It's difficult to maintain the fruit of the Holy Spirit if our lives are dominated with these negative habits. How can we have peace and joy if we are plagued by the things we worry and stress about? We can't. I don't expect you to read this and immediately drop all worrying and stop being anxious. I hope that you are prayerful to demonstrate the fruit of the Spirit more than worry and anxiety. It takes effort, concentration, reading, and prayer. The Holy Spirit's fruit is well worth the effort you put into it. Remember a day at a time.

DEAR LORD, FORGIVE ME FOR BURNING MY ENERGY IN WORRY AND ANXIETY ...

1. Pray to God for the effort to live in the Spirit and be led by the Spirit each day.
2. Pray to God for the attitude to know the blessings that come in doing as the Bible says.

> *"Therefore do not worry about tomorrow, for tomorrow will worry about its own things. Sufficient for the day is its own trouble."* **(Matthew 6:34)**

Day 155

DEAR LORD, I NEED TO SAY NO MORE ...

Do you know one of the longest words in the English language? The word is forty-five letters long. The word is "pneumonoultramicroscopicsilicovolcanoconiosis." According to dictionary.com, it means "a lung disease resulting from inhaling very fine quartz and silicate dust." It would be safe to say that this word is hard to say. I don't believe it's the hardest word. There is another word much smaller but more difficult to say. It is the word no. A child can easily say no to anything. They think it's a game sometimes. When we become adults, the word becomes more difficult to say. We put too much on our plates because we don't want to tell someone no. We push ourselves to the limit because we didn't say no. We can sacrifice time away from family because we didn't say no. What about with bad choices? How many addictions could have been prevented if no was said at the very beginning? How many marriages would be saved if no was said when temptation came? How many souls are lost because of the failure to say no? It becomes tough to say no when the temptation to sin is involved. Jesus said, "Let your 'Yes' be 'Yes,' and your 'No,' 'No'" (Matthew 5:37). The context of this verse is the abusive practice of saying oaths and making promises because our word is not enough. I believe it could apply to all things. We are to mean it when we say yes and no. We mean it for the sake of our families, health, and our awesome God.

DEAR LORD, I CAN EASILY BURY MYSELF IN EXTRA WORK BECAUSE I FAIL TO SAY NO ...

1. Pray to God for the strength to say yes and no and mean it for the sake of yourself and the people you love.
2. Pray to God that if He can tell you no, then how much more can you tell people no when it's too much?

"But above all, my brethren, do not swear, either by heaven or by earth or with any other oath. But let your 'Yes' be 'Yes,' and your 'No,' 'No,' lest you fall into judgment." **(James 5:12)**

DEAR LORD, I CANNOT IMAGINE WHAT YOU FELT WHILE ON THE CROSS ...

What would you do if someone at work or church came to you and said, "I don't want to see you again"? How would you feel? What if your spouse or someone else in your immediate family said, "I never want to see or talk to you again"? That would be unbearable. What is the difference between the two examples? The spouse or family member is someone you have loved longer. This is why the pain would be greater. What was it like for Jesus to feel forsaken by the Father on the cross? They had always been together. Jesus was in the beginning with God (John 1:1). God is not bound by our days and time, so there is nothing we can compare to the length of Their love. It's simply eternal. However, Jesus suffered on the cross when He asked God why. "My God, My God, why have You forsaken Me?" (Matthew 27:46). Jesus felt for a moment rejection from a relationship that dated back to the beginning. In that moment, Jesus felt forsaken by God. Jesus understands when we feel forsaken in this life. I wish I could tell you that every relationship is going to be healthy, helpful, and long-lasting. It wasn't that way for Jesus. He was the only perfect person, and He still faced hateful words. I'm thankful in times when I hear something hurtful that I can go to Jesus. He understands. He also helps.

DEAR LORD, I CANNOT FULLY UNDERSTAND WHY YOU FELT FORSAKEN ...

1. Pray to God, thankful for what Jesus endured for you because He can empathize in your weaknesses.
2. Pray to God to rise above the words people say to you that are hurtful and/or untrue.

"For we do not have a High Priest who cannot sympathize with our weaknesses, but was in all points tempted as we are, yet without sin." **(Hebrews 4:15)**

Day 157

DEAR LORD, I PRAY FOR A BETTER HABIT ...

We live by habits. We're not even aware of it, but we do. It's estimated that about 40 percent of our daily routines is almost the same. Almost half of our lives is run by habit. We look for learned behaviors that work and repeat those actions. Habits also help free up our attention so we don't have to rethink the same decision every day. *Webster's Dictionary* says a habit is "a settled or regular practice, especially one that is hard to give." A habit is so comfortable and automatic for us. Did you give much thought to the habit of brushing your teeth, showering, drinking a cup of coffee or water, taking your medicine, and being on your phone? There is no better time to see how driven we are by habits than in the morning. I wake up at the same time to take my medicine in my seven-day pill container. I sleep some more, knowing I have an extra thirty minutes. I'm very good at touching "snooze" because I do it daily. I get up and go to the bathroom to take a shower. I get dressed and go downstairs to drink a cup of black coffee. Most mornings, I do this without much thought about what I'm doing. Have we created habits in growing in the Lord? It doesn't just happen. It takes effort and consistency. When we start to read and pray daily, we have to think about doing it. Our focus is more on starting a new habit rather than God. When it becomes a habit, we can direct our focus to pursuing God.

DEAR LORD, I PRAY MY RELATIONSHIP WITH YOU IS NOT JUST A DAY OF THE WEEK ...

1. Pray to God to be more intentional in applying spiritual habits in your day.
2. Pray to God to be faithful in your walk with Christ.

"But solid food belongs to those who are of full age, that is, those who by reason of use have their senses exercised to discern both good and evil." **(Hebrews 5:14)**

Day 158

DEAR LORD, I PRAY FOR MERCY ...

My wife and I were newly married when my friend from college came to our house selling a vacuum cleaner. We listened to his presentation. I told myself beforehand that I'm not buying and only listening. He talked about the vacuum and demonstrated it on our carpet. He compared it to our vacuum to show the difference. At the end, he made it sound so easy with the monthly payments. I thought, "Oh, it's not as much when you look at the monthly bill." We bought that overpriced vacuum with credit. We financed it for three years. It wasn't long before I realized I hadn't financed a car, exotic trip, or degree in higher education. It was a vacuum cleaner! We paid it off before the three years. We kept it as a reminder of the cost of a dumb decision. I'm afraid the decisions I've made are worse than that. I'm guilty of sinning against God. That decision cost me separation from the glory of God. If I had remained a sinner, the result would have been spiritual death. I'm thankful for the amazing grace of God. I didn't have to stick with the poor decision I made. I was given the choice to choose Jesus. He offered His invitation to come into Him. I graciously accepted that priceless offer and received forgiveness through Jesus Christ. Like the vacuum, the memories of what I have done are there. They make me appreciate what Jesus has done for us. I'm forever grateful for the cleansing power of Jesus' death. My worst decisions are met by God's best.

DEAR LORD, I'M THANKFUL FOR JESUS AND THE LIFE HE OFFERS ...

1. Pray to God, humbled by the mercy and grace you receive through His forgiveness in Jesus.
2. Pray to God, appreciative of the cleansing power of Jesus' death.

"If we confess our sins, He is faithful and just to forgive us our sins and to cleanse us from all unrighteousness." (1 John 1:9)

Day 159

DEAR LORD, I WANT TO BE AS BOLD AS THE EARLY CHRISTIANS ...

Are you guilty of turning the world upside down? The Christians who met in the house of Jason were given that charge. They were dragged out of the house and brought before the city rulers. What charge required such aggressive behavior? "But when they did not find them, they dragged Jason and some brethren to the rulers of the city, crying out, 'These who have turned the world upside down have come here too'" (Acts 17:6). What does "upside down" behavior look like? What does troublesome behavior to the world do? It's upside down to pray for your enemy and bless those who curse you. It's much more natural just to do to others what has been done to you. It stands out to mention the people in prayer. It's upside down to forgive someone even if that person hasn't asked for it. The world refrains from forgiving or refuses unless the apology is sincere. We are to forgive not because of an apology. We forgive because Christ has forgiven us. Again, it's an upside-down way of thinking and living. What about considering your trials as joy? Many see hardship as a bad thing only. We can see it with joy in Christ as something from which we can learn or come to know God better. May there be more homes and people who, like the house of Jason, are living upside down according to the world. It's right side up according to God.

DEAR LORD, I DESIRE A LIFE DEFINED BY YOU ...

1. Pray to God to be more concerned with what He wants you to say and do rather than the world.
2. Pray to God to demonstrate your uniqueness in your relationship with Christ.

> *"But you are a chosen generation, a royal priesthood, a holy nation, His own special people, that you may proclaim the praises of Him who called you out of darkness into His wonderful light."* **(1 Peter 2:9)**

Day 160

DEAR LORD, I'M THANKFUL FOR THE GIFT OF LIFE ...

I still struggle to find the right words to describe those times in the delivery room with my beautiful, strong wife. She endured the painful process, and I tried to help comfort her. Each delivery was special. I'm so thankful that I was there to witness the births of our three boys. Each time, I left with a greater appreciation of the greatness and awesomeness of God. We naturally look to see what the newborn baby looks like. He has my wife's nose but my chin. The baby smell is so wonderful. They are breathing with their little lungs and are kept warm in the swaddling blanket. They look at you and close their eyes to go back to sleep. It's a humbling experience. I realize not everyone can experience it. Some have, and it goes bad. This makes me more humbled. When our boys were born, I enjoyed thanking God in prayer and saying their given names for the first time. It was the first of many prayers for our boys. They will continue to have prayers as they go through the seasons of life. My parents still pray for me each night. I'm thankful for the prayers of parents. I hope my boys are thankful as they learn more about prayer. They learned that they are a gift from God. We have done nothing but thank Him. One of my favorite times to pray is at night with them. I always thank God for them by mentioning their names.

DEAR LORD, I'M THANKFUL FOR THE OPPORTUNITY TO PRAY FOR MY CHILDREN ...

1. Pray to God to be with your child, helping them make the right choices when you are not around.
2. Pray to God, thanking Him for the gift of life and the opportunities you have because of it.

"I will praise You, for I am fearfully and wonderfully made; marvelous are Your works, and that my soul knows very well." **(Psalm 139:14)**

Day 161

DEAR LORD, I CHOOSE YOU OVER ALL THE TEMPTATIONS ...

Have you ever wondered why there were three crosses that day? Why was Jesus crucified in the center? Could it be that Jesus' death symbolizes one of God's greatest gifts? It's the gift of choice. The two criminals had so much in common. They were convicted by the same judicial system. They both received the same sentence of death by crucifixion. The two robbers saw the same crowd. They were both close to Jesus. They both criticized Jesus. However, the difference came when one thief made the choice to change. All of his bad choices were redeemed by one good choice. We've all made some bad choices in life. Maybe the bad choice was in friends. Was it the bad choice in a declared major in college or in a profession? You may look back and think, "If only I could go back and make up for that bad choice." You can. One good choice for Jesus can offset a thousand bad choices. The choice is yours to make. How could two robbers see the same Jesus and one chose to mock Him while the other chose to acknowledge Jesus? I don't know. How is it that two siblings born of the same mother and father go in two different directions? It comes down to making a choice. Each of us has a choice to make. Today is a great day to make better choices that please God.

DEAR LORD, I REALIZE THE IMPORTANCE OF WANTING TO CHOOSE YOU ...

1. Pray to God to make the choice each day to serve and glorify God in what you do.
2. Pray to God to live in such a way that it helps influence others to make that same choice.

> *"And if it seems evil to you to serve the Lord, choose for yourselves this day whom you will serve. ... But as for me and my house, we will serve the Lord."* **(Joshua 24:15)**

Day 162

DEAR GOD, THANK YOU FOR THE GIFT OF LIFE ...

My grandmother told me the story when I was younger of how someone came into their house through the garage door. At that time, they left the doors unlocked. My grandfather was down at the barn. She assumed it was my grandfather. When the person was in sight, she saw that it was a stranger. She quickly ran out the screened porch door and down the gravel road to my grandfather, barefoot. At the time, I was more amazed by the running on a gravel road without shoes than the stranger. My grandfather came back to the house with her. The stranger was gone, but he had taken some cash hidden in the kitchen. It took some time for my grandmother to feel safe in her own house. Most victims of robbery feel threatened and exposed. How much worse does God feel when we dishonor His creation? We hear of creation harming one other. This was not God's intention in the beginning. God created order and form out of nothing. He looked at everything He had made, and indeed, it was very good. He gave Adam the job to care for creation. He placed him in the garden of Eden to work it and take care of it. The Hebrew word for "care" means to "keep clean; preserve." We have been given the responsibility to take care of God's creation. This includes each other. I wish there were no such thing as robbers, murderers, abusers, and every other harmful person. I'm thankful for Jesus, who helps us have peace in a sinful world. We look for the day when God will restore all things.

DEAR LORD, HELP ME TO LOOK AHEAD ...

1. Pray to God, thankful for the beauty still in creation despite sin.
2. Pray to God to strengthen your faith in Him as you endure the good and bad of life.

"But may the God of all grace, who called us to His eternal glory by Christ Jesus, after you have suffered a while, perfect, establish, strengthen, and settle you." **(1 Peter 5:10)**

Day 163

DEAR GOD, THANK YOU FOR THE REVELATION OF YOUR AWESOME NAME ...

I held a gospel meeting in eastern Tennessee. The second night there, I was invited to dinner at the home of one of the members. After dinner, I noticed, hanging on their wall, a piece of paper with a signature. I was stunned when I realized the identity of the signature. This particular signature is a name well-known in history. In fact, it is a name known throughout the modern world. The name is Adolf Hitler. The signature was recognizing the woman's grandfather, who was the head librarian in Berlin. What comes to mind when you hear the name Adolf? How many people do you know named Adolf? Do you know anyone named Cain or Jezebel? These names carry a negative connotation. I point this out to convey the importance of the name that is worthy of our attention. A name that is the polar opposite of the ones I have mentioned. The name is Jehovah God. "God said to Moses, 'I AM WHO I AM.' And He said, 'Thus you shall say to the children of Israel, 'I AM has sent me to you'" (Exodus 3:14). How do you respond to the name of the Almighty? It's a name not to be used in vain but to be revered. He has graciously revealed Himself by telling us His name. May we go through this day honoring His name in prayer and in living.

DEAR LORD, I GLORIFY YOU BY HONORING YOUR GLORIOUS NAME ...

1. Pray to God to carry the name of Christian in a worthy manner.
2. Pray to God to forgive you when you dishonor Him and His name by your sins.

"Moreover God said to Moses, 'Thus you shall say to the children of Israel: "The Lord God of your fathers, the God of Abraham, the God of Isaac, and the God of Jacob, has sent me to you. This is My name forever, and this is My memorial to all generations."'" **(Exodus 3:15)**

Day 164

DEAR GOD, WE CANNOT HELP WHERE WE ARE BORN ...

Life seems to favor some more than others. Babies are born every day into rich as well as poor families. Some children are blessed to grow up in the nurturing care of sensitive, loving, involved parents while other children hope to survive the horrors of their home lives. Within some families, parents favor one child over the other children. Life is often unfair. Does this excuse bad behavior? Are bad circumstances a free pass for making poor choices? It's difficult to win at life if we don't try. It seems that everywhere Esau turned, he got the raw end of the deal. However, he didn't help it. He gave into instant satisfaction: "... lest there be any fornicator or profane person like Esau, who for one morsel of food sold his birthright" (Hebrews 12:16). What if Esau had accepted his role and embraced God's ultimate plan? Instead, he became desperate and fell for the instant gratifications of life. Was Esau the only one to struggle with impulsive tendencies? What about those who are so desperate to escape their loneliness that they rush into a quick marriage? What about those who flee financial difficulties by entering a bad business partnership? Maybe you feel like you have blown it. It is never too late to make the right choices by repairing a broken relationship, mending a broken heart, and especially restoring a relationship with God. Today is as good of a day as any.

DEAR LORD, HELP GUIDE WHERE WE END UP BY THE CHOICES WE MAKE ...

1. Pray to God to be defined by Him and not the hardship in your life.
2. Pray to God for the strength to ask for His help when you feel the temptation to fall away.

"... looking carefully lest anyone fall short of the grace of God; lest any root of bitterness springing up cause trouble, and by this many become defiled." **(Hebrews 12:15)**

Day 165

DEAR GOD, HELP ME TO DEPEND ON YOU ...

Have you ever felt trapped? Have you been in a situation that seemed inescapable? We call these situations a number of things: in a jam, between a rock and a hard place, hard-pressed, trapped in a corner. The path of life sometimes leads us up, down, and around. It may be that right now you find yourself in a predicament. You might be in that situation because of unwise decisions you have made. You might be in a predicament through no fault of your own. In Exodus 14, the children of Israel were cornered by the Egyptians. God was preparing them for the glory days of the Promised Land. God became significant and real for the children of Israel at the Red Sea. God may be breaking a habit or becoming real to you in your predicament. The children of Israel were trapped between the mighty Red Sea and the massive Egyptian army. "When Pharaoh drew near, the children of Israel lifted their eyes, and behold, the Egyptians marched after them. So they were very afraid, and the children of Israel cried out to the LORD" (Exodus 14:10). They were in a jam, so they looked up. They cried out to God. Sometimes, our predicaments remind us of our inabilities and God's capabilities. God rescued His people, but in His time and in His way. Our prayer lives are not to ask and receive what we want. They're more about depending more and more on God each day. We trust in His will more than our own. There is no greater time to see our dependency on God than in a predicament.

DEAR LORD, I THANK YOU FOR USING THE GOOD AND BAD TO HELP ME GROW MORE ...

1. Pray to God to trust in His will and His timing.
2. Pray to God to forgive you when you grow impatient.

"My brethren, count it all joy when you fall into various trials, knowing that the testing of your faith produces patience. But let patience have its perfect work, that you may be perfect and complete, lacking nothing." **(James 1:2-4)**

Day 166

DEAR GOD, I THANK YOU FOR LOVE AND WHAT IT ENDURES ...

I had a bright spot every day in neuro ICU. I was there for over thirty days. I looked forward to the mornings each night. I knew that my beautiful wife was coming to spend the day with me. I didn't want her to stay the night with me because the boys needed her. She would come in the morning with her bright smile and light up the room. I loved the way she looked at me. It made my pain and situation melt away. She would give me a hug and hold my hand. She told me how things were and how the boys were doing. This was every day. She would leave in the late afternoon, and I would see her again the next morning. It made the stay doable. Our relationship became stronger because of this difficult situation. That is one of the biggest positives that came from my ordeal with my brain tumor. It made my wife and me stronger. I wouldn't want to go back and do it again. However, I wouldn't take anything for it. We have grown closer in a way that I couldn't imagine. I'm so thankful for her love and support for me. I will always remember those days she came and cheered me up. Many have endured and become better for it. There is no greater relationship through the ups and downs than with God. It's in those moments that we find a love that is worth living for and that endures.

DEAR LORD, I HAVE BEEN BLESSED TO BE LOVED BY YOU AND MY SPOUSE ...

1. Pray to God, thankful to love someone in this life the way He has loved you.
2. Pray to God to demonstrate to others what it means to love by your example in the good and bad times.

"Love suffers long and is kind; love does not envy; love does not parade itself, is not puffed up; does not behave rudely, does not seek its own, is not provoked, thinks no evil; does not rejoice in iniquity, but rejoices in the truth." **(1 Corinthians 13:4-7)**

DEAR GOD, I THANK YOU FOR THE REVELATIONS OF YOUR NAMES ...

What makes prayer powerful? Is it the words you say? No, the power of prayer is with God. Our prayer lives may be limited because of our knowledge of God. Have we taken the time to know Him better through the revelation of His names? How do you know people? It starts with their names, and we connect that name to more information about the person. We can apply the same practice with God. Moses learned from the burning bush experience more about God by His name "I AM." The Hebrew word for the capital name is pronounced "Yahweh." It means that God is the eternal One who brought all things into being. Yahweh has been around much longer than your struggles, problems, and concerns. The name for God in Hebrew is *Elohim.* It refers to God being the Creator, Preserver, One who is mighty and strong. God is infinite in His glory and power. The name for Lord in Hebrew is *Adonai.* This speaks to God as the sovereign Lord and Provider of all that exists. There are other names of God throughout Scripture. I would encourage you to see the places where the names of God are mentioned. Is the name mentioned in a prayer? Is it mentioned in a time when God was speaking to His people? It gave the early church strength in a time of threats and persecution. Read and reread how they addressed God. The early church's knowledge of God helped them through the difficult times. It will help us.

DEAR LORD, I PRAY TO KNOW YOU MORE ...

1. Pray to God with the desire to learn more about Him because of the power of prayer.
2. Pray to broaden your view of God by how He has revealed Himself.

> *"For this reason we also, since the day we heard it, do not cease to pray for you, and to ask that you may be filled with the knowledge of His will in all wisdom and spiritual understanding."* **(Colossians 1:9)**

Day 168

DEAR GOD, I SEE YOUR GLORY IN EVERYTHING ...

When I was in Western Samoa in the summer of 1999, we took a break and spent the day and night on a beautiful beach. We swam in the ocean that day, looking for seashells. The best part was at night. We stood with no artificial lights around us. We saw the glory of God's wonderful creation in the nighttime sky. The stars seemed bigger and brighter from our location. The missionary from the island told us that we were the last people on earth to see the sunset. It has changed since then to where they are the first people to see the sunrise. At that time, we were the last to see the day end. I could not help but to see the wisdom, beauty, and majesty of the Father in the night sky. We know that light travels 186,000 miles a second, and a star can be trillions of miles away, but we still see it. Everything that exists from the atom to the infinity of space rests in God. Maybe you struggle to hear God when you pray. You have prayed faithfully but feel like there is no answer. If God can keep up with the stars, moons, galaxies, and constellations, He is mindful and cares for you. Don't give up on prayer. God wants to communicate to you. I would encourage you to keep praying and reading the Scriptures. Do not lose heart when it comes to communication in the most important relationship.

DEAR LORD, HELP ME TO REALIZE THAT YOU CARE FOR CREATION AND FOR ME ...

1. Pray to God to be patient on God's answer when you pray to Him.
2. Pray to God not to grow weary when you are waiting on Him.

"... praying always with all prayer and supplication in the Spirit, being watchful to this end with all perseverance and supplication for all the saints." **(Ephesians 6:18)**

DEAR GOD, I KNOW YOU ARE AT WORK ...

God's silence doesn't mean He is inactive. God is always at work. Do you feel like your prayers have grown cold because of God's silence? You think this because there seems to be no response from your prayers. God is too big for us to confine Him to our concerns and circumstances. Yes, He cares for us, but He cares for everyone else too. Have you ever thought about the times God was silent? After the prophet Malachi, God grew quiet on our end. There were no inspired words between the time of Malachi and the start of the Gospels. No other prophet, priest, judge, or king rose up to make sure God's people stayed on track. God remained silent for four hundred years. That is longer than our country's history. Had the people of Israel sinned so badly that the Lord gave up on them? Did this lack of communication mean God had stopped working on their behalf? We know that the Lord was preparing Israel for the most important event in history—the coming of the Messiah. God was not silent and inactive. He was preparing the people for a sacrifice that would free them from sin completely. In fact, we can receive remission from our sins from the blood of Jesus Christ. Remember that God has used silence to accomplish great things. I would recommend that you think on these times and see that God continues to work on your behalf.

DEAR LORD, I PRAY TO TRUST YOU WHEN I FEEL LIKE YOU'RE SILENT ...

1. Pray to trust the God of the universe with your problems and situations.
2. Pray to trust God in His time and in His will.

"For since the beginning of the world men have not heard nor perceived by the ear, nor has the eye seen any God besides You, who acts for the one who waits for Him." **(Isaiah 64:4)**

Day 170

DEAR GOD, I STAND IN AMAZEMENT OF YOUR WONDROUS PLAN IN THE LIVES ...

My wife and I are close to a couple who asked us to pray for them. They wanted to have another child. We joined them in prayer. We prayed for them to be blessed with another child, if it would be God's will. Sometimes, what we pray is answered but not in the way we expect. Several months later, the husband received a call from his mother. She told him of a young mother putting her baby up for adoption. The young mother knew the family. It wasn't long before the families connected for the sake of this precious baby girl. The birth mom saw that she couldn't provide a stable home for the child. God had answered our friends' prayer in His own way. The prayers of many had opened their home and hearts for this girl to be adopted. This process had its ups and downs, but it ended up being a blessing. The adopted girl has been given the opportunity to grow up in a home with a father, mother, and sister who love her. She will grow up knowing the love of God. I love observing how God providentially cared for the child and this precious family. He did so in a way that no one saw beforehand. We serve an awesome God. He knows what we need. I'm constantly reminded that He has all things under His control. We just need to trust in Him fully and completely.

DEAR LORD, I CONTINUE TO BE IN AWE OF YOU ...

1. Pray to God to forgive you when you begin to doubt or question His will.
2. Pray to God, thankful that His ways are much higher than yours.

"'For My thoughts are not your thoughts, nor are your ways My ways,' says the LORD. 'For as the heavens are higher than the earth, so are My ways higher than your ways, and My thoughts than your thoughts.'" **(Isaiah 55:8-9)**

Day 171

DEAR GOD, THANK YOU FOR THE PEOPLE WHO DEMONSTRATE GREAT FAITH ...

I was asked to go and visit someone special. The person we visited was a 102-year-old woman. I look up to people who show great faith over the age of one hundred. She asked me if I could pray for her son who had cancer. I immediately honored her request and prayed for her son. Afterward, I asked if there was anything else. She said, "No, just prayers." I needed to learn what she knew well. I believe in the power of prayer, but sometimes I feel like it's not enough. I sometimes ask what else I can do. I sometimes fail to realize the power of prayer. What else can help more than prayer? She knew the power of prayer, and for her, that was enough. This godly woman had seen a lot. She lost her home in the May flood. In her ups and downs, she has remained faithful to Jesus Christ. She reminded me of the passage in Hebrews 11. It talks about others whose names are not mentioned in the great chapter. It says of them, "... of whom the world was not worthy. They wandered in deserts and mountains, in dens and caves of the earth" (Hebrews 11:38). I can add more people to that list. This woman of great faith at 102 would be in that list, in my opinion. I'm grateful for their mighty example of living faithfully in this broken world. It helps me to see at my age that living and dying in the Lord is possible. It takes faith and prayer.

DEAR LORD, I'M HONORED TO WITNESS IN OTHERS THEIR ATTITUDE TOWARD PRAYER ...

1. Pray to God to help you see more the One to whom you pray.
2. Pray to God to live and learn from the faith of others who show you it can be done.

> *"And all these, having obtained a good testimony through faith, did not receive the promise, God having provided something better for us, that they should not be made perfect apart from us."* **(Hebrews 11:39-40)**

Day 172

DEAR GOD, HELP ME TO CONSIDER THE WAYS YOU ARE INVOLVED ...

Have you considered the people in your life? What about where you live? Do you ever think about the things that have happened to you? When our first child was born, we prayed for a door to open for us. We wanted to move closer to a set of grandparents. We found an opportunity in west Nashville with a congregation. In our time there, we grew to love the people and the community. While I was there, I had a tumor growing in my brain without my knowledge. It took a special doctor who happened to be a member of the congregation. She led me to the right neurosurgeon. In that first meeting with the neurosurgeon, my doctor and friend was there with me. What are the chances of that happening? I don't believe in chance and luck. I believe in the providential care of God. I can look back and see how a decision made over twelve years ago led to the good. You have your stories too. The people we befriend and the places we go happen to be what we need. If we could stop to look at our present lives, they would look like cobwebs. They would have connections from one person to another. The connections would involve events, jobs, good times, and times we struggled. All of these come together for the good for those who love God and are called according to His purpose.

DEAR LORD, I'M HUMBLED BY YOUR CARE ...

1. Pray to God to help you be more thankful for the things that have happened because of where they have led you.
2. Pray to God to trust in Him during the transitions of life and when you cannot see why yet.

"But now, do not therefore be grieved or angry with yourselves because you sold me here; for God sent me before you to preserve life." **(Genesis 45:5-7)**

DEAR GOD, HELP ME TO BE THANKFUL FOR EVERY SEASON OF LIFE ...

How many Christmas songs are there? I typed the question in a search engine. The first thing that popped up is "The Million Songs of Christmas." I believe it. If my local radio station can play Christmas songs twenty-four hours a day, seven days a week, we have every Christmas song imaginable. A big percentage of Christmas songs are about Jesus' birth. I find it interesting the major difference between songs about Jesus' birth and songs about His death. You won't find a local radio station playing continuous crucifixion songs for thirty days. We are not bombarded with every musical artist making an Easter album each year. We don't have Easter Eve on our calendar. There are no crucifixion movies on the channel notorious for Christmas movies. You know, the ones where it snows at the right time. Why is there more hoopla about the birth of Jesus than His death? It's easier to sing about the birth of a baby than the death of an innocent Savior. We prefer to smile and laugh rather than weep and mourn. We are called to do both. The life of Jesus demonstrates the importance of both. It seems that every great beginning has an ending. "Rejoice with those who rejoice, and weep with those who weep" (Romans 12:15). We need to rejoice in the times of new births. We need to mourn the cost of sin and the consequences of it. The complete earthly life of Jesus shows us how we need to be mindful of all seasons of life.

DEAR LORD, I'M SO COMFORTABLE WHEN IT COMES TO REJOICING WITH OTHERS ...

1. Pray to God to help you mourn with those who mourn.
2. Pray to God to remember the death of Jesus and why He did it.

"Blessed are those who mourn, for they shall be comforted." **(Matthew 5:4)**

Day 174

DEAR GOD, I PRAY TO BE RESPECTFUL ...

We were given the opportunity to take the ferry to the island of Savai'i. It's the biggest island of Samoa but less developed than Western Samoa. The boat ride there was about an hour. It was a lot of swaying back and forth. We went to visit a family of believers. They had prepared for us. We went into their home and sat down on the ground and talked. We got up and went into the kitchen for lunch. I had no idea what was served that day. The meal was a greenish color soup with bones sticking out of it. It was served in a bowl. I like to think it was their version of chicken noodle soup without the noodles. I didn't want to disrespect the host family. I prayed for my life and for the strength to stomach the lunch. If that wasn't enough, I looked up to see children staring at us through a screen door. I realized later that they were waiting for us to finish eating so they could eat. It was their culture for the adults to eat first and the children to eat when they were done. I wanted to invite the children in and let them join us for lunch. However, I wasn't there to change traditions but to encourage and teach. They were more receptive to what we had to say because of our willingness to respect their cultural traditions. We are not called to change traditions if they are not against the Scriptures. We are called to love and respect our differences and share what we have in common through Christ.

DEAR LORD, I REALIZE NOT EVERYONE LIVES THE SAME WAY AS ME ...

1. Pray to God to seek the good of others through your differences.
2. Pray to God, thankful that in all our differences, we are united in Jesus Christ.

> *"... just as I also please all men in all things, not seeking my own profit, but the profit of many, that they may be saved."* **(1 Corinthians 10:33)**

Day 175

DEAR GOD, I PRAY TO BE CONTENT ...

Can you ever do enough to be satisfied? Can you ever have enough to be satisfied? I believe satisfaction is a mirage if it's in things and circumstances. We hear of people with homes full of stuff who are still unhappy. We read of people with extreme wealth who are not satisfied by it. I believe contentment is not based on our circumstances. It comes from within us and not outside of us. In Acts 16, we read of Paul and Silas, who were bound in the inner prison with their feet fastened in stocks. How did they get there? They had been in prayer, and Paul helped the servant girl remove the spirit from her. The town was upset and had them beaten and placed into the inner dungeon. If contentment is based on circumstances, Paul and Silas should have been upset and mad at God. What did they do? "But at midnight Paul and Silas were praying and singing hymns to God, and the prisoners were listening to them" (Acts 16:25). Their singing in the midst of a terrible circumstance shows that contentment is from within. What about us? We focus our attention on our jobs, health, relationships, children's behavior, physical appearance, and so on. *If this would just change, my life would be better.* We see through this story how contentment is more powerful than a change of circumstances. This is why we must get right the greatest commandment: to love God with our whole being.

DEAR LORD, I WILL NOT BASE MY LIFE ON THE CHANGES AROUND ME ...

1. Pray to God to have a love for Him that is greater than the changes in your life.
2. Pray to God for the wisdom to see from within rather than outside of you.

> *"Do not lay up for yourselves treasures on earth, where moth and rust destroy and where thieves break in and steal; but lay up for yourselves treasures in heaven."* **(Matthew 6:19-21)**

Day 176

DEAR GOD, I CANNOT PUT SINS INTO CATEGORIES ...

"How can I forgive that person?" I've gotten that question many times. I had someone tell me that a member of their family had taken advantage of them when they were younger. It made me sick at first to hear that. It made me angry too. I wanted to go to the person and punish them for what had been done years ago. I realized there are other ways that are better for me. The person struggled with forgiveness because the awful memory was still there. "And forgive us our debts, as we forgive our debtors" (Matthew 6:12). We must forgive so that we can deny that individual the power to hurt us. The more we hold on to it, the stronger the individual becomes in our lives. We must look to our own forgiveness because of the love shown by Jesus on the cross. It helps to know that I too nailed Jesus on the cross because I'm a sinner. We need to confess to God in words and feelings our anger, bitterness, insecurity, and hurt. God wants to heal our wounds, but He wants us to tell Him. It helps to tell Him how we feel. We need to lay down any ideas of retaliation by recognizing that only God has the authority to judge each of us. This helps us in knowing that God will handle the situation for us. I'm so thankful that God will be the last word and the last one to settle all debts and accounts.

DEAR LORD, I NEED TO REALIZE THAT ALL SIN HAS THE SAME RESULT ...

1. Pray to God with humility for forgiveness and to forgive all others in your life.
2. Pray to God for a better understanding of what forgiveness is and what it does for us.

> *"For if you forgive men their trespasses, your heavenly Father will also forgive you. But if you do not forgive men their trespasses, neither will your Father forgive your trespasses."* **(Matthew 6:14-15)**

Day 177

DEAR GOD, I LOOK TO YOU AS MY REWARD ...

It seems you can't go anywhere without someone offering a reward card. You purchase six fountain drinks, and you get the seventh one free. You buy ten meals and get the eleventh half off. You spend a certain amount at a store and receive a cash coupon redeemable on the next purchase. Let me not forget those magical power numbers in hopes of millions of dollars. We live in a reward-crazed culture. Are these really rewards? Are you living your life for that free cup of coffee or oil change? What if I told you of a great reward not contingent on numbers, purchases, or stamped cards? It is the reward that exceeds all others because He lives and abides forever. Would you be interested? The Lord came to Abram in a vision. The Lord said, "Do not be afraid, Abram. I am your shield, your exceedingly great reward" (Genesis 15:1). Did you catch that? The Lord referred to Himself as a "great reward." Have you ever thought about God being the reward? The relationship we have with God far exceeds any dollar amount or gift. He is the source of all that is good and right. He is the beginning and the end. He is the great I AM. It's all about God. There is no greater gift than the knowledge and relationship we can have in God.

DEAR LORD, ALLOW ME NOT TO GET DISTRACTED WITH THE TEMPORARY ...

1. Pray to God, thankful for what you know about Him through the Word and world.
2. Pray to God to keep your priorities in the right place with Him being first.

"And whatever you do, do it heartily, as to the Lord and not to men, knowing that from the Lord you will receive the reward of the inheritance; for you serve the Lord Christ." **(Colossians 3:23-24)**

DEAR GOD, I NEED YOUR HELP FOR THE MESS I'M IN ...

When our youngest son was little, he loved to pretend like he was cooking. He wanted to be like his mom. He took out all of the pots and pans and placed them on the coffee table. He dumped his Cheerios into the pots and stirred them with a spoon. When he finished, the pots and pans were everywhere. I found Cheerios lying around for a week. What a mess! Some messes cannot be fixed with wipes, a vacuum, or a mop. It takes something much more than what we can do. David was a man after God's own heart. However, he was not immune from creating a mess. What a mess he made with Bathsheba! David tried to clean it up himself, but it cost the life of Uriah. Nathan's parable caused David to see the only solution to the mess he had made. "So David said to Nathan, 'I have sinned against the Lord'" (2 Samuel 12:13). Messes can leave their mark. David suffered the consequences of his actions, but he was forgiven. God created in him a clean heart. We can get ourselves in some real messes. It is important to know where to go when we find ourselves in a mess. God cares for you. He is willing to cleanse as long as we are willing to come to Him. What a Savior!

DEAR LORD, I AM THANKFUL FOR THE MERCY OF BEING FORGIVEN ...

1. Pray to God to help you lay your pride aside and admit when you're wrong.
2. Pray to God to help you be more tolerant with others because all have sinned.

"... casting all your care upon Him, for He cares for you." **(1 Peter 5:7)**

DEAR GOD, HELP ME TO BE AWARE ...

Have you experienced less than enough? I've never been unable to buy diapers for my children when they were babies. I don't know what it is like not to sleep in a bed. I cannot imagine not knowing where tomorrow's meal will be. I'm able to buy the necessities at the grocery store. We may feel like we have less. I imagine we all have thoughts when it comes to having less than enough. What does God think about it? Jesus considered daily bread as enough. Have you had more than bread today? Jesus mentioned someone with less than enough. His name was Lazarus, and he was a beggar full of sores. He was so poor that he was dependent upon others. This was someone with less than enough to God. A neighbor who had more than enough was aware of Lazarus' needs. Lazarus desired to eat the crumbs that fell from the man's table. What does that say about me? Do you own clothes that haven't been worn in a long while? Have you thrown away dated food? We may think we have less than enough, but chances are we have more. Could others benefit from my extras? When you have a banquet, make a habit of inviting those who can't return the favor. Pure religion includes serving those with less than enough. God's love is best expressed when we serve those who have less.

DEAR LORD, FORGIVE ME WHEN I FOCUS ON WANTS RATHER THAN NEEDS ...

1. Pray to God to open your eyes and heart to the needs of those around you.
2. Pray to God with the desire to serve Him by serving others with the blessings He has given you.

> *"But whoever has this world's goods, and sees his brother in need, and shuts up his heart from him, how does the love of God abide in him?"* (1 John 3:17)

Day 180

DEAR GOD, GIVE ME WISDOM AND STRENGTH ...

A four-year-old girl was read the story of Snow White for the first time. With wide-eyed excitement, she retold the story to her mother. After explaining how Prince Charming arrived and kissed Snow White back to life, the little girl asked her mother, "And do you know what happened next?" The mother replied, "Yes, they lived happily ever after." "No!", said the girl. "They got married." There is no relationship on earth that can bring you more grief or joy than a marriage. Marriage is more than the joining of two lives. Each person brings a unique background and personality into the marriage. Every couple has lived a life prior to the marriage. Their expectations and perspectives of marriage are what they received at home. When marriage becomes difficult, people think that divorce is the cure. Marriage is not a disease but a relationship of two people. If someone is not good at a relationship, divorce will not make it better. The problem is not so much the person but the behavior. I believe marriage is like two streams coming together. What happens when two streams collide? The water is choppy, muddy, and active. As you follow that newly formed river, it becomes one smooth, calm river. I know couples married so long that they know what the other is thinking and they finish each other's sentences. They have become one. Marriage gets better through work and time.

DEAR LORD, I THANK YOU FOR MARRIAGE ...

1. Pray to God for you to bless Him by your dedication to your marriage.
2. Pray to God that you don't run away from people-problems but do your part to work together.

"So then, they are no longer two but one flesh. Therefore what God has joined together, let not man separate." **(Matthew 19:6)**

Day 181

DEAR GOD, I DON'T LIKE THE BAD DAYS …

Have you ever been disappointed by your health? You have something planned, but your body keeps you from doing it. I was invited to speak in Knoxville at a college retreat. On the day I was supposed to leave, I felt awful. I knew by the way I felt that my sodium was low. I was scheduled to be the keynote speaker on Saturday morning and evening. It was Friday, and I felt bad. Many of the college kids whom I knew were excited to see me. They had worked hard in preparing and inviting for the spiritual retreat. My doctor and wife both told me no. My heart wanted to push it and go, but my brain said differently. I felt worse for letting the college students down than I did about my health. They were at an eager age of learning and taking in knowledge of God's Word. They were also young in the faith. They received an important lesson from me. You need to always be ready and prepared because sometimes things don't go according to plan. Sometimes the speaker gets sick and is admitted in the local hospital. I'm thankful that I stayed in the end. I was taken to the hospital and spent the time to adjust my fluid levels back to normal. Everything worked out for them and me. That is the real lesson. Sometimes life goes according to plan. Other times, it doesn't. In the end, it all works out for those who love God.

DEAR LORD, THANK YOU FOR THOSE WHO TELL ME WHAT I NEED TO HEAR …

1. Pray to God not to lose heart due to disappointments that are beyond your control.
2. Pray to God to focus more on the example of Jesus, who endured the death of the cross.

"Many are the afflictions of the righteous, but the Lord delivers him out of them all." (Psalm 34:19)

Day 182

DEAR GOD, I OFFER THIS PRAYER ON BEHALF OF ...

We can say, "I'm praying for you" and "You're in my prayers." It's encouraging to be on the receiving end of someone's prayer. When someone tells me "I've prayed for you," I feel great encouragement because my name has gone before God. It's a challenge to tell someone we are going to pray and forget about it. I'm guilty of doing that. I forget to pray about it, and I don't remember until I see that person again. I've learned to pray in the moment I'm told for that person. I don't want to neglect praying for the one asking. I believe in the practice of not only telling people that you prayed for them but what you prayed for. "I prayed for you last night that God may give you more strength in what you are facing right now." "I prayed that God will make Himself known to you more." How would you feel hearing what someone has prayed for you? This was Paul's practice. He not only prayed for them. He also mentioned what he said to God. "Therefore I ... do not cease to give thanks for you, making mention of you in my prayers: that the God of our Lord Jesus Christ, the Father of glory, may give to you the spirit of wisdom and revelation in the knowledge of Him" (Ephesians 1:15-17). He told them that he prayed for God to give them the Spirit of wisdom and revelation so they could know God better. What a great way to encourage each other!

DEAR LORD, I PRAY THAT THE ONE ON MY HEART MAY HAVE WISDOM TO UNDERSTAND ...

1. Pray to God for others to have a better understanding of the revelation of His Word.
2. Pray to God for others to have a better understanding of God.

> *"Therefore I exhort first of all that supplications, prayers, intercessions, and giving of thanks be made for all men."* **(1 Timothy 2:1)**

Day 183

DEAR GOD, I WANT YOU TO RECEIVE THE GLORY BY …

The Gospel of John gives us an insight into the night of Jesus' betrayal and arrest. We have the Lord's final discourse with His disciples before His arrest and death. In that time, He instituted His Supper. He informed the disciples that He was leaving them. He promised the Helper to come and bring to remembrance all that He had said to them. He closed it out with the Lord's Prayer. It's recorded in the seventeenth chapter of John. He opened this prayer with the words "Father, the hour has come" (John 17:1). The hour was the appointed time of Jesus' death, burial, and resurrection. The hour led Jesus to prayer. He prayed to glorify God through the work He would finish on earth. Each of us has our own hour. How we face it matters. Is it our will or God's that we ask to be done? Jesus prayed to be "glorified," which means "to praise, honor." What was He about to do? He was about to do the most selfless act known in history. He would be lifted up in horrible agony so that we could receive forgiveness. What Jesus asked was for the Father to be glorified. Jesus demonstrated humility during His hour on earth. He wanted God to be glorified through Him. What are you asking? What is your desire? Is it for you? Is it for the glory of God? There is nothing greater than our lives pointing to the glory of God. It begins in prayer.

DEAR LORD, I PRAY THAT I LIVE A LIFE THAT POINTS BACK TO JESUS …

1. Pray to God that it's not about you, and you need to live it.
2. Pray to God, thankful for the humility and sacrifice that Jesus showed in His hour.

"And whatever you ask in My name, that I will do, that the Father may be glorified in the Son." (John 14:13)

Day 184

DEAR GOD, THE UNCONDITIONAL LOVE YOU HAVE HELPS ME TO REPENT ...

On October 31, 1517, Martin Luther challenged the authorities of the church to debate his Ninety-five Theses, which he nailed to the door of the Castle Church in Wittenberg, Germany. Luther proposed a debate about indulgences. The practice of indulgences was doing good works or offering money in order to remove punishment for sin. Luther was displeased how indulgences encouraged people to pay for their forgiveness rather than repent. The first of the Ninety-five Theses was "When our Lord and Master Jesus Christ said, 'Repent' (Mt 4:17), he willed the entire life of believers to be one of repentance." Luther stressed that repentance is the way we make progress with God, not paying to be forgiven. The struggle of repentance continues to be a problem. It's not widely talked about or practiced. If done, it may be for the wrong reason. "I'm sorry because I got caught." We need to remember that none of us is good on our own. We desperately need to repent and be forgiven by God. Does God forgive begrudgingly? He forgives when we repent and confess because God is just. He is merciful and just to forgive because Jesus earned our acceptance. Jesus paid the ultimate debt by offering Himself as the payment. If we understand that and know we are loved, it makes it much easier to repent of our faults. What was needed in 1517 is still needed today!

DEAR LORD, I PRAY TO SEE THE NEED BECAUSE OF YOU TO REPENT ...

1. Pray to God to have the courage to do what you need to do to be forgiven.
2. Pray to God, thankful for the gracious gift of forgiveness.

"If anyone sins, we have an Advocate with the Father, Jesus Christ the righteous. And He Himself is the propitiation for our sins, and not for ours only but also for the whole world." **(1 John 2:1-2)**

Day 185

DEAR GOD, I'M MERELY A JAR OF CLAY ...

In early March of 2016, I was living life at a fast pace. I was on top of my teaching career and ministry. I was involved in multiple things from being on the board of an after-school program to participating in a school play. The last word in my vocabulary was no. I relied too much on my own ability to get through life. After the MRI in the emergency room, I asked the emergency room doctor if I could leave and come back Monday for the surgery. I had the play that weekend, and I needed to be there. I would drive up Monday to have major surgery. I got a strong no for that. My life today is totally different. I cannot go and do like I used to. I'm dependent on medicine. I'm reminded every day how life is weak and fragile. However, I'm more thankful for what I have learned. I've gained a better appreciation of humility. I'm more dependent on God than I was prior to multiple surgeries. If I'm honest with myself, I really was worshiping in the wrong direction. I loved God, but I also believed in myself. Instead of trusting in God's sovereignty, I looked to myself with the ability to get things accomplished. I'm still a work in progress. I'm still working on less of self and more of God. Have you ever questioned your relationship with God? You read your Bible and worship on Sunday. However, the majority of the week, you are leaning on your own understanding and ability. I learned a tough but valuable lesson. None of us is in control except one: God.

DEAR LORD, HELP ME TO OWN YOU MORE IN MY DAY-TO-DAY LIFE ...

1. Pray to God to demonstrate more in your life that God is God.
2. Pray to God to trust in Him more because only He is trustworthy.

"But we have this treasure in earthen vessels, that the excellence of the power may be of God and not of us." **(2 Corinthians 4:7)**

Day 186

DEAR GOD, I SEE HOW BIG YOU ARE WHEN ...

My longest roommate in college was from Sudbury, Canada. It is located in the province of Ontario. A group of us raised money to go there during our December break. The reason for our trip was to work with a local church. We rented a van and made the long trek to Sudbury. On the way, we drove through downtown Chicago around two o'clock in the morning. While in Sudbury, we learned some things about Canada. We have Starbucks, and they have Tim Hortons. We have dollars, and they have "loonies" and "toonies." We have the stars and stripes, and they have the maple leaf. We say "y'all," and they say "eh." The local church was so hospitable and gracious to us. We enjoyed getting to know the people there and learned about other places in the process. We can easily get stuck where we live so that we assume that is the way it is. God made this big, beautiful world. We have different places, different tongues, different ethnicities, different customs, and cultures. When I go somewhere else, I realize the scope of what Jesus said: "For God so loved the world that He gave His only begotten Son, that whoever believes in Him should not perish but have everlasting life" (John 3:16). God's love is so big that every country and citizen couldn't fill it up. Jesus died for the known world then and the world today. It doesn't matter your language, your skin color, or where you are from. God's love was demonstrated to us all through the sending of His only begotten Son.

DEAR LORD, IT'S AMAZING TO CONSIDER THE MAGNITUDE OF YOUR LOVE FOR US ...

1. Pray to God, thankful for the greatest sacrifice for us all.
2. Pray to God, thankful that the gift of Jesus Christ is not contingent upon race, nation, or wealth.

"For God did not send His Son into the world to condemn the world, but that the world through Him might be saved." (John 3:17)

DEAR GOD, THANK YOU FOR MEMORIES ...

We have a wonderful family tradition on Christmas Eve. My wife makes a wonderful meal. Her parents come to spend the evening with us. After eating, the boys, their mom, and their grandmother make sugar cookies for the man up north. They come into the living room for their granddaddy and father to sample. Like any child, our boys are on level ten of excitement. My wife's parents leave to go home and prepare for us coming the next day. We give the boys some time before putting them to bed. One of the last things we do is my traditional read of "The Night before Christmas." I found a picture that my wife took on Christmas Eve 2015. All three boys were looking intently on the same bed. Our oldest son had his hands folded together as if he was praying for Christmas morning. Our middle son was laid back against the wall, watching closely. Our youngest son was squeezing his stuffed animal in anticipation for Santa. I enjoy Christmas Eve traditions more than Christmas Day because of their excitement and anticipation for something to happen. We grow older, but our anticipation is for something greater. The last thing in our Bibles that Jesus said is "Surely I am coming quickly" (Revelation 22:20) Are we looking forward to that day when we will see Jesus as He is? Do we think about the greatest reunion with those who have gone on before us? May we live today with some anticipation that we are closer to heaven than ever before.

DEAR LORD, I PRAY TO LIVE IN ANTICIPATION EACH DAY OF HOW BLESSED I AM TO HAVE ...

1. Pray to God, thankful for the promise of Jesus' coming again.
2. Pray to God, thankful for knowing that the deaths of those you love are not the end.

> *"So Christ was offered once to bear the sins of many. To those who eagerly wait for Him He will appear a second time, apart from sin, for salvation."* **(Hebrews 9:28)**

Day 188

DEAR GOD, I NEED PATIENCE TO ENDURE ...

I was honored to see closure for the body of a fallen War World II pilot, who was found and brought back home. The pilot was from Middle Tennessee, and he was accepted to have been a navy pilot in 1942. He and two other pilots took off from the naval air base on the island of Oahu. During the training exercise, the pilot got separated from the other two. A crashed, burning plane was spotted on July 23, 1945. Almost three days later, a recovery party reached the still-smoking plane in rugged terrain. The recovery party buried the remains of an unidentified body. The parents of that deceased pilot started the process to bring his body back home on May 15, 1948. The story of bringing the body home would be bigger than his life. It would span over seventy years, the administrations of thirteen US presidents, and wars. The parents of the pilot did not see the return of their son's body. The pilot's niece took on the challenge to see an appropriate ending to this ordeal. With strong determination and the help of many, they were able to find and bring back the remains seventy years later. The burial service had highly decorated officers and an honor guard. The mayor of the city proclaimed the day in his honor. It was a great end to years and decades of persevering. I see the parallel with this story and our lives in Christ. We must endure each day and persevere to the end. There are no shortcuts or immediate rewards to Christian living. It's day-to-day faithfulness and dedication.

DEAR LORD, HELP ME TO PERSEVERE ...

1. Pray to God, asking for forgiveness when you grow impatient.
2. Pray to God for a strong determination to endure days, experiences, and events for Him.

> *"For you have need of endurance, so that after you have done the will of God, you may receive the promise."* **(Hebrews 10:36)**

Day 189

DEAR GOD, I NEED TO GIVE MORE THOUGHT ...

I will never, never do that again. I remember early in my ministry that I felt like I wanted my faith to be tested. I wanted to prove myself even more to God. I was in the auditorium of the church building where I had preached at the time. It was during the week, and I was alone with God. I prayed for my faith to be challenged so that I could grow more. I cannot stress this enough: be careful what you pray for. Several months later, I was hit with an extreme issue. I struggled mentally. I don't blame God for it. I wanted to cave in because of how heavy it was. I confided in a friend with my struggle. He listened as I wept openly about my problem. I was a wreck. I lost weight, and I dreaded the nights when I struggled to sleep. I prayed as if my life depended upon it. Thankfully, through prayers and support, I gradually overcame the problem. It took months, and I still think about it sometimes. I go back to that prayer that I foolishly prayed. What I said was not the problem. How I said it was. I did so with complete confidence in myself. I was so arrogant and foolish. I was younger and believed that I could endure almost anything. We should be careful with what we say and how we say it to God. We are talking to an eternal God who knows us better than we do. Whatever the situation, we need to keep our eyes on God.

DEAR LORD, I REALIZE THE EVIL ONE IS LOOKING TO BRING US DOWN ...

1. Pray to God, asking for forgiveness when you seem independent of Him.
2. Pray to God, humbly approaching His awesome throne and recognizing your weaknesses before His strengths.

> *"Humble yourselves in the sight of the Lord, and He will lift you up."* **(James 4:10)**

Day 190

DEAR GOD, IT SHOULD BE AN HONOR TO PRAISE AND GLORIFY ...

Isaiah prophesied, "Therefore the Lord Himself will give you a sign: Behold, the virgin shall conceive and bear a Son, and shall call His name Immanuel" (7:14). By the time of Mary and Joseph, it had been a long time since this writing. For over seven hundred years, there was no sign from the Lord. Then it happened. It happened at a time far removed from the prophecy that was long-forgotten by many. God sent Gabriel to a city of Galilee named Nazareth, where Mary lived. This heavenly announcement changed Mary and the world forever. What would Mary say to us today? Would she be astonished how little we praise and honor the Son of God? Mary was so moved by the news that it led her to worship. The birth, life, death, and resurrection of Jesus should move us to worship. This alone should get us out of bed and prepare us to assemble with God's people as we honor and glorify Him. If we only think of Jesus during this time because of the giving and receiving of gifts, we have missed the boat. Those touched by the birth of Jesus were led to worship. Those touched by His ministry were led to worship. Those touched by His death and resurrection were led to worship. Our response should be no different.

DEAR LORD, I EMBRACE THE BLESSING OF WORSHIP ...

1. Pray to God, thankful that you have reason to sing and praise because of the life of Christ.
2. Pray to God, thankful to worship God with your lips and heart among God's people.

> *"God is Spirit, and those who worship Him must worship in spirit and truth."* (John 4:24)

Day 191

DEAR GOD, THANK YOU FOR THE LIFE I LIVE ...

I find each year that the holiday of Thanksgiving is celebrated less and less. It seems that Black Friday is quickly erasing Thanksgiving. There is the parade on television, a meal, and some football. However, many are strategizing their shopping route for Thanksgiving night and into Black Friday on that day. If other things are taking over a day proclaimed in 1789 to be thankful, we can easily allow other days to distract us from being appreciative and thankful. Did you know that giving thanks is the will of God? "In everything give thanks; for this is the will of God in Christ Jesus for you" (1 Thessalonians 5:18). How many thank-yous have you heard this week? Is our reason for giving thanks based on our circumstances? Only ten percent gave thanks to Jesus. That ten percent was one out of ten lepers. All were sick. All were healed. All but one went on living as if they had never been sick. Would the percentage be higher among ten patients healed by doctors? Would the percentage be greater for ten civilians rescued in war? Are we good enough to remember the disease of sin and how good it feels to be cleansed? Paul stated, "In everything give thanks." This includes the good times and bad. We are to give thanks in every situation and circumstance. Be thankful on Thanksgiving. Be thankful on Black Friday. Be thankful for every day because of Jesus Christ.

DEAR LORD, MY REASON TO SAY THANKS IS NOT BECAUSE OF MY CIRCUMSTANCES ...

1. Pray to God to be more thankful for the life you have in Christ.
2. Pray to God to help you go through today being appreciative and grateful.

"Oh, give thanks to the Lord, for He is good! For His mercy endures forever." (Psalm 107:1)

Day 192

DEAR GOD, I STRUGGLE WITH WHAT I SEE ...

I find it difficult to observe someone not having a basic need met. I want to do something about it when I see it. I was on a service trip to New York City through a school. We served at various food pantries and soup kitchens. We had finished serving at a food pantry in Coney Island when we saw someone digging through a trash can for food. Someone from our group gave some food to the hungry person. He was appreciative of the food. We went about our way and turned around to see him digging in another trash can. He had no shame. He was digging in public for others to see. His concern was not an audience. He was hungry, and food was his concern. It's difficult to imagine being so hungry that I'm digging in a public trash can for anything to eat. I believe the smell alone would be enough to drive my hunger away. I struggle with life problems that are too big for me to fix on my own. I'm reminded of Jesus coming into a world that was plagued with problems. When He ascended into heaven, the problem of hunger, shelter, and sin was still here. The harvest has always been plentiful. I realized even more as we walked away from him digging in the trash can that our help was so limited. It didn't solve his problem. The only one I know who can solve the problems of this life is Christ. It starts and builds with Christ, but it continues with the church and community. I cannot fix everything, but I can do something.

DEAR LORD, HELP ME TO BE MORE LIKE THE SAMARITAN ...

1. Pray to God to be open and active to do what you can for the needs of others.
2. Pray to God that your community can be more involved in making sure basic needs are met.

> *"For the poor will never cease from the land; therefore I command you, saying, 'You shall open your hand wide to your brother, to your poor and your needy, in your land.'"* **(Deuteronomy 15:11)**

Day 193

DEAR LORD, HELP ME TO LISTEN BETTER ...

It took me several years to listen to my body. I'm still a work in progress. I was used to getting up and running through life without giving much thought prior to my first surgery. The complications that came from multiple surgeries forced me to listen to my body. I ended up back in the hospital because I failed to listen to my body many times. I pushed myself too far, thinking that I could do it. I believe the most difficult part of any type of health condition is the recovery time. It takes a lot of patience to go through a recovery. The recovery process goes against our fast-speed, drive-through culture. We want to get better as quickly as possible. It's frustrating to take months and years to figure out what the new normal is. Our bodies speak to us when we are tired, hungry, thirsty, or have done too much. What if we listened to our bodies better? What if we stopped to address the need at that time? What if we all did a better job of listening to and taking care of the one body God gave us? How can we do better when it comes to listening to what is important? It takes time, a positive attitude, and constant prayer. I cannot think of any recovery where prayer and God should not be involved.

DEAR LORD, I NEED YOUR HELP WHEN IT COMES TO LISTENING IN MY LIFE ...

1. Pray to God that even though you cannot change yesterday, you can change today when it comes to hearing Him.
2. Pray to God for the right measure of patience to endure the day as you recover.

"My son, give attention to my words; incline your ear to my sayings. Do not let them depart from your eyes; keep them in the midst of your heart; for they are life to those who find them, and health to all their flesh." **(Proverbs 4:20-22)**

Day 194

DEAR GOD, HELP ME TO KNOW YOU ENOUGH TO GIVE ...

I called a family friend a day after he had served his time in prison and a halfway house. He was thankful to be done and had a newness of life. He shared with me what he experienced while in prison. He said that several inmates are religious. However, many are angry and question God and Jesus. My friend was shocked by the number of people who denied the Sonship of Jesus Christ. While in prison, he was questioned by another inmate whether Jesus was the Son of God. He said he didn't know how to answer him. It bothered him that he couldn't answer him. He wants to learn how to help others know that Jesus is Lord. I was encouraged by his passion for the Lord. I pray the devil doesn't quench his passion for Christ. "But sanctify the Lord God in your hearts, and always be ready to give a defense to everyone who asks you a reason for the hope that is in you, with meekness and fear" (1 Peter 3:15). Do you love the Lord enough to explain it to someone who has a question? Can you provide an answer as to why you believe what you believe? Can you answer how Jesus is the Son of God? My conversation with my friend made me question myself. There will be moments in our lives when someone may question what we believe.

DEAR LORD, I PRAY THAT MY FRIEND'S PASSION DOESN'T DIE OUT ...

1. Pray to God that you, too, can be zealous for Him.
2. Pray to God to be ready to provide a biblical answer to those who ask.

"And this is eternal life, that they may know You, the only true God, and Jesus Christ whom You have sent." (John 17:3)

DEAR GOD, I'M HUMBLED BY JESUS' DEATH WHILE WE WERE SINNERS ...

A family set their hearts to adopt a troubled teenage girl. The girl was destructive, disobedient, and dishonest. One day, she came home from school and ransacked the house looking for money. The father came home to see the girl gone and the house in shambles. Friends urged the couple not to finalize the adoption. "Let her go," they said. "She is not your daughter." The couple responded, "We know. But we told her she was." God made a covenant to adopt us. This covenant doesn't become invalid in our rebellion. It's one thing for God to love us when we are strong, courageous, and obedient. It's another to love us while we are sinners. "But God demonstrates His own love toward us, in that while we were still sinners, Christ died for us" (Romans 5:8). God didn't say, "Christ will die for you when you deserve it." God's love goes beyond our finest hours and failures. We represent that rebellious girl. We've been adopted, but we continue in sin. We need to remember the love that died in our place. His love saved us even when we didn't deserve it. His love provided a way to be completely forgiven. His love demands us to surrender our will to His. His love calls on us to follow in His steps. We realize what God could have done to us. However, He loved us enough to save us from ourselves. Don't let your day get you down. You are loved by God.

DEAR LORD, I'M GRATEFUL FOR YOUR LOVE EVEN WHEN I FALL SHORT ...

1. Pray to God to be more understanding of those you love.
2. Pray to God to help you demonstrate your love in return through your faithfulness.

> *"And now abide faith, hope, love, these three; but the greatest of these is love."* **(1 Corinthians 13:13)**

Day 196

DEAR GOD, HELP ME TO TAKE BACK MY DAY BY SEEKING YOU FIRST ...

All around us, we see frustrated couples, exhausted workers, and families juggling multiple schedules. It's no different than a hamster in a wheel. We exert all this energy in a day for what? Life records the passing of years on our faces and in our bodies. It passes too quickly to waste any portion of it. We must manage today better by making the most of our time. If we want to change, it begins with today. What should we make sure to do today? We need to make time for God today. If we are too busy for God, we are too busy. I sometimes wonder what we mean by "too busy." Are we busy with the distractions we engage in each day? I'm not too busy to use my phone for recreational use each day. I'm not too busy to watch my shows or a game. I'm not too busy to do what I want to do each day. We need to reevaluate our priorities and eliminate the excess of our days. Jesus helps us with what we should do today. He said, "But seek first the kingdom of God and His righteousness, and all these things shall be added to you" (Matthew 6:33). Ask yourself, "Are all the activities that scream for my time really important?" Are you missing a "burning-bush moment" by keeping your chores in order? We cannot do everything we want to do in a day. We can do the things God expects us to do. He asked for us to seek Him first.

DEAR LORD, HELP ME TO REALIZE YOU HAVE GIVEN US ENOUGH TIME ...

1. Pray to God for help to change some habits in your day.
2. Pray to God for strength to make better use of your day.

"Therefore, as the Holy Spirit says: 'Today, if you will hear His voice.'" **(Hebrews 3:7)**

Day 197

DEAR GOD, GIVE US THE STRENGTH TO KEEP YOUR WORD TODAY ...

Many years ago, a professional football game was canceled due to weather. The football field was covered with five inches of snow, and the forecast called for more accumulation. The governor of the state was upset that it was canceled. He commented that the country had become too soft. I realize the comment was over a game of football, but have we grown too soft? Are we soft when it comes to morality and Christianity? Are we living courageously? The Word of God has called us to be strong and courageous. "Have I not commanded you? Be strong and of good courage; do not be afraid, nor be dismayed, for the LORD your God is with you wherever you go" (Joshua 1:9). The book of Joshua begins with God. He was commanding His newly appointed leader, Joshua. A successful campaign starts with the word of God. God commissioned Joshua to go to the land He was giving them. The land of Canaan was God's gift to His people. Most of the land remained to be taken, but God had already given it to them. In a way, Israel possessed the deed to the land. They were waiting for God's word to proceed. The key to a successful life is to be faithful to the word of God. It requires strength. It also requires courage. Life can be tough and unbearable sometimes. We need the strength to endure and lean on our faith to overcome the day.

DEAR LORD, THANK YOU FOR YOUR PRESENCE ...

1. Pray to God to be like Joshua—strong and courageous as you battle through this day.
2. Pray to God to be led by the Holy Spirit this day by the Word.

> *"Only be strong and very courageous, that you may observe to do according to all the law which Moses My servant commanded you."* (Joshua 1:7)

Day 198

DEAR GOD, THANK YOU FOR THE MEMORIES BUT HELP US TO ...

I came across some pictures of playing Thomas the Train with my oldest son when he was three years old. He loved Thomas. We had the shows, trains, and tracks, and we could sing the opening song: "They're two they're four they're six and eight, shunting trucks and hauling freight ..." Our son was so precise about setting up the track on our cedar chest. He had certain engines doing different things. I tried to play with one of the engines, but he corrected me. I remember listening on CD to show after show from the library in the car. Everywhere we went was Thomas. If we were visiting family, we packed the car and prepared the trip with a Thomas fest of almost every episode on audio. I was driving down the interstate listening to Thomas, Percy, Henry, and Sir Topham Hatt. At the time, I was sick of Thomas and wished for this stage to be over. Now, I look back, missing that phase of life. Why do we wish for things to pass when we later want them back? We can easily wish our lives away before we realize we don't have much of it left. Today will be over before we know it. We need to embrace every stage and moment we have. We need to give every day and moment a chance. Each day deserves it. Today, I'm wishing to be back in 2009 playing Thomas with my oldest son. That day is only a memory. I can't go back. I can focus on today and be thankful for the moments I have in it.

DEAR LORD, WE CANNOT GO BACK, BUT WE CAN TAKE ADVANTAGE OF THE PRESENT ...

1. Pray to God to continue to make memories with family.
2. Pray to God to better appreciate all moments and phases of life.

> *"Let the peace of God rule in your hearts, to which also you were called in one body; and be thankful."* **(Colossians 3:15)**

Day 199

DEAR GOD, I FIND MYSELF NOT KNOWING WHAT TO SAY ...

The hard times in our lives can sometimes hit in waves. I have two good friends to tell me at different times of someone close to them who lost a young baby. They wanted me to pray for the families and the situations. I'm thankful to them for allowing me to pray. How do I pray? "Dear God, thank You for Your goodness and greatness and being with these families." "Dear God, thank You for answered prayers." Both prayers are true, but the timing doesn't sound right. It's difficult to pray about all the wonderful things about God when we are hit hard by life. It's not God's fault. It's hard not to speak out when we are questioning why and hurting. I struggle to read the third chapter of Job. He endured more than anyone I know. He lost his ten children at once. Job spoke harshly about how he felt. He cursed the day He was born. I cannot imagine the trouble of Job and the trouble of others whom I hear about and see in my lifetime. Job was calling out because his three friends heard him. They were offended by his words. They should have been more focused on what Job had been through rather than what Job said. I'm so thankful for God's patience in those moments of prayer when our feelings are raw because of the brokenness of this life. Am I patient enough to hear people in their suffering?

DEAR LORD, I'M HURT WITH THOSE WHO GO THROUGH HARD SITUATIONS ...

1. Pray to God, thankful for His patience as you work through your feelings in difficult times.
2. Pray to God for the Holy Spirit to help you with your words in those vulnerable times.

"For we do not know what we should pray for as we ought, but the Spirit Himself makes intercession for us with groanings which cannot be uttered." **(Romans 8:26)**

Day 200

DEAR GOD, PEOPLE ARE FULL OF ANSWERS, BUT MAY WE SEEK YOUR WORD ...

I want to challenge my students, as a teacher, in areas of life that go beyond the classroom. I sometimes ask a question that challenges their sense of following directions. On a history test, I had a question asking them to circle the number twenty-five and stand up to tell me the answer to two plus two. I could see some of them look at me when they came to that question. I specifically said in the directions that you cannot come and ask me, or it will not count. All it took was one brave soul to stand up and say "four." It was a female student, and she bravely stood up by herself and said "four." She quickly sat back down. Several students looked around with a confused look on their faces. I could easily read their nonverbal communication. "What is going on?" "What just happened?" Then, it happened. It was a chain reaction of "fours" throughout the room. They were almost harmonious in following directions. How well do you follow directions? How many times do we buy a product and only use the manual if we get stuck putting it together? Do we get to a point in God's Word where we struggle to follow the directions? We love God, but not with all of our heart. We want to follow Christ, but we are not willing to fully surrender ourselves by taking up our crosses and following Him. In life and especially in matters of salvation, always read the directions.

DEAR LORD, YOU KNOW WHAT IS BEST ...

1. Pray to God to be more diligent in your time and effort in knowing His directions.
2. Pray to God to be faithful to Him by being faithful to His words.

"Be diligent to present yourself approved to God, a worker who does not need to be ashamed, rightly dividing the word of truth." **(2 Timothy 2:15)**

DEAR GOD, I THANK YOU FOR THE NEWNESS OF EACH DAY AND YEAR ...

New York City has a fairly new tradition called "Good Riddance Day." It takes place in Times Square and involves a giant shredder. On the selected day, people from all over the city bring something to shred. One person brought all the negativity she experienced throughout the year. Another person carried a large shoulder bag stuffed with medical bills and bank statements. One woman shredded a pushcart full of old personal records. When asked why, she said, "I'm here to shred my whole life and start fresh." There is something irresistible about saying goodbye to the past and welcoming the present. Many people look for a way to start over. Despite all the traditions, rituals, and cleansing processes, every new year is the same. Everyone—rich and poor, famous and unknown—have exactly 1,440 minutes a day, 168 hours a week, and 8,760 hours in a year. Time is one of life's greatest values because when it's gone, it can never be recovered. Time is too slow for those who wait, too fast for those who fear, too long for those who grieve, and too short for those who rejoice. The truth about our lives is not found in the resolutions we make or good intentions. It's in the things we do day after day. What matters is what we choose to spend our time doing. Do we see the new year as an opportunity to know God better? Do we approach it with becoming more in love with Him?

DEAR LORD, WHAT MATTERS IS WHAT I DO ...

1. Pray to God to use the day you have wisely for Him.
2. Pray to God not to go through a day or year without knowing Him better.

"See then that you walk circumspectly, not as fools but as wise, redeeming the time, because the days are evil." **(Ephesians 5:15-16)**

Day 202

DEAR GOD, I'M HUMBLED THAT YOU ARE NOT ONLY MINDFUL OF ME ...

How would you respond if Jesus took off your shoes and began to wash your feet? I might feel unworthy and ask, "Why are You washing my feet?" I might say, "Please, You have served me too much. Let me give back to You." This is the heart of Christianity. God humbled Himself to serve and die for us. "The Son of Man did not come to be served, but to serve, and to give His life a ransom for many" (Matthew 20:28). God wants us to resemble His Son. Do we gather together looking to serve? We live busy lives, and many times we come already tired. We naturally want to come to rest and be fed spiritually. Imagine gathering with a group of people who were trying to out-serve one another. Have you ever been in a room filled with humble people who count others more significant than themselves? When servants gather together, everyone is built up. Why? We resemble the Son. It goes against the self-centered culture and world we live in. It goes against how most of us were brought up. We are used to having the attention or being the center of it. We like to be noticed and receive the praise. We are used to winning and receiving something. Now, we are called to serve, and the reward is to help someone else? When Jesus served His disciples, it stood out to them. If you stop receiving and start serving, it too will stand away from us and out to God.

DEAR LORD, I'M INDEBTED TO YOUR WILLINGNESS TO SERVE US ...

1. Pray to God that you can resemble Jesus more today by serving.
2. Pray to God for opportunities, no matter how big or small, when it comes to serving.

"For God is not unjust to forget your work and labor of love which you have shown toward His name, in that you have ministered to the saints, and do minister." **(Hebrews 6:10)**

Day 203

DEAR GOD, I STRUGGLE IN THE HARD TIMES ...

Have you received unfair treatment? Have you been at the end of unmerited misfortune? "For what credit is it if, when you are beaten for your faults, you take it patiently? But when you do good and suffer, if you take it patiently, this is commendable before God" (1 Peter 2:20). What is commendable before God? If we suffer for doing good, we need to be able to endure through it. Peter's words described Joseph's example in an Egyptian dungeon. Joseph was a young man with life all in front of him. The next moment, he was the property of some stranger named Potiphar. Joseph trusted God, and he found favor in the Lord and Potiphar. Then, he was falsely accused and placed in a dungeon. How would you feel? You do everything right, and the result is a nice spot in the dungeon. We can all agree that Joseph didn't deserve prison. What Joseph deserved is not the point. He endured it all for the good. He endured it for many years. The idea of what we deserve or don't deserve is not from God. There is no verse that says, "Follow Me, and you will get what you deserve in life." There is no immunity from life and its hardships. The point of following Christ is not to have shelter from all wrongdoings. The point is to be faithful, committed, and dedicated to following Him no matter what. I admire the Josephs of our day who continue to endure hardships of this life for the good.

DEAR LORD, HELP ME TO DO WHAT'S RIGHT ...

1. Pray to God to trust even more as you endure the times when you don't understand or have an answer.
2. Pray to God to be a support for those who struggle with life by your presence and prayers.

"The Lord was with Joseph and showed him mercy, and He gave him favor in the sight of the keeper of the prison." (Genesis 39:21)

Day 204

DEAR GOD, HELP ME TO LEARN THAT HOLDING ON ...

Have you ever messed up? I mean really messed up? In 2006, an airline made a slight mistake on its website. They advertised business-class seats from Toronto to the island of Cyprus for $39. The price was supposed to be $3,900 a ticket. An employee left off two zeros, and customers bought 2,000 tickets, costing the airline $7.7 million. Somebody messed up. Messes can be as simple as spilling a glass to something more complicated and costly like sin. The Bible doesn't sugarcoat sin. "If we say that we have no sin, we deceive ourselves, and the truth is not in us" (1 John 1:8). One of the most comforting qualities about Jesus is the way He pursued the outcast. He was willing to help anyone, even if they didn't realize they needed Him. Much like today. We have no use for Jesus unless we see the need. The Gospel of John provides the longest recorded conversation Jesus had with someone. Who was the person? It was a Samaritan woman in a mess with relationships. Jesus' encounter with the Samaritan woman changed her. Are you in a mess? Do you feel it's too big for God? Jesus showed through this encounter how far His grace and love could reach. I would encourage you to read John 4. It's a message of hope for us all who mess up one time or another.

DEAR LORD, I NEED TO SEE THAT JESUS CAN HELP ME ...

1. Pray to God to realize and accept His role as Lord and Savior.
2. Pray to God, confessing your faults and asking for God's mercy.

"In Him we have redemption through His blood, the forgiveness of sins, according to the riches of His grace." **(Ephesians 1:7)**

Day 205

DEAR GOD, THANK YOU FOR HELPING ME IN THOSE UNSPEAKABLE MOMENTS ...

Have you felt so overwhelmed that you didn't know what to pray? One of the hardest times in my early years in ministry was being with a family in intensive care after a bad car wreck. The family had a minivan, and it slammed into a telephone pole. The sliding door came unhinged, and it flew back and hit their five-year-old daughter. I saw her all beaten and bruised in intensive care. We prayed and prayed for her to pull through. She didn't make it. I was asked to do the funeral. I barely got through before falling apart emotionally. It was overwhelming. There are times when "we do not know what we should pray for" (Romans 8:26). Praise be to God for the Holy Spirit to help us. When our human understanding and vocabulary are insufficient, the Holy Spirit intercedes with unspeakable language. The Holy Spirit intercedes for us according to the will of God. He prays in line with God's plan and purpose. The Holy Spirit intercedes from the heart. We pray to God through Jesus with the help of the Holy Spirit. He does so with wordless groans. In other words, it's too deep for words. Doesn't knowing all of this make praying more important? When we find ourselves in moments where we don't know what to say, we have the Holy Spirit to intercede for us when we pray.

DEAR LORD, I'M GRATEFUL FOR THE PARACLETE'S HELP IN OUR PRAYERS ...

1. Pray to God, thankful for the intercession of the Spirit and the mediation of the Savior.
2. Pray to God for help when you struggle with words and thoughts in unspeakable moments.

> *"Now He who searches the hearts knows what the mind of the Spirit is, because He makes intercession for the saints according to the will of God."* **(Romans 8:27)**

Day 206

DEAR GOD, I NEED TO LOOK BEYOND WHAT I SEE TO WHAT IT REALLY IS ...

I know it's fall when I hear the phrase "pumpkin spice." It seems each year we get more things that are pumpkin-spice flavored. There are pumpkin-spice ice cream sandwiches, pumpkin-spice almonds, pumpkin-spice Cheerios, pumpkin-spice doughnuts, and pumpkin-spice lattes. I'm afraid "pumpkin-spice flavored" does not mean a piece of pumpkin is used in the item. It is more of a concoction of natural and artificial flavors. They even use an ingredient to give the product that pumpkin-orange color. Isn't that advertising? When summer ends and the season of fall starts, we think of falling leaves, pumpkins, hayrides, and pumpkin spice. It doesn't have to be real pumpkin poured into the drink. It's the thought of drinking a pumpkin-spice latte. I wonder if we treat matters of life like that. We can easily say what we don't mean. It's not "I love you" but "I lust for you." It's not "I forgive you" but "I will hold on to it and bring it up again." It's not "sin" but "what makes me happy." There are several things that are subjective. You can like or dislike pumpkin-spice flavor. However, there are some things that are objective. What God calls wrong is wrong. Time doesn't make it right. People don't make it right. It's right or wrong because of God.

DEAR LORD, HELP ME TO HAVE A HEART THAT SEEKS YOUR RIGHTEOUSNESS ...

1. Pray to God to have a heart to discern right and wrong.
2. Pray to God to be loyal to His word in all matters of life and salvation.

"Woe to those who call evil good, and good evil; who put darkness for light, and light for darkness; who put bitter for sweet, and sweet for bitter!" **(Isaiah 5:20)**

Day 207

DEAR GOD, YOU ARE THE ONE TRUE LIGHT IN THIS DARK WORLD …

I was slowly losing my vision in my late thirties. I thought it was my age. I was reaching forty, and I needed glasses. We realized after failing several eye tests that my problem was not on the outside but the inside. An MRI showed a tumor pressing on my optic chiasm. The doctors believed it had been growing for about ten years. The first choice was to have surgery and remove the tumor in order to see. The second choice was to forgo the surgery and allow the tumor to take my vision. The thought of not seeing scared me. I thought about losing my vision and being unable to see my three boys. I wouldn't see how they looked as they grew older. I thought about not seeing my beautiful wife's smile and face. I gave up many things in order to see. I was used to seeing, and I didn't want to lose it. How much more are we willing to sacrifice for the true Light, Jesus Christ? John gave his life. He was sent by God to bear witness of the Light as a forerunner. He was beheaded because of a foolish birthday wish. Was his humiliating death in vain? No, he had the Light and was able to see through the darkness. He stands as a witness to the Light, Jesus Christ. We are to "walk in the light as He is in the light" (1 John 1:7). The Light is still shining! Can you see Him?

DEAR LORD, YOU ARE THE SOURCE OF ALL THAT IS GOOD AND HOLY …

1. Pray to God to give you the wisdom to see past your present problems to the glory of Him.
2. Pray to God to work on presenting your body, time, and life as a living sacrifice.

"Then Jesus spoke to them again, saying, 'I am the light of the world. He who follows Me shall not walk in darkness, but have the light of life.'" **(John 8:12)**

Day 208

DEAR GOD, I'M THANKFUL FOR YOUR CONSTANT PRESENCE IN MY EVER-CHANGING LIFE ...

I had a funeral for a woman who lived to be 107 years old. She was three weeks from turning 108. Can you imagine all the things she saw in the past century? When she was born, the president of the United States was William Taft, and there had been no World Wars. She was born in a rural part with no running water or electricity. She endured the Great Depression, World Wars, and eighteen presidents. As a baby, milk was nine cents, and eggs were thirty-three cents. I cannot imagine all the changes she experienced and endured in over a century of living. She lived through an ever-changing world. Some of the changes were for the good, and some for the bad. I cannot imagine what it was like for those living through the Great Depression. What about our country during the early years of both World Wars? It's easy for us to look in hindsight, but it's another thing for those who experienced it. How does a person endure all the changes and events for one hundred years? It requires faith. The world changed, but she remained faithful to God and His love. We cannot know what tomorrow will be, let alone one hundred years from now. What we can know is that God will be the same. He can be a constant presence in our lives if we let Him.

DEAR LORD, HELP ME TO SEEK YOU IN THE CONSTANT CHANGES OF THIS LIFE ...

1. Pray to God, thankful for the Word that never changes but abides forever.
2. Pray to God, thankful that time and changes don't change who He is.

> *"Jesus Christ is the same yesterday, today, and forever."* (Hebrews 13:8)

DEAR GOD, FORGIVE ME WHEN I GET PICKY ABOUT YOUR ANSWERS ...

A woman was watching her grandson play on the beach when a huge wave came in and swept him out to sea. She fell down on her knees and pleaded, "Please, God, save my only grandchild. Please, I beg You, bring him back." Suddenly, another wave came in and delivered the boy onto the beach, as good as new. The grandmother looked up to heaven and shouted, "He had a hat!" This fictitious story points to how ungrateful we can be if it's not how we want it. Our special order of coffee or constant requests to the server about our meal can easily spill into other areas of life. We forget about what God has already done and look to what God hasn't done for us. We can pray for God to help us find a job to provide for our family. We find a job, but it's not a high-paying job with a lot of benefits. We can pray for God to heal us, but we are not at 100 percent. Do we have high standards with God? We may not voice them, but we might feel that way. We want a child, but we want the child to be a specific gender. What about a healthy child? "And whatever you ask in My name, that I will do, that the Father may be glorified in the Son" (John 14:13). The point of asking is doing so "in My name." Christ is not giving us a blank check to get whatever we want. He doesn't want to be a genie. He wants to be Lord and Savior. Be thankful that we have access to God because of Jesus.

DEAR LORD, I NEED TO BE GRATEFUL FOR ALL THAT YOU DO FOR ME ...

1. Pray to God to have the faith to accept the answer He gives you.
2. Pray to God to be more grateful for what He has already done.

"Oh, that men would give thanks to the Lord for His goodness, and for His wonderful works to the children of men! For He satisfies the longing soul, and fills the hungry soul with goodness." **(Psalm 107:8-9)**

Day 210

DEAR GOD, I NEED THE STRENGTH TO STOP MY BUSY LIFE AND BE ...

In the days of creation, God worked to create this life that exists for us to see and explore. I'm still amazed by how little we know about creation. The sun is almost ninety-three million miles away. Light travels at 186,282 miles per second. At that speed, it takes light from the sun eight minutes and twenty seconds to reach the earth. The sun is that far away, yet we cannot look directly at it without squinting. We can easily get burned on a hot summer day if we are not slathered in sunblock. God created it all, and He rested on the seventh day. Does God get tired or worn out? I believe He rested for our benefit. The nation of Israel was commanded to remember the Sabbath and keep it holy because God rested. They were to rest from their work. How well do we rest? I don't mean going to sleep. I mean resting our bodies, minds, and spirits. We take vacations, but we come back more tired because we were on the move. Jesus spent time away from His busy schedule by going on the mountainside to pray all night. If God rested and Jesus took time to rest away from the craziness of life, how much more should we make the time to rest? I challenge you to make time for quiet moments to rest your mind and spirit from the day. Center your thoughts on God in that moment.

DEAR LORD, I NEED TO UNDERSTAND THE IMPORTANCE OF REST ...

1. Pray to God to help you seek time in your day to rest in Him and His Word.
2. Pray to God for strength to concentrate on Him and not allow the thoughts of this world to interfere.

"Be still, and know that I am God; I will be exalted among the nations, I will be exalted in the earth!" **(Psalm 46:10)**

Day 211

DEAR GOD, I CANNOT HIDE MY FEELINGS WITH YOU ...

I like to dress up. I don't mean a shirt, tie, and sports coat. I mean costumes with a mask. I spoke at an elementary chapel as a Jedi. I hid behind the curtains until my time to speak. I came out with my face covered by my robe. I was swinging my lightsaber around. The kids were watching intently. I jumped down from the stage and continued to swing my lightsaber as if I were fighting hundreds of Stormtroopers. If we are not careful, we can put on a mask without wearing a mask. We can pretend by our faces that everything is fine when our hearts are broken and hurting. We can have the appearance that everything is okay when we've been spreading things about someone because they hurt us. I believe we wear masks more than we think. We pretend to be happy when we are sad. We pretend to be okay when we are not. We pretend to be spiritual when we don't live it. The Greek word *hypokrites* means "an actor or stage player." It was used to refer to a Greek actor wearing a mask to play a character. The word took on a figurative meaning to refer to someone pretending to be something they were not. We know this word. It's hypocrite. Jesus condemned the practice of hypocrisy. He condemned pretending to be something that they were not. We need to examine ourselves. Am I transparent to God and others?

DEAR LORD, I PRAY TO LIVE WITH TRANSPARENCY ...

1. Pray to God to be genuine in heart and not to pretend to be something you are not.
2. Pray to God for the wisdom to use better judgment when it comes to your feelings.

"And when you pray, you shall not be like the hypocrites. For they love to pray standing in the synagogues and on the corners of the streets, that they may be seen by men. Assuredly, I say to you, they have their reward." **(Matthew 6:5)**

Day 212

DEAR GOD, I'M SCARED AND ANGRY ...

He was a Nazirite child living in the wilderness. His walls were the mountains, and the stars were his roof. That changed for John. His next home was a dingy, dark dungeon. He was a prisoner of the king. We can read what happened and think John deserved better treatment. He was in a cell because the king didn't like what John had to say. John was given a chance to ask Jesus a question while stuck in a cell. He heard the works of Christ, so he sent two of his disciples with the question, "Are You the Coming One, or do we look for another?" (Matthew 11:3). John was on death row, and Jesus was outside preaching, teaching, and healing. Is this what Messiahs do when trouble comes? We can relate to John's question. We face unwarranted attacks from others because of our faith, and we struggle to find God in it. "God, where are You in all of this?" Jesus sent a message back to John. He informed John that miraculous things were happening. The blind could see, the lame could walk, and the lepers were cleansed. It takes a Messiah to do that. The preaching and work continued even though one of His workers was unfairly locked up. Jesus wanted John to know that everything was going to God's plan. God cares about our situations and circumstances. Remember there are things far greater than our unpleasant moments. They are righteousness, salvation, and eternity.

DEAR LORD, WHY AM I FACING PERSECUTION ...

1. Pray to God to help you see Him for Him and not for someone that you want Him to be.
2. Pray to the Lord when you struggle with bad things happening to good people. Ask Him to help you remember what happened to Jesus.

> *"Blessed are you when they revile and persecute you, and say all kinds of evil against you falsely for My sake. Rejoice and be exceedingly glad, for great is your reward in heaven, for so they persecuted the prophets who were before you."* **(Matthew 5:11-12)**

Day 213

DEAR GOD, I PRAY TO LET GO ...

"Grudge" is one of those words that defines itself by the way it sounds. Say it slowly. It starts with a growl: "Grrrr!" It sounds like a bear waking up from hibernation. Don't you just love being around a person nursing a grudge? Aren't their words so delightful to hear? We know that the only things bubbling over are resentment and anger. If you remove the first and last two letters of the word "grudge" and add the letter "m," you have "mud." Mud is thrown with someone bearing a grudge. Their words are slung, names are called, circles are drawn, and characters are attacked. Let's say the person holding a grudge gets even. The person is able to get the person back. Will that free the person holding the grudge? "Blessed are the merciful, for they shall obtain mercy" (Matthew 5:7). The purpose of mercy is not to inflict pain but to relieve it. I believe mercy is forgiveness in action. It's getting what we don't deserve but what we desperately need. Mercy helps us see that our situations before God are no different from the person's we don't like. We both need a Savior to show mercy by forgiving us of our trespasses. My position of holding a grudge doesn't give me an advantage with God. We must be merciful to one another if we want God to show mercy to us. If someone hurts you, don't forget your situation with God.

DEAR LORD, FORGIVE ME FOR FORGETTING THE THINGS I HAVE DONE AGAINST YOU ...

1. Pray to God to give you the strength to squash resentment, bitterness, and anger with mercy.
2. Pray to God, thankful that mercy triumphs over judgment. Ask for help to remember that when showing mercy is difficult.

"For judgment is without mercy to the one who has shown no mercy. Mercy triumphs over judgment." (James 2:13)

Day 214

DEAR GOD, THERE IS NO OTHER WAY ...

A man was driving home from work when his wife called him on the phone. "Josh!" she shouted in a panic. "Please be careful! I just heard on the news that some lunatic is driving the wrong way on the interstate." "You won't believe it," he replied. "It's not just one car; it's hundreds of them!" There is a reason the direction of traffic is one-way. What happens if we disobey? We find ourselves in trouble by heading straight into another car. We understand this when it comes to driving. Do we understand when it comes to Jesus? "Jesus said to him, 'I am the way, the truth. and the life. No one comes to the Father except through me'" (John 14:6). Jesus said "the way." The definite article points to Jesus as the one way and not many ways. The one way to the Father is through Jesus. That way is not through you or me. It's not through a building. It's not through a certain location on earth. It's not through something that hasn't been revealed yet. It's through Jesus. I sometimes watch people in a busy place. Everyone is engaged and focused on where they are going. Everyone is going to different places in different directions. Some are talking to someone on the phone. A few are looking straight down at their phones. Others are speed-walking in hopes of getting there faster. Do we all realize that when it comes to the Father, there is only one way? It's through Jesus. I'm thankful that we have a way to go and for Jesus going that way for us.

DEAR LORD, I'M THANKFUL YOU PROVIDED A WAY ...

1. Pray to God to humbly obey His directions on how to go to Him even when you think you have a better way.
2. Pray to God to be watchful each day in checking to see where you are on the way to the Father.

> *"My foot has held fast to His steps; I have kept His way and not turned aside."* (Job 23:11)

Day 215

DEAR GOD, ENOUGH IS ENOUGH WHEN IT COMES TO ALL THIS STUFF ...

Enough. It's a complicated word. We use the word almost daily without thinking consciously about it. Do I have enough gas? Do I have enough money to go out to dinner and a movie? Do we understand "enough" when it comes to our stuff, finances, and daily schedule? How much house is enough? How much car is enough? How much money will be enough to make me feel secure? We can easily define "enough" when it comes to filling up our vehicles, but we struggle when it comes to filling up our lives. How do you know when you have enough? "Now godliness with contentment is great gain. For we brought nothing into this world, and it is certain we can carry nothing out. And having food and clothing, with these we shall be content" (1 Timothy 6:6-8). We brought nothing into this world, and we will carry nothing out when it comes to stuff. What is enough in-between our beginning and end? We are to be content with the basic necessities of food, clothing, and shelter. What if we have more than that? We shouldn't grumble or complain because we have more food, clothing, and shelter. We need to draw a line in our hearts and say enough is enough. "God, I have enough today, right now." Jesus modeled what we needed daily by praying, "Give us this day our daily bread" (Matthew 6:11). Be thankful for what you have, and remember the grass is not always greener on the other side.

DEAR LORD, I NEED STRENGTH TO BE CONTENT ...

1. Pray to God for the wisdom to see that in the end the only thing that matters is your relationship with Him.
2. Pray to God to be more thankful when you realize that you have more than enough and no reason to complain.

"I know how to be abased, and I know how to abound. Everywhere and in all things I have learned both to be full and to be hungry, both to abound and to suffer need. I can do all things through Christ who strengthens me." **(Philippians 4:12-13)**

Day 216

DEAR GOD, I CAN CHOOSE TO FORGIVE ...

Have you ever looked behind the celebrated day? Saint Patrick's Day is filled with parades, green-tinted rivers, green beer, and shamrocks. Who was Patrick? Patrick was born in Scotland. When he was sixteen, he was captured by raiders and became a slave in pagan Ireland. He was forced to tend to his master's sheep and spent six years in slavery and in prayer. He was able to escape and returned back home. When Patrick was in his forties, he went back to Ireland to teach about Christ. I have no idea what it's like to work as a slave for six years. I cannot imagine the horror he faced working for his master. If Patrick wanted to spread Christianity, he shouldn't have gone to the place that enslaved him. Patrick faced those demons as an adult with the help of the gospel. He went back to Ireland, and he was successful in spreading the good news. Many people were converted to Christianity. What a lesson for us to face our horrible pasts with the love of God! "Do not be overcome by evil, but overcome evil with good" (Romans 12:21). Patrick could have taken what happened to him and been bitter for the rest of his life. He could have chosen not to forgive. He could have overcome abduction with evil. He didn't. He chose to overcome evil with good. On a day known for drinking and partying, the real lesson is forgiveness and to overcome evil with good.

DEAR LORD, I CHOOSE FORGIVENESS BECAUSE OF YOUR EXAMPLE ...

1. Pray to God for the strength to seek what is right when wrong is done.
2. Pray to God for the mindfulness of those in history who chose good rather than evil.

> *"Beloved, do not avenge yourselves, but rather give place to wrath; for it is written 'Vengeance is Mine, I will repay,' says the Lord."* **(Romans 12:19)**

DEAR GOD, I'M AFRAID I WON'T HAVE ENOUGH TIME ...

Worry is informing you, through the news, that there is data breach in a chain of stores where you recently shopped. Worry thinks your child needs a bigger coat because the weather predicts the day will not be above freezing. Worry wakes you up at 4:30 a.m. Worry cannot go back to sleep, so worry climbs out of bed to get dressed and quietly slips out of the house in the dark to work at the office. "Therefore I say to you, do not worry about your life, what you will eat or what you will drink; nor about your body, what you will put on. Is not life more than food and the body more than clothing?" (Matthew 6:25). Do you fear running out of time, luck, or credit? Fear of running out is synonymous for worry. Worry won't fill a bird's belly with food or a flower's petal with color. We can dedicate the entire day with anxious thought to fear of running out, and we will not extend life by a single second. How can we better respond to worry today? Start with prayer and write down all your worries. Look and see if there are themes with the things you wrote down. Is the majority of your fear with life, finances, or performance? Place your energy into today and share with others when you start to look beyond the day. In everything, let God be enough. Ask for God's help and lean on Him more. Don't let worry rob you of the joy you can have today!

DEAR LORD, HELP ME COMBAT WORRY ...

1. Pray to God to focus on today and trust in Him.
2. Pray to God for forgiveness when you doubt His word or allow this world to overtake your knowledge of God.

"But seek first the kingdom of God and His righteousness, and all these things shall be added to you. Therefore do not worry about tomorrow, for tomorrow will worry about its own things. Sufficient for the day is its own trouble." **(Matthew 6:33-34)**

Day 218

DEAR GOD, HELP ME NOT TO LIVE IN FEAR ...

I remember when I was scared by something I watched at my grandmother's house. I was a young boy, and we were visiting her in Alabama. I remember calling out in fear, and my father came and sat in the room until I fell asleep. Imagine your whole life untouched by fear. What if faith, not fear, was your response to life? Do you know what Jesus' most common command was with fear? It's ahead of His commands to love. The commands about fear are mentioned over 60 percent more than "love God" and "love your neighbor as yourself." Jesus doesn't want us to live in fear, but neither do you. Fear may fill our world, but it doesn't have to reign in our hearts. We have Jesus' words and example. When Jesus was in the garden of Gethsemane, waiting for His betrayer and the arresting mob, He prayed. How do you face your worst-case scenario? Jesus was open about His feelings in His prayer to the Father. "And He said, 'Abba, Father, all things are possible for You. Take this cup away from Me; nevertheless, not what I will, but what You will'" (Mark 14:36). Prayer is the practice of placing our trust in God. It is also an opportunity to ask God. We can pray for God to "take this cup away." Our cup could be disease, betrayal, or conflict. Prayer equipped Jesus to stare down His worst-case scenario and fulfill God's will. Jesus was open about His cup. If we are open as well, it will help us to see the light of God. Don't react in fear, but respond in prayer and bring to light your cup before God.

DEAR LORD, I GIVE YOU MY CUP ...

1. Pray to God that His will, not yours, be done with your scenario.
2. Pray to God for a spirit of power and love and a healthy mind that is not compromised by fear.

"For God has not given us a spirit of fear, but of power and of love and of a sound mind." (2 Timothy 1:7)

DEAR GOD, I CAN EASILY LET MY SURROUNDINGS DEFINE YOU ...

There is a 125-foot statue of Jesus on top of a mountain in Rio de Janeiro, Brazil. The original idea for the statue came from a group of Brazilians during World War I. They feared an advanced tide of ungodliness, so they made the statue as a way of reclaiming the city. Do people standing around the statue really know "Christ the Redeemer"? Jesus has often been misunderstood. At the age of twelve, Jesus informed His parents of His real identity when they lost him. Jesus' hometown of Nazareth rejected Him. We can easily misunderstand Jesus by making Him into something He is not. Is the Jesus you're following of convenience or commitment? The only Jesus from the Scriptures is not a Savior that anyone made up. He contradicts, convicts, challenges, and transforms us into His image. We surrender to Him and not Jesus to us. We are the jars of clay made from the dust of the earth. What we believe about Jesus doesn't make Him who He is. If no one on earth believed in Jesus, He still would be the Son of the living God. We don't make Jesus. He didn't come to this world to live and die so that He could be a convenience for you. He came for us to deny ourselves and surrender all to follow Him. We live each day following the Jesus of the Scriptures and not of culture.

DEAR LORD, I NEED TO ALLOW YOUR WORDS TO PAINT THE PICTURE IN MY MIND ...

1. Pray to God for the strength to be transformed, not conformed, into His image.
2. Pray to God to forgive you for the times when you need Him out of convenience rather than an absolute need.

> *"Do not be conformed to this world, but be transformed by the renewing of your mind, that you may prove what is that good and acceptable and perfect will of God."* **(Romans 12:2)**

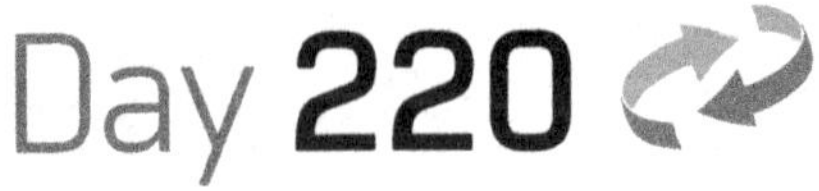

Day 220

DEAR GOD, IT'S MY FIRST DAY BACK AT WORK THIS WEEK, SO PLEASE HELP …

Don't you just love Monday? I do daily announcements at school and end them by telling the kids, "It's a Marvelous Monday, our favorite day of the week." I usually hear a lot of groans. I don't know if there is a single student or teacher who would say "Monday is my favorite day of the week." "Hello, Monday. May I ask you a question? Why are you here so quickly? Don't you have a hobby?" "If each day is a gift. I'd like to know where I can return Monday." Poor Monday. It doesn't have a chance with Friday, Saturday, or Sunday. Doesn't Monday deserve a chance? It's a chance for us to approach the day with a better attitude and perspective. A day to know how blessed we are to experience the day by doing something rather than be confined to a bed, unable to get out. We should use each Monday to be productive rather than waste it away. How would our week end if we began Monday grateful and thankful for it? When the alarm goes off on Monday morning, get up and read a verse from God's Word and pray that verse for your life. I find reading and praying helps direct my thoughts on what is positive. It helps my attitude as I walk out the door and into my car. "For every creature of God is good, and nothing is to be refused if it is received with thanksgiving" (1 Timothy 4:4). God created day and night. He gave us each day, including Monday. It would be a shame to go through it wishing it was over.

DEAR LORD, I'M GRATEFUL FOR MONDAY …

1. Pray to God to appreciate every day as a gift and to treasure it by glorifying God.
2. Pray to God for forgiveness for rushing through a day and not taking advantage of how you can love Him and others.

"Give thanks to the Lord, for He is good! For His mercy endures forever." (1 Chronicles 16:34)

Day 221

DEAR GOD, I PREPARE MYSELF TO WILLINGLY ACCEPT YOUR WILL ...

When I was in Western Samoa, I witnessed a Christian woman who had surrendered all. My friend and I stayed at the church building at night to sleep and shower. We noticed a hut in the back. It was simple—four posts with a roof. There were no doors, windows, or walls. It was a flat, wooden surface for someone to sit or lie down. We noticed a woman taking a small branch-like broom and sweeping the entire church building. We asked the missionary about her, and he told us her story. She was converted in a nearby village. The chief of the village banished her from her family and community because of her faith. She surrendered all. She gave up her family, heritage, and community. It cost her everything to follow Christ. She lived in the hut behind the church. She worked around the building and was given food as payment. She surrendered all by giving up her identity with her people to be a part of the people of God. The cost of surrendering all is not a catchy song, phrase, or T-shirt. It's totally and completely accepting the thoughts, ideas, teachings, and will of Jesus Christ. We no longer live for ourselves but for the One who lives within us. It requires devotion and, sometimes, comes at a great cost. It did for that godly woman who surrendered all. It's one thing to sing it. It's much different to live it out at any cost.

DEAR LORD, I SURRENDER ALL ...

1. Pray to God to love Him more than anything that keeps you from following Him.
2. Pray to God to know no other way but His way, will, thought, and teachings.

"I have been crucified with Christ; it is no longer I who live, but Christ lives in me; and the life which I now live in the flesh I live by faith in the Son of God, who loved me and gave Himself for me." **(Galatians 2:20)**

Day 222

DEAR GOD, HELP ME TO WAIT PATIENTLY ...

"Then it came to pass, at the end of two full years" (Genesis 41:1). What could you do for two full years? Could you work a terrible job, if the pay was right, for two full years? Could you be in a bad relationship for two full years? What about prison? Could you be an inmate for two full years in another country? This was Joseph. However, he didn't have a choice. I could do several things for two years, but prison is not one of them. I don't know what it's like an hour let alone a day in prison. Joseph was there because of mistreatment and false accusation. His brothers mistreated him by selling him to Midianite traders. Joseph had an opportunity to get out of an Egyptian dungeon. He interpreted the chief butler's dream. "Yet the chief butler did not remember Joseph, but forgot him" (Genesis 40:23). What about having to wait? I prefer doing something rather than waiting for someone. I don't like waiting. I go to my ten o'clock doctor appointment only to wait for another hour. We are waiting for our turn to order in the drive-through. We are waiting for the results of a test. We are waiting to turn sixteen to drive. We can all relate to waiting. How does this apply to "Now is the time"? Joseph shows us the need to trust in God and wait. I don't know what he thought about every day for two more years in prison. I do know that the Lord was with him. I don't know the answer to a lot of "why" questions. I do know that if God is for us, who can be against us? Sometimes we work. Other times we wait.

DEAR LORD, I STRUGGLE ...

1. Pray to God to wait on His timing in your life.
2. Pray to God to help you understand, like Joseph, that He knows the overall picture.

"Therefore be patient, brethren, until the coming of the Lord. See how the farmer waits for the precious fruit of the earth, waiting patiently for it until it receives the early and latter rain." (James 5:7)

DEAR GOD, I CANNOT DO WHAT CHRIST HAS DONE FOR US ...

"For I delivered to you first of all that which I also received: that Christ died for our sins according to the Scriptures, and that He was buried, and that He rose again the third day according to the Scriptures" (1 Corinthians 15:3-4). I don't think I'll forget one woman's response to realizing that her sins could be forgiven. She had been a slave to her addiction to drugs. She couldn't stop shaking from what her body had endured. She thought she had gone too far. We talked about forgiveness and the gracious act of Christ alone. He did what she and no one else could do. She realized that forgiveness was only possible through Christ alone. It hit her, and she broke down in tears. She was so humbled by the gracious act of Christ. It touched me to see this raw emotion of someone being pricked by the love of God. I can take for granted "in Christ alone." I can go through life feeling forgiven but not appreciative because it happened when I was younger. I can easily get distracted and miss the point. It's in Christ alone. There are people who feel that God's love cannot help them. They continue to spiral downward. They do more damage to themselves because help isn't possible for them. It's in Christ alone. Salvation and forgiveness are possible because of the life, death, and resurrection of Jesus.

DEAR LORD, THANK YOU FOR THE LIFE, DEATH, AND RESURRECTION FOR MY SAKE ...

1. Pray to God not to take for granted the cost of being forgiven for all your sins.
2. Pray to God, thankful that all you will ever need is found in Christ alone.

"Nor is there salvation in any other, for there is no other name under heaven among men by which we must be saved." (Acts 4:12)

Day 224

DEAR GOD, I COME TO YOU AS I AM TODAY …

Charlotte Elliott was born in 1789 in London. She suffered a serious illness at the age of thirty-two that left her disabled the rest of her life. She had a spiritual friend to console her anger and inner conflict with peace. She turned to writing hymns. She would go through moments of depression due to her disability. In 1834, she moved to live with her brother. One day, everyone in her family left her to go to a fundraiser for a school. She felt alone, useless, and depressed. She recalled the message from her friend: "Come to Christ just as you are." This helped her to overcome her dark moment and write the hymn "Just as I Am." "All that the Father gives Me will come to Me, and the one who comes to Me I will by no means cast out" (John 6:37). Jesus was trying to tell the crowd that He fed with loaves and fishes to receive Him as the "Bread of Life." All they had to do was come to Him as they were. Many didn't do that. They turned away, never to follow Him again. The exodus from Jesus was so great that He turned to His disciples to see if they were leaving too. Peter confirmed their position with the Lord. "Lord, to whom shall we go? You have the words of eternal life" (John 6:68). There is no greater day than today to come just as you are. The only thing stopping you from doing that is you. We feel we are not ready. We need to get things in order. We do all of that knowing that it's "just as I am."

DEAR LORD, THANK YOU FOR MAKING YOURSELF AVAILABLE AND ACCESSIBLE …

1. Pray to God for the constant invitation to come to Christ just as you are.
2. Pray to God for the strength not to be proud and selfish, but to come willingly to Him.

"Come to Me, all you who labor and are heavy laden, and I will give you rest." **(Matthew 11:28)**

DEAR GOD, HELP ME NOT TO COMPLAIN ...

I would be telling only half of the story if I said Thanksgiving is a time of giving thanks and being thankful. The truth is everyone is not thankful. Some choose to live an unthankful life. They live a life of complaining and grumbling. They choose to pick things apart. The flow of this current seems stronger toward complaining than praising. The heart easily drifts toward complaining. We assume complaining to be a reasonable response to disappointing events. If practiced long enough, it becomes familiar to us. With every complaint, we become like the Israelites murmuring in the desert. A spirit of complaining should not be the norm or acceptable. Israel forgot God's goodness. They experienced the parting of the Red Sea, manna from heaven, and water from a rock. They responded to it all by complaining and grumbling. God has been good to us too. He loves us, cares for us, shows mercy to us, and forgives us. If all we think about is what we don't have or what we want, we are no different than those before us in the wilderness. Life is too short, and God is too good for us to be in the habit of complaining or grumbling about our lives. We have more than enough reasons to be thankful and live in thanksgiving.

DEAR LORD, FORGIVE ME FOR OVERLOOKING YOUR GOODNESS ...

1. Pray to God to possess the wisdom to handle things in a better way that avoids complaining.
2. Pray to God for the strength to stand against the strong current of complaining and, instead, to live a life of thanksgiving.

"Do not grumble against one another, brethren, lest you be condemned. Behold, the Judge is standing at the door!" (James 5:9)

Day 226

DEAR GOD, I STAND IN AMAZEMENT OF YOUR CREATIVE HAND ...

On our way to the Samoan Islands, we had a couple days layover on the island of Oahu. One morning, we got up and drove a rental car to Hanauma Bay. It's a natural pool created in a volcanic crater. It is home to over four hundred species of fish. I was enjoying the underwater scenery through a snorkel mask. I came across a group of giant sea turtles. They were so graceful underwater. I was able to get close and touch a sea turtle's flipper. The turtle didn't seem to mind. I was mesmerized with these gentle creatures. I swam with them for a few minutes. It was my first time experiencing coral life like that. I thought about a completely different world from what I'm used to on a day-to-day basis. I find it interesting that we seem to discover more about this planet. We are discovering new species, new plants, and unknowns of the deep. I was grateful to have that experience. It gave me a better appreciation of God's world. "In His hand are the deep places of the earth; the heights of the hills are His also. The sea is His, for He made it; and His hands formed the dry land" (Psalm 95:4-5). The more we know about our planet, the greater God is. We are still finding out all the things God made in the beginning. If God can make and know this complex world, He can know you. There is not a day that goes by of which God isn't aware.

DEAR LORD, THE WISDOM OF CREATION CONTINUES TO DISPLAY YOUR GLORY ...

1. Pray to God to grow your faith by the evidence around you and in you.
2. Pray to God, thankful that He is mindful of you.

> *"But the very hairs of your head are all numbered. Do not fear therefore; you are of more value than many sparrows."* **(Matthew 10:30-31)**

DEAR GOD, I'M GRATEFUL FOR THE PICTURE OF A WEDDING WHEN ...

It was a long center aisle on that first day of July in the year of our Lord two thousand. There were hundreds of family and friends sitting on both sides of the aisle. When the song was played, everyone stood and admired the most beautiful bride in a flowing white dress. I was twenty-three years young when I saw a picture from heaven. The beautiful bride was escorted with her father. One of the greatest moments of a wedding is the processional of the bride. She appears to her groom for the first time in the ceremony. The invited guests look at her with great joy. The moment is of a great celebration with the bride and the groom. This earthly experience is how history as we know it will end. "I, John, saw the holy city, New Jerusalem, coming down out of heaven from God, prepared as a bride adorned for her husband" (Revelation 21:2). The end of time is described as a wedding feast. Who is the groom? Jesus is the bridegroom. The bride of Christ is the people of God. The husband and wife relationship is compared to Christ and His church. We, the bride, will soon be united with Him. Doesn't that put the end in a more pleasant thought? Sometimes we can feel frozen in fear as we wonder how it all will end. It will be the feast of all feasts. Doesn't that seem more inviting when it comes to the end?

DEAR LORD, MAY WE BE FAITHFUL IN ALL ...

1. Pray to God to be devoted to Christ in your heart, soul, and mind.
2. Pray to God to be devoted to Christ by loving your neighbor as yourself.

"Watch therefore, for you know neither the day nor the hour in which the Son of Man is coming." **(Matthew 25:13)**

Day 228

DEAR GOD, WHAT DID YOUR PRECIOUS SON SEE THAT DAY ...

The Hebrew "Golgotha" has a dark tone to it. The location was known as the place of the skull, where Jesus died. The instrument of death was a square-hewn beam of wood with a crosspiece. It's estimated to have been ten feet in length. The reason to lift up the executed was to send a strong warning to others and to make a spectacle of the condemned. Whom did Jesus see as He was lifted up? His friends. Those who stood near the cross were Mary the mother of Jesus, Mary the wife of Clopas, Mary Magdalene, and the disciple whom Jesus loved. The other disciples fled. What was it like for Mary the mother of Jesus to see her firstborn and Savior dying in front of her? She had comforted Him when He cried as a baby, rejoiced over His first words, and assisted Him in taking His first steps. She also knew, through the virgin birth, that He was the Son of God. Yet she looked on as He was lifted up on the place of the skull. There is a well-known hymn that speaks to us surveying the cross. What did Jesus see that day? He saw friendly faces. I'm thankful that there were some who believed Him on that horrible day. Can Christ who was raised on that third day and who ascended to the right hand of God still see friendly faces? Is Jesus more than our Savior and Lord? Is He our friend?

DEAR LORD, I CANNOT IMAGINE WHAT IT WAS LIKE TO DIE THE WAY YOU DID ...

1. Pray to God that He sees in you a friend who is loyal and committed to Him.
2. Pray to God to never forget the gracious act of Jesus, showing what it means to be a great friend.

"And He, bearing His cross, went out to a place called the Place of a Skull, which is called in Hebrew, Golgotha, where they crucified Him, and two others with Him, one on either side, and Jesus in the center." **(John 19:17-18)**

Day 229

DEAR GOD, I WANT TO FINISH MY DAY THE WAY I BEGAN IT ...

Have you heard of Eleazar, the son of Dodo? He was one of David's mighty men. Eleazar arose and attacked the Philistines, fighting so long and hard that "his hand stuck to the sword." He continued to fight when the army of Israel retreated. Why didn't he leave with them? He stayed behind because he was committed to finishing the job. He was tired and weary, but he kept on fighting. Do you have commitment like Eleazar? Do you keep on pushing yourself because the cause is greater than your own? We can learn from Eleazar to stay committed to what we need to do even if others have left us. Eleazar wasn't worried about the lack of numbers on his side. He didn't leave because he was left alone. He was devoted to getting the job done. Are we as dedicated about our day? We start something only to quit or move on to something else when we grow tired of it. The older I get, the more I value others' commitment and consistency. It seems people who are dependable and get the job done are not in the majority. I believe we can be mighty in our character in being determined to follow God no matter what. We are not swayed with numbers or weariness. We are devoted to the cause of Christ because it's bigger than us. Let me challenge you to go through today with the mindset to complete and finish what you have started. Don't give up on living for God today.

DEAR LORD, I WANT TO HOLD MYSELF TO WHAT I HAVE PRAYED ...

1. Pray to God to be mighty in faith in the way you live it out all day.
2. Pray to God to be mighty in faith in the way you commit to following God.

"Watch, stand fast in the faith, be brave, be strong." **(1 Corinthians 16:13)**

Day 230

DEAR GOD, MY MARRIAGE IS WORTH ...

My counseling professor in my graduate work shared with us an equation to see if a marital relationship will stay together. The equation is attractions + barriers – alternative attractions = the likelihood of staying together. The attractions refer to the things that brought you together as a couple, the ways you are attracted to your spouse. If you're someone who has been married for several years, go back to the wedding album and remember what led you to say "I do." Are you attracted to physical looks, companionship, shared interests, or desires? There is tremendous power in remembering and bringing up things for the good. The barriers are any obstacles that prevent you from ending the relationship. They are mental blocks that discourage the person from leaving the marriage. They could be religion, children, economic dependency, family, and community. The idea is to have barriers so great that you cannot get over them. If attractions and barriers are great, it's not likely to end in divorce. The "alternative attraction" is the perceived reward. It's the "grass is greener on the other side" mentality. If our alternative attraction is greater, then the likelihood of divorce is great. The key is to be committed to remembering your attractions and building up your barriers. A marriage is worth fighting for. It's worth digging in and saving the relationship. I realize there are exceptions to the rule. God gave us the gift of marriage. It is to be lovely and good. It can be if God is involved in our marriages.

DEAR LORD, I'M THANKFUL FOR RELATIONSHIPS ...

1. Pray to God that your faithfulness with others is a reflection of your relationship with Him.
2. Pray to God to be committed to your family, friends, and spouse.

"Mercy and truth have met together; righteousness and peace have kissed." **(Psalm 85:10)**

Day 231

DEAR GOD, FORGIVE ME WHEN YOU SAY THAT I ...

Children are masters at finding out the missing link. They quickly learn the right time and the right person to ask for something. Our three boys are strategic in getting what they want. If Dad is in a good mood or seems really busy, ask him, and he will more likely say yes. If he seems upset about something, don't ask him. If Mom is kissing me and giving me hugs, ask her because she is in a great mood. I can see them think this way because I did the same. We grow up learning how and when to ask for something. If Mom said no, we go to Dad, and vice versa. We still do this as adults. "Please, we really need a cat!" "I really could use a new car." "We deserve a vacation!" Do we sometimes carry that learned behavior over to prayer? Do we try to serve God more in order for Him to say yes? Do we think the beginning of our day is a better chance with God than at the end of the day? If we pray for others long enough, will God finally reward us? We need to remember an important principle with God and prayer. "Every good gift and every perfect gift is from above, and comes down from the Father of lights, with whom there is no variation or shadow of turning" (James 1:17). When we pray, God gives us what is good and perfect for the occasion of our request. God always knows our hearts. He knows our intentions. We must always trust in His answer. His will, not mine.

DEAR LORD, YOU WERE HERE LONG BEFORE ME, AND YOU ALWAYS KNOW WHAT IS BEST ...

1. Pray to God to receive His answer as the best answer for you in your life.
2. Pray for wisdom from above to understand that what you receive today is sufficient.

"If you then, being evil, know how to give good gifts to your children, how much more will your Father who is in heaven give good things to those who ask Him!" **(Matthew 7:11)**

Day 232

DEAR GOD, I'M THANKFUL THAT YOU LISTEN ...

How does God answer our prayers? He can say yes. God said yes to Hannah's prayer to have a child. Hannah prayed for God to remember her and give a male child that she could give back to the Lord. Hannah spoke in her heart and only moved her lips. The priest thought she was drunk. He even asked her, "How long will you be drunk? Put your wine away from you" (1 Samuel 1:14). He hadn't seen someone pour their soul out to the Lord in prayer. I'm guessing he had never poured his soul out to God in prayer. God remembered Hannah's prayer, and she gave birth to Samuel. She kept her vow and gave Samuel back to the Lord. God blessed her with five more children. I've prayed for a godly woman in my life. A woman I could love and be with for the rest of my life. I know God has said yes to that prayer because of my beautiful wife of nineteen years. She is not only an answer to my prayer, but my parents' as well. They prayed for me to find and marry a godly woman. I'm thankful for her and how God blessed me through His answer to my prayer. I see more and more why God said yes. She has helped me more spiritually. In times where I have fallen, she has been there to pick me up. I'm thankful for the times when God says yes to our prayers. I am one of billions of people, but He is mindful of me.

DEAR LORD, I'M HUMBLED BY THE TIMES YOU HAVE SAID YES TO MY PRAYERS ...

1. Pray to God with an understanding that your time in prayer is about God and not an answer.
2. Pray for the courage to take the answers given and know that God knows what is best.

"The Lord has been mindful of us; He will bless us." (Psalm 115:12)

Day 233

DEAR GOD, I STRUGGLE WITH THE BROKENNESS …

I hate addiction. I know that sounds strong, but I have seen the damage it does firsthand. It affects much more than the addict. It's like throwing a rock into a pond. The splash is made because of the impact. What happens next? There is a ripple effect that moves throughout the whole pond. I hear it. "It's my life, and I'm only hurting myself." That is not true because we belong to God. It's not true because we are connected as family members, friends, and communities. I try to help those who are fighting addictions by meeting a need. I leave feeling overwhelmed by how big of a problem it is. I cannot be upset with the addict because we are all broken. Whom do you know who is put all together perfectly? I can find myself feeling I have everything in control only to break. We all need God whether we are addicted to something or not. We all need His help and constant presence in our lives. Life is hard. I believe it's impossible without Jesus. May we not only focus on those whose lives are broken but on our own brokenness as well. I'm thankful that God cares for us. Let Him know your cares today in your prayer.

DEAR LORD, HELP ME TO LEAN ON YOU MORE …

1. Pray for the brokenness of this world and the part you play.
2. Pray for healing that can come only from the blood of Jesus.

> *"The Lord is near to those who have a broken heart, and saves such as have a contrite spirit."* **(Psalm 34:18)**

Day 234

DEAR GOD, I'M GRATEFUL THAT YOU DO MORE THAN HEAR ...

How does God answer our prayers? God can say no. God said no to Moses when he prayed for the forgiveness of his rebellious people. The people had made a false god out of gold. They put something false in the place of God. David prayed for the life of his son, but God said no. The child came as the result of adultery and murder. David pleaded, fasted, and prayed fervently. On the seventh day, the child died. I prayed for no more surgeries, but that was not to be. My oldest son was upset by my health problems. I told him that everything was fine and the surgeries were done. He said, "I don't believe you." I wanted so badly to be right to comfort his young heart. I had three more surgeries. It was a tough time, but we got through. I'm thankful for the times when God says no to our prayers. I realize He could say yes or to wait. I'm thankful for Him taking the time to answer my request. I am one of billions of people, but He is mindful of me. I have learned to value the gift of praying more than the receiving. I didn't see it then, but I know now that I needed those surgeries to function in life today. Sometimes it's difficult to see in the moment. We understand God said no, but His word seems to point to yes. I'm not God; He is. My perspective, knowledge, and understanding are limited. That's the reason I need God every day. He sees what's best for me better than I do.

DEAR LORD, I STRUGGLE WITH THE TIMES YOU SAY NO TO MY PRAYERS ...

1. Pray to God to take the answer and trust in God's judgment.
2. Pray for patience in not getting what you want but settling for what you need.

"He who did not spare His own Son, but delivered Him up for us all, how shall He not with Him also freely give us all things?" **(Romans 8:32)**

Day 235

DEAR GOD, WE CAN GET SO FOCUSED ON ONE EVENT WHEN WE SHOULD ...

I've read that the average cost of a wedding is between $33,000 and $40,000. This is the average. Some are much higher, and others are way lower. Imagine all the time spent planning and preparing for a wedding. It's hours, weeks, and months. What about the time spent on a marriage? What are couples doing for their marriages after they say "I do"? Many states offer a sizable discount on a marriage license to couples with hours of premarital counseling. The states see the great need of thinking of a marriage rather than the wedding. We see God's concern for marriage prior to the wedding in Genesis. The longest chapter in Genesis is a wedding story. Only thirty-one verses are devoted to the creation account, and twenty-four verses describe the destruction of the world by water. The story of Abraham finding a godly bride for Isaac is sixty-seven verses. According to the Bible, there is more to marriage than planning a wedding. Only one verse in Genesis 24 is dedicated to the wedding: "Then Isaac brought her into his mother Sarah's tent; and he took Rebekah and she became his wife, and he loved her" (v. 67). The chapter shows us the importance of marriage over a wedding. What if we invested in a marriage as much as a wedding? Would the divorce rate shrink? Would couples have the tools to handle the first fight, conflict, or disagreement? Weddings are nice, but a marriage is better.

DEAR LORD, THANK YOU FOR MARRIAGE ...

1. Pray to God to continue what you have started in your marriage, home, and friendships.
2. Pray to God, thankful for the people in your life.

"Set me as a seal upon your heart, as a seal upon your arm; for love is as strong as death, jealousy as cruel as the grave; its flames are flames of fire, a most vehement flame." **(Song of Solomon 8:6)**

Day 236

DEAR GOD, HELP ME TO KEEP MY HEART IN YOU TODAY ...

"Some people are here to see you," a church member said as he came into my office. The tone in his voice wasn't pleasant. I was unaware that this member had a gun pulled on him at a convenience store a quarter of a mile from the church building. I was shocked when the visitors following him were FBI agents. They entered my office and flipped out their wallets to show their identification. One agent was wearing a suit and tie, and the other was covered in black apparel and wearing a bulletproof vest. Other agents were out of sight, armed by my office and prepared to fire. I quickly realized their interest in seeing me was not for a Bible study. I was asked, "Were you at this bank around this time?" I nodded yes. He informed me that the bank had been robbed around the time I was there. An eyewitness claimed the escaped robber was driving the same make, model, and color of my car. I was having a major identity crisis. Jesus gave a shocking statement to those in the upper room. "Most assuredly, I say to you, one of you will betray Me" (John 13:21). We can easily point our fingers at Judas and shake our heads at him. Judas gave Jesus away, but Jesus died for all of our sins. Like Judas, we can follow Him for a while and allow our hearts to belong to something else in time. We need to be Christians whose identities are in Christ.

DEAR LORD, TEMPTATIONS CAN LEAD ME AWAY ...

1. Pray to God for the strength to withstand temptation and for deliverance from Satan.
2. Pray to God to demonstrate to those around you an identity in Christ by being salt and light.

> *"... knowing this, that our old man was crucified with Him, that the body of sin might be done away with, that we should no longer be slaves of sin. For he who has died has been freed from sin."* **(Romans 6:6-7)**

Day 237

DEAR GOD, I'M THANKFUL FOR A PLACE CALLED HEAVEN ...

Our son drilled us with questions about heaven. His concern was with the kinds of food in heaven. This generally came at the supper table. He surveyed his plate and then asked us about heaven's supper table. I don't know if he hoped that what he was having for dinner would not be served in heaven. He may have thought that anything green belongs somewhere else. On the other end, he would love some heavenly pizza and desserts. I hope my son's questions about heaven will not stop with food. I hope he will continue asking about heaven because it shows his interest in it. It's our desire as parents for our boys to love God and have the same desire as us to be with God forever. The apostle Paul wrote about some exciting events about heavenly things. He talked about Jesus Himself descending from heaven with a shout. There will be the voice of an archangel and the trumpet of God. The dead in Christ will rise, and those who are alive will meet the Lord in the air. Then, Paul concluded, "We shall always be with the Lord" (1 Thessalonians 4:17). These words were written so that we could comfort each other. We should take an interest in them by investing our minds, hearts, and words. When was the last time you asked, "What will we eat in heaven?" Heaven will surely be worth it all!

DEAR LORD, MAY WE HAVE FAITH LIKE A CHILD WHEN IT COMES TO HEAVEN ...

1. Pray to God, thankful for the debt Jesus paid that makes heaven possible.
2. Pray to God, thankful for knowing what will soon happen and not being in the dark.

"For God did not appoint us to wrath, but to obtain salvation through our Lord Jesus Christ, who died for us, that whether we wake or sleep, we should live together with Him." **(1 Thessalonians 5:9-10)**

Day 238

DEAR GOD, I'M REMINDED OF WHEN I WAS SEPARATED FROM THOSE I LOVE ...

I have a strong memory of being separated from my mom in a store. I'm guessing my mother had her list and wanted us to follow right behind her. I probably saw the toy section and wandered off to look. When I turned around, my mother was gone. I ran from aisle to aisle, looking for a familiar face. I panicked and became upset. A "good Samaritan" employee saw me and took me to customer service. They asked my mother's name and did the all call. My fear melted away when I saw my mother running toward me. I learned early how painful and scary separation is. The greatest separation is from God. He doesn't leave us, but we leave him because of sin. Sin separates us from God because God is holy, good, and right. Do we realize the pain we bring to ourselves because of sin? How would you feel if what you are doing pushed those you love away from you? It would be unbearable for me to be away from my beautiful wife and three boys because of my actions. How much more to the One who gave Himself up to die on the cross? We are not always going to do things right and get it right each day. Sometimes we make a decision that we know is not right. Are we willing to reconnect back to God? There is no better time than today.

DEAR LORD, I SEE MY SEPARATION FROM GOD BECAUSE OF SIN ...

1. Pray to God to repent and be forgiven of your sins as you forgive those who have sinned against you.
2. Pray to God to see more quickly the need to be forgiven when you separate yourself from Him.

> *"At that time you were without Christ, being aliens from the commonwealth of Israel and strangers from the covenants of promise. ... But now in Christ Jesus you who once were far off have been brought near by the blood of Christ."* **(Ephesians 2:12-13)**

Day 239

DEAR GOD, I'M AMAZED AT YOUR TIMING ...

I believe in a God who puts the right people in our lives. I was adjusting to my new life after surgeries. I wanted to do what I once did before my health situation. I learned the hard way that I couldn't. It took me three years to adjust to my medicine and keep my levels from going too high or low. I was given a co-teacher at school because of some students. We clicked immediately. I came to love her as a sister. She has a wonderful husband and two beautiful girls. She helped me with some of my classes when I was wiped out by the day. She filled in for me when I was back in the hospital. I felt at ease knowing that she knew the classroom and what to do. It allowed me to focus on my health and get better. This person was a former Disney princess and worked in theater on Broadway. She has more talent in one finger than I do period. She could have followed that track, but she didn't. She has a passion for teaching kids in volleyball and theater. This desire to teach brought us together. The timing was perfect, and I look back and see God's providential hand. I can think of many more lives God placed in my life that I needed more than I realized at the time. God's goodness can involve the people we know and encounter on a daily basis. I'm thankful to God for the right person and the right time. God is good.

DEAR LORD, THANK YOU FOR HELPING WITH THE RIGHT PEOPLE ...

1. Pray to God to be the hands and feet of Him to someone in need today.
2. Pray to God, thankful that He is mindful of your needs today.

"Even to your old age, I am He, and even to gray hairs I will carry you! I have made, and I will bear; even I will carry, and will deliver you." **(Isaiah 46:4)**

Day 240

DEAR GOD, I KNOW THAT WITHOUT YOU, LIFE AS WE KNOW IT WOULD BE ...

What is greater than God and eviler than the devil? The poor have it, the rich need it, and if you eat it, you'll die. What is it? The answer is nothing. Nothing is greater than God, nothing is eviler than the devil, the poor have nothing, the rich need nothing, and if we continue to eat nothing, we will die. God's greatness and goodness should leave nothing but praise and gratitude on our lips and heart. The largest book in the Bible is the book of Psalms. One of the greatest contributors of psalms was David. He knew the source of his musical gift. "Now these are the last words of David. Thus says David the son of Jesse; thus says the man raised up on high, the anointed of the God of Jacob, and the sweet psalmist of Israel: 'The Spirit of the Lord spoke by me, and His word was on my tongue'" (2 Samuel 23:1-2). David thanked God and expressed his gratitude in psalms. The last five psalms begin with the same expression: "Praise the Lord!" Are the same words on our lips at the end of a day? God is the reason for our success. Where would we be without Him? Nowhere. If God took away all His blessings, what would you have left? Nothing. When we sing and praise God's awesome name, we are expressing our thankfulness for Him. We know that without God, we would be nothing. With God, we have everything.

DEAR LORD, WHEN I SURVEY ALL THE THINGS YOU DO FOR ME, I'M LEFT TO ...

1. Pray to God to possess the same spirit as those before you when it comes to gratitude for God.
2. Pray to God with an understanding that your day doesn't take away God and who He is.

> *"The Lord is good to all, and His tender mercies are over all His works."* **(Psalm 145:9)**

Day 241

DEAR GOD, I'M SURROUNDED BY NOISES ...

My oldest son typed out a sermon. His opening sentence said, "Listen to counsel and receive instruction that you may be wise in your ladder days." I foresee a lot of climbing in the future. "Listen to counsel and receive instruction, that you may be wise in your latter days" (Proverbs 19:20). The Greek Stoic philosopher, Epictetus, is known for the famous quote, "We have two ears and one mouth so that we can listen twice as much as we speak." What if Epictetus lived today? Did they have the noises like we have today? The decibel or loudness level for a normal conversation is between 60 to 65 decibels. The loudness of a power mower is around 107 decibels. The loudness of a rock concert is 115 decibels. The loudness of a jet engine at 100 feet in the air is 140 decibels. God is trying to get to us through all the noise. Are we listening to His Word? There are so many noises trying to get our attention and capture our hearts. We can stand beside someone and not hear. We have zoned out and into something else. When questioned, we respond, "What was that?" or "Huh?" Do we find ourselves zoning out in prayer and reading God's Word? We start off praying, but our minds wander off to something unrelated. I would suggest focusing on a verse and letting that verse be your reference when you pray.

DEAR LORD, HELP ME TO CONCENTRATE ON YOUR WORD TODAY ...

1. Pray to God for help to block out or redirect thoughts that distract you from God.
2. Pray to God for strength to continue listening to God's counsel as the words influence your life.

"He who heeds the word wisely will find good, and whoever trusts in the LORD, happy is he." **(Proverbs 16:20)**

Day 242

DEAR GOD, MY PLACE OF REST SHOULD HAVE ...

When you walk into our home, the presence of family is strong. We have pictures of our family in frames throughout the house. We have the dates of our wedding and the births of our boys on the wall. We have pictures up from our last Disney trip. We have Bible verses framed in different areas of the house. The presence of family is strong in our home. Do you know of a home where anything about God cannot be found? In the Old Testament, the ark of God symbolized the presence of God. He gave special instructions on how to build it. The ark was carried to war because it was a symbol to the people that God was with them and fighting for them. The ark of God was captured in war by the Philistines. They had it for sixty-seven years. David decided to bring the ark of God back home. God is not confined to an ark. He is everywhere; however, we can be unwelcoming by the way we live at home. Our environment can shape the way we think and act. If we are leaving God at the church building, what does that say about our homes? David saw the need to bring the ark back home. It represented God and His presence. We have a translated copy of the written Word. It's a reminder of God and His wonderful plan of redemption. Today or this week, you will bring things home: homework, food, household items, ideas, and possibly problems. What about God? We need to bless our homes with God.

DEAR LORD, I PRAY THAT MY HOME IS A PLACE WHERE EVERY MEMBER CAN THRIVE IN YOU ...

1. Pray to God to be in the daily practice of reading, praying, and talking about God.
2. Pray to God to be an example in Christ to your younger family members.

> *"For every house is built by someone, but He who built all things is God."* (Hebrews 3:4)

Day 243

DEAR GOD, THANK YOU FOR YOUR SON ...

I love the tradition of giving and receiving Christmas cards. My favorite ones are with babies. I love to see the precious babies dressed up for the season. The photographer always has the best poses and expressions. We generally put those cards on the refrigerator for an entire year. We see their sweet faces every day. I don't know when the tradition of picture cards of families started. It's nice to go to the mailbox in December and see the cards addressed to you. We have adopted a grandmother who never had any children. We have sent her a picture card for over ten years. She has kept every one of them. She has framed several. I sometimes like to visit her and remember the cards we made because we gave all of ours away. She currently has our latest one by her bedside. It's amazing what a simple picture card can do for someone. It means more than you might think to many people. The picture card is a reminder that people love us and care for us. They invite us to share with the family. It's a blessing to be loved by others and have friends. When God looked on Adam's loneliness, He said it was not good (Genesis 2:18). It's still not good to be left alone and not connect with anyone. The simple act of a card, call, or visit means a lot to that person who doesn't have anyone. The greatest thing about the Christmas season is giving back to others.

DEAR LORD, I'M THANKFUL FOR THE PEOPLE WHO LOVE ME ...

1. Pray to God to value your friendships with people and, more importantly, with Him.
2. Pray to God to help you spread cheer to someone who is alone this season.

> *"The sweetness of a man's friend gives delight by hearty counsel."* **(Proverbs 27:9)**

Day 244

DEAR GOD, THE CHALLENGES IN THIS LIFE DON'T COMPARE TO YOU ...

The "Elf on the Shelf" is a book with an elf. The children name the elf and get up in the morning to see where the elf is. They cannot touch the elf according to the book. The elf is supposed to go back to the North Pole and give Santa an update. Our boys, many years ago, received an Elf on the Shelf and named him "Josh." *Why did they do that?* One year, a few of my coworkers challenged each other to have the best Elf on the Shelf setup. I can't turn down a challenge. I found out how difficult it was to create a bigger and better setup than the night before. I spent over an hour setting up. Why? I didn't want to be the first one to quit or lose. I recreated scenes from movies with the elf. I created a house of cards with our elf sleeping on top. Our youngest son loved waking up and seeing what new creation was on display. I wondered if he thought something was off from the regular, simple setup to the elaborate competition setups. The things we do for our kids. I guess I should say, the things we do to win. Do you have a winning spirit? You can't stand to lose? I'm thankful we don't have a competition when it comes to our faith. Christ came and provided a way to live victoriously. We just need to follow in His steps. I cannot say the same when it comes to Elf on the Shelf.

DEAR LORD, I'M THANKFUL FOR THE VICTORY WE HAVE IN JESUS ...

1. Pray to God to take a day at a time walking in Jesus' steps.
2. Pray to God to be reminded that it's not a competition when it comes to our faith.

"... looking unto Jesus, the author and finisher of our faith, who for the joy that was set before Him endured the cross, despising the shame, and has sat down at the right hand of the throne of God." **(Hebrews 12:2)**

Day 245

DEAR GOD, HELP ME TO UNDERSTAND WHY "NO" IS NECESSARY …

I forgot how mobile small children are. A precious baby girl was walking around our house, touching everything and trying to put it in her mouth. She walked around to see the stairs going to the second floor. She tried to climb them, but I told her no and redirected her. Did she forget those stairs? No. She walked away, but eventually found herself back at those stairs. Again, I said no and blocked her from climbing them. I imagine we did this more than ten times. I don't know what she was thinking. Did she think my "no" was too weak and, eventually, I would break? Did she think she could get to the stairs before me? I don't know, but she was determined to climb the stairs. She was unsuccessful, but she'll try again another day. I can't blame her. We all struggle with "no." Maybe it goes back to the first people. They were told no when it came to the tree of the knowledge of good and evil. They were able to eat from every other tree. The one tree that they couldn't eat from was the tree that did them in. It's the things we are told not to do that we later try and do. We sometimes learn the hard way when it comes to the "no." We were raised not to do something, and we do it. We read from God's Word what we should and shouldn't do. We go against it because of the temptation to do what is wrong. Why are we told no? It's to live our best lives away from sin. Maybe the next time you read a "no," realize it's because it is what's best for you.

DEAR LORD, FORGIVE ME FOR THE TIMES I DO WHAT I KNOW I SHOULDN'T …

1. Pray to God for a desire to please Him, not disobey Him.
2. Pray to God for a heart to trust in His way of life more than your own.

"But each one is tempted when he is drawn away by his own desires and enticed. Then, when desire has conceived, it gives birth to sin; and sin, when it is full-grown, brings forth death." **(James 1:14-15)**

Day 246

DEAR GOD, I PRAY FOR WISDOM AND PATIENCE ...

"LORD, I pray, open his eyes that he may see" (2 Kings 6:17). The prophet Elisha said this prayer on behalf of his servant. His servant arose early in the day and went out to see an army with horses and chariots surrounding them. He came to Elisha and said, "What shall we do?" (v. 15). I can relate to the servant of Elisha. When something unexpected happens, I am alarmed and don't know what to do. I've called out to God many times for an answer to what I am facing. Elisha didn't rebuke his servant for his lack of faith. He immediately went to God in prayer. His unselfish prayer was for the servant's eyes to be opened to what Elisha was able to see. The Lord immediately opened the servant's eyes to see the mountains full of horses and chariots of fire all around. The best thing we can do for someone is pray. Maybe the individual is struggling with a temptation or having a lack of faith. Before we open our mouths to give an answer, let us go to God in prayer. We can pray for God to open the person's heart to receive the words of God. We can ask God for wisdom to guide them with the right words. The story also shows the reality of God. We can allow our problems to become bigger than they are. Nothing is greater or bigger than God. In times we forget, we need to pray, "Lord, open my eyes that I may see."

DEAR LORD, I PRAY TO SEE YOU ...

1. Pray to God to focus on the needs of others and for the understanding to help them.
2. Pray to God to have faith like Elisha, knowing that in the heart of a problem, God is bigger and greater.

> *"This is the confidence that we have in Him, that if we ask anything according to His will, He hears us."* **(1 John 5:14)**

DEAR GOD, I'M INDEBTED TO MY FAMILY ...

My grandparents on my mother's side changed their family tree. My grandmother and grandfather were saved when they were married with young children. They fell in love with a godly man who walked what he believed. He was a gospel preacher and former president of a Christian university. What if he hadn't taken the time to influence them in the gospel of Jesus Christ? I wouldn't be here, spiritually speaking. My grandparents raised their children in the Lord. My mother was influenced by their godly example and fell in love with Jesus. The ripple effect continued with my siblings and now with great-grandchildren. The seed that was planted landed on good soil and produced a crop that reaches five generations. I look to my godly grandparents and thank them for being an example to my mother. I cannot think of a greater gift to leave a family than one's faith and example in the Lord. When Jesus told the parable of the sower, he mentioned four types of soil that the seed fell on. Only 25 percent of the soil was good. How the seed is planted and what it produces is up to the person. We can only plant the seed. I would love to look back someday and see generation upon generation of believers in my family. I would love to hear great-grandchildren praying to God. It only takes one generation to see the need to lean on God and live in prayer. The greatest legacy we can leave is our faith. One day at a time, trust in God and be devoted in prayer.

DEAR LORD, I'M THANKFUL FOR THOSE WHO HAVE SHOWN ME HOW TO FOLLOW CHRIST ...

1. Pray to God to walk in the same steps as those family members ahead of you.
2. Pray to God to leave the same legacy when it comes to faith and prayer.

> *"... when I call to remembrance the genuine faith that is in you, which dwelt first in your grandmother Lois and your mother Eunice, and I am persuaded is in you also."* **(2 Timothy 1:5)**

Day 248

DEAR GOD, I'M IN AWE AND WONDER WHEN I MEDITATE ON YOU ...

We have an ever-increasing need for wonder. If I were to tell my children the same fairy tale, notice the different reactions. If I told my oldest son that his younger brother opened the back door to an angry, red, and fire-breathing dragon hungry for people, his eyes might get bigger. If I told my middle son that his younger brother opened the back door to an angry, red, fire-breathing dragon, his eyes might get wide then. If I told my youngest son that he opened the back door to something angry and red, his eyes would be wide. Do you see the difference? My oldest son needed "fire-breathing dragon hungry for people" to show emotion. My middle son needed "fire-breathing dragon." My youngest son needed a door to something angry and red. The older we get, the more it takes to fill our hearts with wonder. This is why we need God. He is big enough to fill our hearts with wonder. Praise is one of the wonders that becomes bigger, better, and greater as we grow into the faith. "The genuineness of your faith, being much more precious than gold that perishes, though it is tested by fire, may be found to praise, honor, and glory at the revelation of Jesus Christ" (1 Peter 1:7). We need to be in the habit of praising God until Christ comes (Hebrews 13:15). We need to be consistent in our praise to God. There is nothing that can fill our wonder other than God. May our days be filled with praise and prayer.

DEAR LORD, I CAN NEVER KNOW ENOUGH ...

1. Pray to God, grateful for what He has revealed to you through creation and His Word.
2. Pray to God for a hunger and thirst for righteousness.

"I will extol You, my God, O King; and I will bless Your name forever and ever. Every day I will bless You, and I will praise Your name forever and ever. Great is the Lord, and greatly to be praised; and His greatness is unsearchable." **(Psalm 145:1-3)**

DEAR GOD, I STRUGGLE WITH WHY ...

The story of Job fascinates me. We see behind the scenes in the trial of someone's life. It wasn't God who caused Job to suffer greatly. It was Satan. I wonder if we blame the wrong one when it comes to our trials. We assume God is causing our trouble when the devil is trying to accuse us. Job's three friends didn't help him. They assumed he did something wrong, which caused him to lose so much. They even accused him of committing sins that he hadn't done. Job wanted God to come and answer him. He pictured a courtroom where he gave his defense before God. God appeared to Job in a great whirlwind. The Almighty hurled over seventy questions to Job. He presented to Job the perspective and knowledge of God. Can you guess how many questions Job got right? None. Job endured much. He suffered the loss of all his children and his own health. It was Job who realized that he could not answer God. Job wanted to know why he was suffering. Instead, he found out, through the questions, who God was. We are a "why" culture. We want to know why to everything. We struggle when we can't know. Sometimes things will happen to you, and you may never know the answer. Are you willing to trust God for who He is? We must realize our limitations when it comes to God. Are you willing to trust Him no matter what today?

DEAR LORD, HELP ME TO TRUST YOU MORE ...

1. Pray to God for His greatness and ability to know everything.
2. Pray to God to be Job-like and trust in God even though you may not know why.

"Then Job answered the Lord and said: 'I know that You can do everything, and that no purpose of Yours can be withheld from You. ... Therefore I have uttered what I did not understand, things too wonderful for me.'" **(Job 42:1-3)**

Day 250

DEAR GOD, I WANT TO BETTER MY COMMUNICATION WITH YOU ...

A man and his wife were having some communication problems at home. They were both upset, giving one another the silent treatment. The husband realized he would need his wife's help to wake up early for a flight. He wrote on a piece of paper, "Please wake me at 5:00 a.m." The next morning, the husband woke up and noticed it was 9:00 a.m. He was furious that his wife didn't help wake him. He noticed a piece of paper beside the bed. It said, "It's 5:00 a.m. Wake up." I believe we can all agree that communication is necessary for a relationship. This is no different in our relationship with God. We can only go so far in gazing at the stars and observing a beautiful landscape. We must look in other places for God's revelation. It's amazing to consider the number of ways we have access to God's Word. I have a Bible app on my phone, tablet, and computer. I have multiple hard copies of the Scriptures. With all this access to the Word, are we better for it? God has spoken to us through His last voice, Jesus Christ. We can read and respond to Him through prayer and actions. Examine your prayer life. Is it routine at the beginning and end of the day and before a meal? Do you seek God only when a problem is happening? Every good relationship involves constant communication. We need to be connected to God in His Word and in prayer daily.

DEAR LORD, I'M GOING TO TAKE THE TIME TODAY TO READ AND RESPOND IN PRAYER ...

1. Pray to God to work on your communication with Him.
2. Pray to God, thankful for the Scriptures and not to take them for granted.

"But you must continue in the things which you have learned and been assured of, ... which are able to make you wise for salvation through faith which is in Christ Jesus." **(2 Timothy 3:14-15)**

Day 251

DEAR GOD, I PRAY FOR THOSE WHO ARE POOR AND SICK ...

I enjoy hearing my boys pray. They mention "the poor and sick" most of the time when asked to pray. They know "sick" a little bit with my health and the joys of getting a virus. It seems like every year we share a virus with one another. Obviously, there is greater sickness, and they will soon be aware as they get older. They don't know poor yet. Most people don't know poor in a first world country. I cannot forget those simple mud homes in the bush of Tanzania. A woman invited us into her home to hear about Jesus. There was nothing but a roof and a floor. I was humbled by her warm hospitality. She had nothing but was grateful to hear us. I'm thankful that my boys are thinking about "the poor and sick" in their prayers. They are mindful of others less fortunate. I pray that they will continue to be prayerful and helpful when they get older. I want them to always be mindful of the world around them. They will always be aware that there is someone in need of prayers and help. I also don't want them to take for granted what they have physically and spiritually. We are all rich in Christ Jesus. The places and things we have on earth are only temporary. They do not last. I've officiated many funerals. I've seen no one bury a house, car, or money with the deceased person. I pray that I'm more mindful of others in my prayers like my boys.

DEAR LORD, I PRAY TO BE OPEN TO THOSE WHO ARE LESS FORTUNATE AROUND ME ...

1. Pray to God, thankful for the riches we receive in Christ Jesus.
2. Pray to God for your heart to be set on things above and on those in need on earth.

> *"But when you do a charitable deed, do not let your left hand know what your right hand is doing, that your charitable deed may be in secret; and your Father who sees in secret will Himself reward you openly."* **(Matthew 6:3-4)**

Day 252

DEAR GOD, I THANK YOU FOR LOVING US ENOUGH TO ALLOW US TO CHOOSE ...

How can two siblings have the same father, mother, and upbringing but choose two different paths? Edwin Thomas Booth was a master of the stage. He performed Hamlet in New York City for one hundred consecutive nights. He had two brothers who were also actors. They all three performed in Julius Caesar. Edwin's brother, John, took the role of Brutus. He was the assassin in the play. John was also the assassin of President Lincoln in Ford's Theatre in 1865. Edwin was ashamed of his brother's action and retired from the theater. At a local train station, Edwin noticed a well-dressed man who lost his footing and fell between the platform. Edwin helped untangle and free the man before the coming train. Edwin received a letter, notifying him that he had saved the life of the son of the late Abraham Lincoln. One brother takes a life, and the other brother saves it. How? How did Cain and Abel come from the same parents, but one chose murder and the other obedience? How did Peter and Judas both deny the Lord, but one sought mercy and the other took his own life? I don't know. I do know that God has given us the choice. We can choose to love Him or deny Him. We can choose to serve Him or serve ourselves. We can pray to Him or trust in ourselves. We can choose to live today for ourselves or for God. The choice is yours.

DEAR LORD, HELP ME TO MAKE THE RIGHT CHOICES TODAY ...

1. Pray to God to choose Him always in whatever you do.
2. Pray to God for strength to make wise choices that will help your relationship with Him.

"Enter by the narrow gate; for wide is the gate and broad is the way that leads to destruction, and there are many who go in by it." **(Matthew 7:13)**

Day 253

DEAR GOD, THANK YOU FOR THE CHANGING OF THE SEASONS, ESPECIALLY SPRING ...

Whether you realize it or not, gardening is in your blood. Life began in a garden. The garden of Eden was the first garden where life as we know it began. The garden had the necessary ingredients. It had soil, seed, and water. It was in the garden where humans were created, marriage began, homes were established, and sin had its start. Life was reconciled in a garden. In the garden of Gethsemane, Jesus agonized over the Father's will, surrender came, salvation was coming, and all that was lost in Eden was being restored. In Eden, humans fell because of sin. In Gethsemane, humanity was reconciled back to God. Every spring, when the flowers bud, trees bloom, and the smell of freshly cut lawns fills the air, we are reminded of the renewal of creation with the regrowth from the dormant winter. It's in this time of year that I'm mindful of the major historical events in a garden. All is not lost because of the garden of Gethsemane, where Jesus accepted the Father's will. I don't know what this spring will bring. All is well as long as we are in the Lord. It's in Him that we can be renewed.

DEAR LORD, I AM MINDFUL OF THE RENEWING OF OUR MINDS ...

1. Pray to God, thankful for Jesus, who began His reconciliation in the garden.
2. Pray to God for help to bear much fruit in Him this season.

"Do not be conformed to this world, but be transformed by the renewing of your mind, that you may prove what is that good and acceptable and perfect will of God." **(Romans 12:2)**

Day 254

DEAR GOD, I WANT TO BE MORE MINDFUL OF YOU TODAY ...

What are you thinking about today? It's said that the average number of thoughts we have each day is around seventy thousand. Every time you recall a memory or have a new thought, you are creating a new connection in your brain. Memory is formed by associations, so if you want help remembering things, create associations for yourself. I believe visual aids can help with this. What do you think about when you see a Dr Pepper can? I imagine our thoughts are different about it. We think of something. What do you think about when you think of Alabama football? I can feel the "boos" in your mind. I expect cheers from those who are fans. What do you think about a Bible? Do you think of how often you read it? Are you comfortable with what you know in it? Several years ago, I stayed with some friends from college. The couple was learning Spanish. They had a Spanish word on every item in their house. They had to say and know the word before they could use the item. If they wanted food in the refrigerator, they had to say *el refrigerador*. What if we take a pack of sticky notes and stick a Bible verse in the rooms of our homes? The verses would remind us of God's Word and how our thoughts should be on it more. I believe the more our minds are on God's Word, the better our lives and prayers will be. We are in tune with God's Word.

DEAR LORD, I NEED TO SET MY MIND ON THINGS ABOVE BY MY THOUGHTS AND MEMORIES ...

1. Pray to God to be more mindful of His Word in your life each day.
2. Pray to God to be determined every day to know more in prayer and in word.

"Let this mind be in you which was also in Christ Jesus." **(Philippians 2:5)**

Day 255

DEAR GOD, HELP ME TO FOCUS ON YOU ...

"I have a mountain of credit card debt," one man said to another. "I have lost my job. My car is being repossessed, and our house is in foreclosure. But I am not worried about it. I've hired a professional worrier. He does all the worrying for me, and that way I don't have to think about it." "That's fantastic. How much does your professional worrier charge?" "Fifty thousand dollars a year." "Fifty thousand dollars a year! Where are you going to get that kind of money?" "I don't know," said the man. "That's his worry!" Have you ever been so anxious about tomorrow that you felt keyed up, fatigued, and irritable? Did you find it difficult to sleep because your mind was racing with thought and your muscles were tense? Maybe you can relate to what I'm talking about. If God is of peace, shouldn't His people be? How can we be "anxious for nothing"? This doesn't mean we don't care or have concerns. It is referring to a way of life where we allow worries and anxieties to take over. The problem with this is that it takes away from the power of the Lord. What are we to do? We are to pray. This is not a one-time prayer to fix all things. It's a practice of bringing all our concerns to God and leaning on Him. We trust Him more than ourselves when it comes to the situations that worry us. It's not easy to do, but we can do it with a faithful prayer life.

DEAR LORD, I TRUST YOU WITH MY PROBLEMS ...

1. Pray to God to lean on Him continuously as life attacks you with things to worry about.
2. Pray to God for the faith not to live with anxiety, but to free yourself from it by the habit of talking to Him.

"Be anxious for nothing, but in everything by prayer and supplication, with thanksgiving, let your requests be made known to God." **(Philippians 4:6)**

Day 256

DEAR GOD, I NEED YOUR HELP TO BE CONTENT ...

Contentment is not false peace or pretending that a circumstance is good when it's bad. It's not trying to see the positive side of every problem. Contentment is realizing the resources within are more than our circumstances from without. How many believe that a change in circumstances would make them happy? "If I had more money ..." "If I had a good spouse ..." "If I had less responsibility ..." We can be content regardless of these things. How is this possible? It's because of Christ. In the context of contentment, Paul said, "I can do all things through Christ who strengthens me" (Philippians 4:13). This verse is not about playing sports, getting a job, or passing an exam. It's referring to contentment. We can be satisfied or at peace because of our relationship with Christ. We have something more valuable than anything on earth. Paul experienced highs and lows. It's not natural to be content during difficult situations. Who jumps out of bed and runs to experience a terrible day? Paul was not immune to problems. He prayed for his thorn in the flesh to be removed three times. Paul learned contentment. He was not dependent upon circumstances to be satisfied. He learned that what he had was far greater than what he experienced. We can too. It starts and ends with Christ.

DEAR LORD, I'M THANKFUL FOR THE RELATIONSHIP I CAN HAVE WITH YOU ...

1. Pray to God that because His love is better than life, you will seek Him early and late.
2. Pray to God, praising and thanking Him for giving you the strength you need when it comes to your relationship with Him.

"Not that I speak in regard to need, for I have learned in whatever state I am, to be content." **(Philippians 4:11)**

Day 257

DEAR GOD, IT'S NOT ABOUT ME ...

Can you recall every trophy, award, certificate, diploma, or promotion in your life? Do you still possess tangible trinkets of achievements? We recently moved, and I came across a box in the attic with awards I had won. It was upstairs, collecting dust. We live in a culture motivated by achievements and rewards. We think in terms of "best" and "first." We have books that collect the best of the best at doing things. I sometimes hear people who have won the championship in an interview say, "I like to thank God for this." I wonder what the losing team thinks. Is God not thankful for them? There is nothing wrong with being successful in something. It's a problem if we allow it to influence the way we see God. Our personal accomplishments don't determine our salvation. If they did, Paul would have been first in the line. He was circumcised on the eighth day, the stock of Israel, and of the tribe of Benjamin. Paul was racially, culturally, and ritually accomplished. However, he considered everything profitless compared to Jesus. Paul gave up all for the knowledge of Jesus Christ. We can be Paul-like in any field. We can be successful in a business or in a sport. We can hold many degrees and have a lot of endings at the ends of our names. All of it is useless unless we have a relationship with Christ Jesus.

DEAR LORD, I'M LOST WHEN IT COMES TO SAVING MYSELF FROM MY OWN SINS ...

1. Pray to God for the forgiveness of your sins as you forgive others who have sinned against you.
2. Pray to God for humility as you look at what the world values and the difference in Christ.

"Yet indeed I also count all things loss for the excellence of the knowledge of Christ Jesus my Lord, for whom I have suffered the loss of all things, and count them as rubbish, that I may gain Christ." **(Philippians 3:8)**

Day 258

DEAR GOD, THANK YOU FOR BEING ATTENTIVE TO MY REQUESTS AND CONCERNS …

I was visiting my adopted grandmother when one of the workers asked to speak to me. She knew that I was a preacher, and she wanted to unload her feelings on me. We sat down away from people, and she poured her broken heart out to me. She told me that her eighteen-year-old daughter had left her. She moved in with another family. She was crying and upset. She said it happened the day before. She was lost and didn't know what to do. I was overwhelmed by her story. She had been living out of a motel because of financial burdens. She wanted me to stop and listen to her troubles. I left wondering how many people I pass just want someone to listen. They feel like the world is on their shoulders. I feel weighed down. I cannot imagine the weight of the cross. I'm not talking about the literal weight of the beams. I'm talking about the burdens, sins, and cares of the world on Jesus' shoulders. It's one thing to bear the load of someone's problems by listening to them. It's another thing to bear the sins of the world. He did it for you and me. It helps me to bear the cares of others. I look to Jesus, who is the master at bearing the weight of sins. Maybe someone doesn't need you to say anything. They need an ear to listen just as God listens to our cares.

DEAR LORD, I'M HUMBLED BY THE WEIGHT YOU BORE ON THE CROSS …

1. Pray to God to help you bear the burdens of others, knowing that Jesus carried your sins.
2. Pray to God to be attentive and open to listening to others' cares and concerns.

> *"He was numbered with the transgressors, and He bore the sin of many, and made intercession for the transgressors."* **(Isaiah 53:11-12)**

Day 259

DEAR GOD, BE WITH ME AS I WALK CLOSER TO THEE ...

There are several fascinating things about the first genealogy in Genesis. We read that the people lived longer. Adam lived to 930 years. Methuselah lived 969 years. The genealogy mentions people having children at a much older age. Enosh was 90 years old when he had a son. In the same genealogy, we have Enoch. He walked with God for 365 years. "Enoch walked with God; and he was not, for God took him" (Genesis 5:24). Enoch was the first person to bypass the penalty of sin through death. *Peripateo* is the Greek word for "walk." It means the way we conduct ourselves. We are to walk in love, by faith, and in wisdom. Most of us looked up to our parents when we were young. We wanted to be like them because we did as they did. My youngest son wants to do what I do because he thinks he is big enough. Our oldest son wants to eat an adult portion like us. They are still at an age of wanting to be like us. As children of God, we are to be concerned with imitating Christ. One of the ways we can imitate Christ is in the way we love. We need to love someone enough to forgive them. We need to love someone enough to be willing to give of our time to others. May we consider walking in the steps of Christ today in the way we love one another.

DEAR LORD, I'M GRATEFUL FOR THE EXAMPLE OF CHRIST WHEN IT COMES TO LOVE ...

1. Pray to God to love Him with all your heart, soul, mind, and strength.
2. Pray to God to love Him enough to demonstrate a Christlike love for others.

"Beloved, let us love one another, for love is of God; and everyone who loves is born of God and knows God." (1 John 4:7)

Day 260

DEAR GOD, YOUR LOVE IS SO GREAT THAT YOU GAVE YOUR ONLY BEGOTTEN SON ...

His mother, grandmother, and aunt raised Nikolaus. His father died when he was six weeks old. He graduated from Wittenberg University. He toured Europe afterward. He had a life-changing experience in an art museum. He saw a painting by Domenico Feti called "Behold the Man" (translated). It was a painting of the thorn-crowned Christ gazing at the viewer. Underneath the painting were the words "I have done this for you; what have you done for me?" The young man said to himself, "I have loved Him for a long time, but I have never actually done anything for Him. From now on I will do whatever He leads me to do." Jesus gave His life. What have we given to Him? The one thing He wants, and we struggle to give it, is our spiritual heart. Another young person saw the same painting on a different date. She sat and read the words underneath. She started to put together a few words of a hymn. She finished the poem, and it was published. The words of her poem became the hymn "I Gave My Life for Thee." Whether in a painting, song, or passage, do we have something that moves us to give to Christ? Today is a good day to give your time, love, devotion, service, or prayer to God.

DEAR LORD, I'M GRATEFUL FOR WHAT YOU GAVE FOR ME ...

1. Pray to God to show your love back today in an act of service or kindness.
2. Pray to God to be humbled today, remembering the cost of a redeemed life.

"For even the Son of Man did not come to be served, but to serve, and to give His life a ransom for many." **(Mark 10:45)**

Day 261

DEAR GOD, THANK YOU FOR GRACE ...

Robert had a rough beginning. His father died when he was young, and his mother sent him to London to learn barbering. What he learned was drinking and gang life. When he was seventeen, his friends went to a fortune-teller after drinking. Something about that experience bothered Robert. He attended a church meeting held by George Whitefield. The preacher's words haunted Robert for three years until He became a follower of Christ. He entered into the ministry and, three years later, started serving a local congregation. He wrote a song for his Pentecost Sunday. It was a prayer that the Holy Spirit would flood into the hearts of the church with streams of mercy, enabling them to sing God's praises and remain faithful to Him. Robert is not the only one whose wild life was changed by the gospel of Christ. I think of Paul. He was a religious terrorist. He had persecuted Christian men and women. He was breathing death threats when Christ took a hold of him on his way to Damascus. Paul was forever changed. He spoke a lot about the blessings in Christ. He was grateful for the transformation in Christ. There is no greater blessing than knowing you have been saved from all of the sinful things you have done. May we be guided by the Spirit's words to streams of mercy as we praise God in our lives.

DEAR LORD, I'M FOREVER GRATEFUL FOR YOU BEING THE SOURCE OF EVERY BLESSING ...

1. Pray to God that you are moved to produce the Spirit's fruit today.
2. Pray to God for the power of the blood of Jesus to transform your old self into a new creation.

"We were buried with Him through baptism into death, that just as Christ was raised from the dead by the glory of the Father, even so we also should walk in newness of life." **(Romans 6:4)**

Day 262

DEAR GOD, OUR NEED FOR YOU IS CONSTANT ...

The words to the hymn were written in June 1872. Annie wrote, "One day as a young wife and mother of thirty-seven years of age, I was busy with my regular household tasks. Suddenly, I became so filled with the sense of nearness to the Master that, wondering how one could live without Him, either in joy or pain, these words, 'I Need Thee Every Hour,' were ushered into my mind, the thought at once taking full possession of me." Annie's husband died sixteen years after the words were published into a hymn. The words she wrote comforted her in a time of grief. Many people look to the same words in a time of significant loss. It's when we lose something great that we feel the strongest need for God in every moment. The passing of time seems slow, and the nights drag out. It's in those moments that we cry out to God in pain, needing Him more than ever. I'm mindful at a funeral of the surviving family members when they are alone at night with nothing but their thoughts. I'm mindful in prayer for God to be with them even more. I pray for a presence of peace in a time of loss. I'm thankful for the words of Annie. She reminds us of the need for God at every hour or moment. I'm thankful for the avenue of prayer, where we can go to God in moments of sadness and loss.

DEAR LORD, I PRAY FOR THE COMFORT ONLY YOU CAN PROVIDE ...

1. Pray to God that you will be comforted by His care and love for you at this time.
2. Pray to God that you can have the peace that surpasses this moment and understanding of it.

"If we are afflicted, it is for your consolation and salvation, which is effective for enduring the same sufferings which we also suffer. Or if we are comforted, it is for your consolation and salvation." **(2 Corinthians 1:6)**

Day 263

DEAR LORD, MAY MY LOVE FOR YOU SHOW ...

Steel Vengeance is one of the tallest, fastest, and longest hybrid coasters in the world. It holds the world record for airtime on a roller coaster. This is where the rider feels like flying rather than riding. I was sitting in the middle of the coaster. The person sitting beside me looked at me with excitement. He had ridden it one hundred times. He went on to talk about how he knew every twist and turn. He knew everything about the coaster. He knew who built it and how much it cost. He said that Steel Vengeance was his favorite ride in the world. It was his baby. He was so passionate about roller coasters and riding them. Here is someone very passionate about something. The excitement and thrills of riding a roller coaster don't compare to our great and awesome God. Am I excited about knowing and loving God? Do I express a love for God that is noticeable to others? I'm not saying that we cannot have fun in this life. Do we express a greater joy in serving our God? The greatest commandment is not there for us to consider. It's to be followed and shown. I wonder if someone were paired up with me, would they see how much I love God?

DEAR LORD, I LOVE YOU AND I WANT TO SHOW IT MORE ...

1. Pray to God to be mindful of the message you send out to others about Him.
2. Pray to God to reciprocate more the love He has graciously shown to you.

"Let your light so shine before men, that they may see your good works and glorify your Father in heaven." **(Matthew 5:16)**

Day 264

DEAR GOD, HELP ME TO SEE BEYOND MY NEGATIVE VIEW OF MYSELF …

Do you recognize the name Roy Ratcliff? If not, you know the person he helped convert to Christ. Jeffrey Dahmer was a serial killer and sex offender. While in prison, Roy studied with Dahmer and he became a born-again Christian. Many people had a hard time believing, let alone, accepting it. How could someone as evil as Dahmer be saved by God? One member where Roy preached said, "If Jeffrey Dahmer is going to heaven, I don't want to be there." We struggle that God's grace can reach a depth to save someone like him. What about the conversion of religious terrorists like Saul of Tarsus? Saul had "persecuted this Way to the death, binding and delivering into prisons both men and women" (Acts 22:4). How could God's grace cover the sins of someone like Saul? We know the rest of the story. He was blinded with the "Light" on the way to Damascus. He gave his life to the Lord. At first, many disciples were leery because of his bad reputation. When I think of notorious people like Jeffrey Dahmer and Saul, I see the power of God's amazing grace. What the world cannot forgive, God can because of the amazing grace in Jesus Christ. Unless we give into God, we are as lost as Saul or Dahmer. Lost is lost regardless of the sins. May we live out the day, knowing the love and grace that God has shown to us.

DEAR LORD, HELP ME TO REALIZE THAT YOUR GRACE IS GREATER THAN MY SINS …

1. Pray to God that you will continue to follow His plan for your salvation.
2. Pray to God, humbled by the grace He has shown in providing forgiveness for your sins.

> *"Let us therefore come boldly to the throne of grace, that we may obtain mercy and find grace to help in time of need."* **(Hebrews 4:16)**

DEAR GOD, I HAVE SINNED AND FALLEN SHORT OF YOUR GLORY ...

Imagine taking a nice walk on a beautiful spring day. You come to a running creek and notice that someone has dumped trash into the water. There is a cloudy film on top of the water in a certain spot. You examine some cans in the river and realize that the trash has been there a while. You can't just leave it, so you take the time to clean it out. Once it's clean, you step back to admire the job you've done. When you come back the next day, there is more trash to be found. You walk upstream to find a garbage dump. If you want the creek to be clean, you have to go to the source. How much of our lives is spent in dealing with the visible garbage and forgetting the source? If you have an anger problem, taking a deep breath and counting to ten isn't going to work. If you have a marriage problem, a date night and gift will not fix it. The problem is a spiritual one. We want to focus our attention on what's outside when the problem is on the inside. Jesus knows that the problem is a heart issue. We need to address the problem and not the symptoms. It's not easy to do this. We must be open and honest with ourselves, others, and God. We cannot pretend that everything is all right when it's not. We cannot smooth it over and ignore it. Have you kept something from God? There is no better time than today to address the problem you have to Him.

DEAR LORD, I REALIZE I HAVE A PROBLEM AND NEED HELP ...

1. Pray to God to create in you a clean heart.
2. Pray to God to help you address and solve your problem. You need His forgiveness.

"Do you not yet understand that whatever enters the mouth goes into the stomach and is eliminated? But those things which proceed out of the mouth come from the heart, and they defile a man." **(Matthew 15:17-19)**

Day 266

DEAR GOD, I BELIEVE, BUT HELP MY UNBELIEF ...

A research company polled people about suffering and faith in God. The question was, "How do you feel about God when suffering occurs that seems unfair?" Thirty-three percent said, "I trust God more." Twenty-five percent said, "I'm confused about God." Sixteen percent said, "I don't think about God in these circumstances." Twenty-six percent struggled with anger or doubt in God. Many great people in the Scriptures struggled with their faith. Elijah had the blues (1 Kings 19). Jeremiah wept and felt that his work had been ineffective (Jeremiah 9). Peter's faith couldn't stay above water (Matthew 14). There was a desperate father who cried out to Jesus, "Lord, I believe; help my unbelief!" (Mark 9:24). The father had asked Jesus to heal his son. Jesus said, "If you can believe, all things are possible to him who believes" (v. 23). No topic is more central to Christianity than faith, and no need is more crucial than the strengthening of faith. We are told repeatedly in the New Testament that the righteous shall live by faith. This comes from the Old Testament. It was the answer God gave to his prophet Habakkuk. His prophet questioned God as to why bad things were happening. God told him to write His answer down for others to read it. God told him, "Behold the proud, his soul is not upright in him; but the just shall live by his faith" (Habakkuk 2:4). Our answer as to why is to live by faith. We are to trust in the Almighty and not lean on our own understanding.

DEAR LORD, I STRUGGLE WITH WHY QUESTIONS ...

1. Pray to God to help you trust in Him and in His answer of living by faith.
2. Pray for the Holy Spirit to bring you love, joy, peace, goodness, kindness, faithfulness, gentleness, patience, and self-control today.

"For in it the righteousness of God is revealed from faith to faith; as it is written, 'The just shall live by faith.'" (Romans 1:17)

Day 267

DEAR GOD, I WANT TO GROW IN THE FAITH ...

In the parable of the sower, the sower cast out seeds, and they landed on four types of soil. Seventy-five percent was not good enough for the seed to grow, develop, and mature. Imagine being in a room with twenty people. Only five will be fruitful and faithful in their faith. I believe the number could be higher if we still had the childlike attitude of wanting to grow. I remember well how our three boys wanted to be big enough to do like the rest of us. They wanted to be big enough to get out of their car seats. They wanted to be big enough to ride the rides at the amusement park. They wanted to be big enough to order from the adult menu. How many times did we hear our children say, "When I get big enough, I will ..."? Our desire to grow up doesn't always last. We grow older, and our passion to grow up changes. We tend to focus on where we have been rather than where we are going. One of God's greatest gifts is the unlimited potential to grow spiritually. My father grew up going to church. His preacher had a lofty goal. He memorized the entire New Testament. He could quote any part or all of it to you. Yet his desire to learn more didn't stop there. He kept on studying and learning. We can never learn too much when it comes to God and His Word. I'm growing more when it comes to my prayers. We need to be as we once were when it comes to growing up in the Lord.

DEAR LORD, I CAN NEVER KNOW ENOUGH WHEN IT COMES TO YOU ...

1. Pray to God, amazed in His presence and how He loves you the way that He does.
2. Pray to God for the desire to keep on learning and growing in the faith.

"Brethren, I do not count myself to have apprehended; but one thing I do, forgetting those things which are behind and reaching forward to those things which are ahead." **(Philippians 3:13)**

Day 268

DEAR GOD, I WANT TO BE AN ENCOURAGER ...

Is there such a thing as a self-made person? Did any of you get to where you are all by yourself? Did you do it without any guidance, assistance, help, or support? Everyone who has ever done a kind deed for us or spoken one word of encouragement to us has entered into the makeup of our characters and our thoughts, as well as our successes. My list is long of the people who have helped and influenced me in my life. My senior year of college, I traveled on the weekend to preach to a congregation in Kentucky. I've looked at some of my sermons that I preached then, and I cringe to think that people sat and listened to them. I would have run out the door. They didn't do that. Instead, they supported, encouraged, and loved me during that year. I grew and learned a lot during that experience. Encouragement is needed for us to be successful physically, emotionally, and spiritually. It doesn't take much to encourage someone. I believe small acts of kindness go a long way. We can pray for someone and let the person know. We can bake something out of love for someone. We can write them a letter, email, or text. We can be positive with our words in building them up. Let me encourage you today to be an encourager to someone. Pray about it and be intentional to let them know they are appreciated.

DEAR LORD, THANK YOU FOR THE ENCOURAGEMENT I RECEIVE FROM YOU ...

1. Pray to God, thankful for the people that He has put in your life to encourage you.
2. Pray to God to be mindful of those around you on a daily basis and to let them know they are appreciated.

"But exhort one another daily, while it is called 'Today,' lest any of you be hardened through the deceitfulness of sin." **(Hebrews 3:13)**

DEAR GOD, I PRAY TO SEE THE WORLD THROUGH YOUR WORD AND SON ...

My youngest son is fascinated by people jaywalking. We were in some traffic, and I was looking to move over into the right-hand lane so I could turn right at the next stoplight. He yelled, "Jaywalking!" and I began to brake as if we were about to hit a car. I didn't say anything, but I thought, "Why are you yelling?" This is a common law that people break. In other words, it's no big deal. At his age, it's a big deal because he has recently learned about it. He doesn't know why someone would break the law. He feels like if the law says it, we should follow it always. It made me think about sin. I can easily desensitize sinful behavior. We read and hear about it so much that it doesn't seem like a big deal. My young son reminds me of God. He doesn't hold the attitude that it's no big deal. Sin is a big enough deal that He gave His only begotten Son. How would you feel if someone close to you died for a cause and others didn't respect that cause? We would be upset. Have we seen something so long that we just accept it? We are called to be a holy, living sacrifice, denying ourselves and following Him. This requires us to see the world through the lens of the gospel.

DEAR LORD, I SOMETIMES ALLOW THINGS AROUND ME TO BE NO BIG DEAL ...

1. Pray to God to strive to see sin for what it is and separate yourself from unholy things to be holy.
2. Pray for God's Spirit to breathe into you that your thoughts might be holy.

> *"As obedient children, not conforming yourselves to the former lusts, as in your ignorance; but as He who called you is holy, you also be holy in all your conduct."* **(1 Peter 1:14-15)**

DEAR GOD, I'M HUMBLED BY THE GIFT OF FORGIVENESS THAT IS FREELY GIVEN ...

Have you heard of Homer and Langley Collyer? The brothers hoarded everything. They were born in the late 1800s to an affluent Manhattan couple. They lived in the luxurious three-story mansion at the intersection of Fifth Avenue and 128th Street. Homer earned a degree in engineering, and Langley became a lawyer. Everything was going good until their parents divorced in 1909. Homer and Langley retreated into their mansion and locked the doors. They were unheard of for forty years. In 1947, someone reported the smell of something dead at their address. It took seven policemen to break down the door because of all the stuff. The police found the body of Homer with gray hair to his shoulders. It took fifteen days and 103 tons of junk for them to find Langley. He was collapsed under all the stuff he had held onto. Who wants to live with yesterday's junk? Do we pile up old things in our hearts? Is a pile of rejection stockpiled in my heart? Have I built up a pile of pain? Doesn't it make sense to get rid of the trash in our hearts? We all choose what lives in us. Forgiven people forgive people. The people who refuse to forgive continue to pile in their hearts the hurt and pain. May you choose forgiveness every day!

DEAR LORD, HELP ME TO BE JUST AS FORGIVING TOWARD THOSE WHO HAVE OFFENDED ME ...

1. Pray to God to be justified by His grace through the redemption in Christ.
2. Pray to God to find within Him the strength to forgive the pile of hurt and pain in your heart.

> *"Let no corrupt word proceed out of your mouth, but what is good for necessary edification, that it may impart grace to the hearers."* **(Ephesians 4:29)**

DEAR GOD, I KNOW LOVE DEMANDS THAT I DEMONSTRATE FORGIVENESS ...

Love "does not seek its own, is not provoked, thinks no evil" (1 Corinthians 13:5). A husband messed up in his marriage. The wife was angry, upset, and quick to let him know it. He apologized, repented, and was forgiven by his wife. However, from time to time, she would bring up what he had done. "Honey," said the husband. "Why do you keep bringing it up? I thought our policy was to forgive and let go." "It is," she said. "I just don't want you to forget that I've forgiven and forgotten." What is forgiveness? Jesus practiced forgiveness while on the cross. "Father, forgive them, for they do not know what they do" (Luke 23:34). Jesus showed that forgiveness is not always easy. It can be hard work. This should not stop us from doing what Christ has asked and shown us. I believe forgiveness is a process. You may say, "I forgive," but it takes time to let go of the harm that has been done. It doesn't happen overnight. You may start out feeling strong about the person. You can think, "I hate you and wish you weren't around." As we let go, we think, "I don't feel any ill will against you." In time, we feel in our hearts the words we have said: "I forgive you." The point is to let go and not hold on to the act done against us. What good is it to hold on to it? Will it help us out? Does it give us peace? We are not in a competition, so there is no need to keep score.

DEAR LORD, HELP ME TO LET GO OF THE THINGS THAT CAUSE HARM TO ME ...

1. Pray to God to be more like Him when it comes to forgiveness.
2. Pray to God to understand the importance of resolving conflict and not holding on to it.

> *"And whenever you stand praying, if you have anything against anyone, forgive him, that your Father in heaven may also forgive you your trespasses."* **(Mark 11:25)**

Day 272

DEAR GOD, I'M NOTHING BUT A JAR OF CLAY, YET YOU LOVE ME ...

I've done it. I did what my parents did to me. I told my boys, "Because I said so." This ended all discussion and debate. They didn't like it just like I didn't when I was younger. They would rather have a better answer, but it's what I choose to use. Why? I'm the parent, and sometimes I don't need to explain my answer. It's yes or no because I said so. What about our relationship with God? I sometimes hear people say, "I could never love a God who would ..." I want to say, "Who would what? Who would disagree with you? Who would allow bad things to happen to good people?" I believe questioning or critiquing God makes as much sense as the clay looking up to the Potter and complaining. God is perfect, and I'm not. My thoughts and ways are far less than His. He has never and will never ask us to figure out why something works. There will be many times when we won't figure out completely what God knows. We struggle and wrestle with God because of what happens to us. I've come to the conclusion, through experiencing life, that I may not completely understand hell, why we are made like this, and why God allowed this to happen. I am clay to God. I will joyfully submit to Him because He is much greater and more knowledgeable than me. God is the Potter, and He said so. Will you have the faith and trust to accept what He has said?

DEAR LORD, HELP ME TO BE SATISFIED WITH TRUSTING IN YOU ...

1. Pray to God to forgive you when you get impatient with Him or question His judgment.
2. Pray to God to humbly accept His will as Jesus did.

"For as many as are led by the Spirit of God, these are sons of God. For you did not receive the spirit of bondage again to fear, but you received the Spirit of adoption by whom we cry out, 'Abba, Father.'" **(Romans 8:14-15)**

DEAR GOD, HELP ME TO BE SATISFIED ...

"Now godliness with contentment is great gain. For we brought nothing into this world, and it is certain we can carry nothing out" (1 Timothy 6:6-7). The Bible is filled with people who got into trouble for wanting more than they had. Every other tree was not enough for Adam and Eve. They wanted the fruit from the forbidden tree. The victory of Jericho was not enough for Achan. He wanted more. He stole from God some silver, gold, and a robe. Everything in Jericho belonged to God. Achan stole from God. Simon wasn't satisfied with the message of God. He wanted the miraculous measure of the Holy Spirit. He offered money to have the power of the Holy Spirit. Peter said to him, "Your money perish with you, because you thought that the gift of God could be purchased with money!" (Acts 8:20). Greed and discontentment are a deadly disease. I'm afraid our world is filled with people not satisfied with what they have. We are bombarded with advertisements for more. After Christmas, I'm flooded with emails from businesses, encouraging me to get the gift I deserve or didn't get. When archaeologists unearthed the city of Pompeii, they uncovered many bodies. Scientists found a preserved body of a woman holding in her hands precious stones. It seemed as death rained down from the mountain above, she risked her life, trying to save a handful of stones. In the end, what seems priceless will be worthless.

DEAR LORD, YOUR LOVE IS BETTER THAN LIFE ...

1. Pray to God to be more connected to Him than stuff.
2. Pray to God to be content in your relationship with God, family, and friends.

"Two things I request of You (deprive me not before I die): Remove falsehood and lies far from me; give me neither poverty nor riches—feed me with the food allotted to me." **(Proverbs 30:7-8)**

Day 274

DEAR GOD, I'M THANKFUL FOR THE SHELTER I RECEIVE IN CHRIST ...

Augustus was born in Farnham, England, in 1740. His father died in a war, his mother spoiled him, his friends thought he was "sick and neurotic," and his relatives disliked him. He began writing hymns at the age of fourteen. In 1776, he wrote an article about God's forgiveness. He ended the article with the poem "Rock of Ages," which has been turned into a beloved hymn. He died two years later. He was only thirty-eight years old. A cleft is a hiding place. There is a human shadow etched in stone in Hiroshima. The stone steps led to the entrance of a bank eight hundred and fifty feet from the hypocenter of the atomic bomb. The person sitting was waiting for the bank to open when the full force of heat rays killed the person on the spot. The only security we have from the wrath of God is the cleft of the Rock of ages. What Jesus did on the cross was an act of double cure. He provided salvation from the wrath of God and made us pure. His wounded side was broken for us. We shouldn't remember what Jesus did on Sunday only. Every day, we should look to the cross and the shelter we find in Jesus. "Much more then, having now been justified by His blood, we shall be saved from wrath through Him" (Romans 5:9).

DEAR LORD, I AM GRATEFUL FOR BEING SAVED BY THE BLOOD OF JESUS ...

1. Pray to God with a humble heart, thanking Him for loving you enough to save you while you were ungodly.
2. Pray to God to always remain in the Lord until your eyes shall close in death.

> *"But God demonstrates His own love toward us, in that while we were still sinners, Christ died for us."* **(Romans 5:8)**

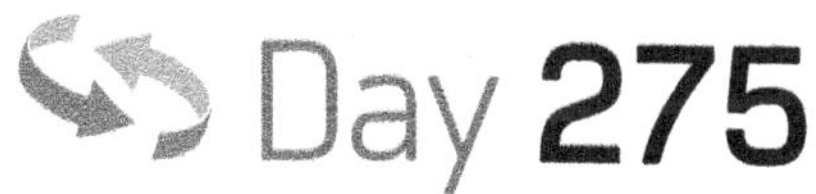

DEAR GOD, I'M LEFT WITH THE CONCLUSION "HOW GREAT THOU ART" ...

The title of the hymn "How Great Thou Art" is a declaration of truth. Stuart was a missionary when he was moved at hearing the hymn in Russian. He modified and expanded the words and made his own arrangement. He said that the first three verses were inspired by Russia's rugged Carpathian Mountains. The first verse was composed when he was caught in a thunderstorm in a Carpathian village. The second verse came from hearing the birds sing near the Romanian border. Has nature moved you or inspired you? You don't have to write a poem or the lyrics to a song to be inspired. "I see the stars." We have only one star in our solar system, and we call it the "sun." The sun is ninety-three million miles away and affects our seasons, ocean currents, weather, and climate. The nearest star to our sun is Proxima Centauri. This star is 4.2 light-years away. A light-year is the distance light travels in one year. One light-year is about 5.88 trillion miles. The nearest star is four times that many miles away. The next time you look at the sky and see all the stars, imagine that the second closest star is 4.2 light-years away. Science, technology, satellites, and missions help us to see more "how great Thou art." What we know is confirmation of God's greatness and power.

DEAR LORD, THE HEAVENS DECLARE THE GLORY OF GOD ...

1. Pray to God about how wonderful it is to see, touch, feel, hear, and taste His creative world.
2. Pray to God with gratitude that He is still mindful of you when you consider all the stars, planets, galaxies, solar systems, people, and animals.

"For since the creation of the world His invisible attributes are clearly seen, being understood by the things that are made, even His eternal power and Godhead, so that they are without excuse." **(Romans 1:20)**

Day 276

DEAR GOD, THANK YOU FOR THE GREAT POWER MADE CLEAR IN JESUS ...

Have you ever sat down to pray and found your mind wandering? Think of all the distractions in your day. We are buried in distractions. I can start to pray, and my mind wanders off to "Did I remember to pay that bill?" or "Do we have enough money for the week?" I can lie down for the night and start my prayer and then go off in the direction of work and what I need to do the next day. We can be busy and worried about many things. Prayer reveals how unfocused our lives are. We need to examine our lives. What is the purpose of my day? What am I striving for? What we do day in and day out is not unimportant or useless. We need to center our focus and attention more on the main thing. When Jesus told His listeners to seek first the kingdom of God, He was telling them that instead of worrying about many things, we should concentrate on the one necessary thing. Our minds can be single-minded. Have you ever noticed a dog at the dinner table? It's sitting patiently, waiting for something to drop from the table or someone to give him some food. The dog is so focused that nothing else matters but the piece of meat on the table. The dog has no other wishes, hopes, or thoughts. If only we were that concentrated in our prayers. I believe we can be when we keep the one necessary thing in our daily lives.

DEAR LORD, KEEP ME FOCUSED ON THE NECESSARY THING TODAY ...

1. Pray to God to give you clarity in all your distractions.
2. Pray to God, who loves you with a greater love than you can love yourself, to help you today.

"But seek first the kingdom of God and His righteousness, and all these things shall be added to you. Therefore do not worry about tomorrow, for tomorrow will worry about its own things. Sufficient for the day is its own trouble." **(Matthew 6:33-34)**

DEAR GOD, GUIDE MY THOUGHTS AND HEART ...

We can easily look at prayer as a kind of magic wand. We look to God like a genie asking for our three wishes. We want growth without the cost, results without effort, answers without the work of searching and asking. If we are not careful, our prayers sound like one big Band-Aid to our problems. Yet God has called on us to ask Him. He has invited us to participate through prayer. He already knows what we tell Him. The asking is for our sake and the sake of others. God listens, moves, and acts as we pray. "Only God can move mountains. But faith and prayer move God." Moses was with God on Mount Sinai. He was there to receive the Ten Commandments; however, the people were at the foot of the mountain, melting gold for an idol. God knew their sin and told Moses to go down. He said, "Now therefore, let Me alone, that My wrath may burn hot against them and I may consume them" (Exodus 32:10). Moses pleaded with the Lord. He spoke of the history of God with Abraham, Isaac, and Israel. "So the LORD relented from the harm which He said He would do to His people" (v. 14). It seems hard to imagine that God looks to us to do things. In prayer, we look to God to listen to our requests as a loving parent listens to the request of a child. Asking demonstrates that we need Him. It's not that we ask and He gives, but we ask because we trust and hope in Him.

DEAR LORD, GUIDE MY LIPS THAT I WILL ASK FOR THE THINGS THAT GIVE YOU GLORY ...

1. Pray to God, thankful that He listens and considers your requests in connection to His awesome will.
2. Pray to God to trust in His sovereignty as He guides you in the way you should go.

"And now, O Lord GOD, You are God, and Your words are true, and You have promised this goodness to Your servant. Now therefore, let it please You to bless the house of Your servant." (2 Samuel 7:28-29)

Day 278

DEAR GOD, MAY I SEEK YOU IN THE EVENTS OF MY DAILY LIFE ...

It would be nice to afford the time to get away more in seclusion out at sea or by a deep wooded mountainside. We can get away from the noises of our every day and enjoy the silence and sounds of nature. We can stay in our cabin in the woods and meditate all day because of no normal workday pressures. However, everyday life is our main setting for spiritual growth in life and in prayer. It's on the way to work where we can say a prayer for God's guidance and wisdom and for what we do to glorify Him and bring Him honor. It's in those moments of quick rest at work that we look to God to help us be a light to the person we see on a daily basis. Ask God for wisdom for the right encouraging word that will aid them to finish out their day as well. There are so many ways we can use our time in prayer. We can write reminders or set our phones to alarm us at a certain time to pray. These things help when daily activities and pressures lure me into forgetting my spiritual resolve. Prayer and reading the Scriptures keep me grounded and centered in-between Sundays. Our souls need constant attention. We are not made for the weekends and retreats only. We are to endure each and every day. This is done one step at a time and one prayer at a time.

DEAR LORD, I'M THANKFUL FOR THE DAILY REMINDERS THAT I HAVE OF YOU ...

1. Pray to God to seek Him every day and not only on weekends or at special events.
2. Pray to God to teach you to seek Him in all things and to do all things for Him.

"Your kingdom come. Your will be done on earth as it is in heaven. Give us this day our daily bread." **(Matthew 6:10-11)**

Day 279

DEAR GOD, THANK YOU FOR MY SWEET, GODLY MOTHER ...

My mother had a tremendous influence on my life. Her influence was not in her degrees because she never finished college. Her influence was not in her profession because she raised us at home. Her influence was not because she was famous. Her influence was because of her faith. When I was younger, I thought all mothers were like mine. They easily said no and didn't take any back talk. I'm so thankful for my mother and the example she set for us. Mothers are special, but godly mothers are priceless. Anna Jarvis loved her mother. She conceived of "Mother's Day" as a way of honoring the sacrifices mothers make for their families. Anna recalled her mother tending to the needs of the wounded in the Civil War. Anna wanted Mother's Day to be personal and with family. When Mother's Day took off with merchants, Anna denounced the commercialization of Mother's Day with cards, flowers, and candies. I'm thankful for the national holiday Mother's Day. However, I believe we should take every day to thank Mom for her dedicated love for the family. I'm grateful to the mothers who work tirelessly and sacrifice greatly for their families. I'm honored with the mothers who show the love of Christ every day. Thank You, God, for mothers like this.

DEAR LORD, THANK YOU FOR ALL GODLY WOMEN AND MOTHERS ...

1. Pray to God, thankful for the home and family because you can see His love for you through mothers.
2. Pray to God, asking for protection and safety for your home from temptation from the evil one.

"As one whom his mother comforts, so I will comfort you; and you shall be comforted in Jerusalem." (Isaiah 66:13)

Day 280

DEAR GOD, I PRAY FOR THE ONES READING THIS RIGHT NOW ...

A young girl said to her mother, "I suppose up in heaven they think I'm dead." Her mother replied, "Why do you suppose they think you are dead?" "Because," said the girl, "I haven't said my prayers for a week." The young girl is right. We are spiritually dead without prayer. How long can you go without hearing from your family? We get concerned after so long of not hearing from our families. It's a greater concern with God when it comes to us not talking to Him. He has accepted the high cost of sin and paid it with His only begotten Son. Why? So we can freely and openly talk to Him because of our relationship to Him as our heavenly Father. Paul believed in talking to God in prayer. I find it interesting that Paul and the disciples had the power of the Holy Spirit to heal, cast out demons, and cure ailments. However, they were dedicated to learning more about prayer. Paul wanted the Christians to know that he was praying for them. How did they feel, knowing that someone like Paul was praying for them? I can only imagine that they were encouraged by it. I'm encouraged when someone tells me that they prayed for me. It warms my heart and soul that someone else took the time to mention my name to God. Let me encourage you to pray for someone and let them know.

DEAR LORD, HELP ME TO THINK OF OTHERS ...

1. Pray to God, lifting up ________________ to His awesome throne on high.
2. Pray to God, asking that He consider, comfort, and surround ________________ with His love, mercy, and grace.

"May the Lord make you increase and abound in love to one another and to all, just as we do to you." **(1 Thessalonians 3:12)**

DEAR GOD, I KNOW THAT MY SINS PLACED ME AT ODDS WITH YOU ...

The Bible introduces the friendship of David and Jonathan by saying, "The soul of Jonathan was knit to the soul of David, and Jonathan loved him as his own soul" (1 Samuel 18:1). Do you have a friendship like that? Have you ever described a friendship as "my soul is knit to the soul of ____________"? This type of friend is someone willing to sacrifice. Jonathan freely gave David his robe, bow, sword, armor, and belt. Jonathan was not selfish with his things. He gave something meaningful to his friend, David. I believe a key to a great friendship is a relationship where unselfishness prevails. Jesus said, "Greater love has no one than this, than to lay down one's life for his friends" (John 15:13). Jesus sacrificed Himself for His friends. We know the feeling of receiving a gift. We may have received so many gifts that we don't think a lot about it. No gift reaches the height, depth, and weight of Jesus. God gave His only begotten Son. He didn't sell, trade, or finance Jesus to us. He gave the greatest gift so we could have everlasting life. Why should I let loneliness take control of my heart and day when I know there is someone who demonstrated "greater love" to be our friend? There's not a friend like the lowly Jesus.

DEAR LORD, I'M THANKFUL THAT I CAN LOVE YOU AND BE ACCEPTED BY THE FATHER ...

1. Pray to God, thanking Him for the people in your life who have helped you love Him.
2. Pray to God, humbled that He still wants your friendship despite your sinful nature.

> *"A man who has friends must himself be friendly, but there is a friend who sticks closer than a brother."* **(Proverbs 18:24)**

Day 282

DEAR GOD, YOUR LOVE IS SO AMAZING ...

"When I Survey the Wondrous Cross" is a hymn written by Isaac Watts. He wrote it in 1707 for the use at a communion service. The original title was "The Crucifixion to the World by the Cross of Christ." The title of the hymn accurately describes the event that Jesus endured. As Jesus walked, bearing the weight of the world, He could hear the crowds cry out, "Crucify, crucify." He could feel the hatred in their voices. They were His chosen people. He loved them, and they wanted Him dead. He was beaten, bloody, and bruised. The harshness of the world was depicted on the body of our Lord. His heart was heavy, but He walked to His death. Crucifixion was the harshest form of punishment allowed under Roman law. The purpose of the cross was to terrorize, humiliate, and torture. Why do we sing about the "wondrous cross"? Jesus was the best heaven had to offer, and the crucifixion was the worst mankind had to offer. The cross was the testimony of the unconquerable love of almighty God. The crucifixion showed God's length to which He would go to redeem the sinful world:

> "Forbid it, Lord, that I should boast,
> Save in the death of Christ my God;
> All the vain things that charm me most,
> I sacrifice them to His blood."[3]

DEAR LORD, I LOOK TO THE CROSS AND SEE ...

1. Pray to God about any struggles you have while thinking and reading about what your Lord did for you because of your guilt.
2. Pray to God with humility and sincerity for the love of God while you were a rebellious sinner.

> *"For Christ also suffered once for sins, the just for the unjust, that He might bring us to God, being put to death in the flesh but made alive by the Spirit."* (1 Peter 3:18)

Day 283

DEAR GOD, I LOOK BACK TO THE NIGHT IN THE GARDEN ...

Abraham Lincoln sits on his stone chair in our nation's capital. George Washington is stretched to the last cent, war heroes are etched in rock, great athletes retire their jersey numbers, and streets are named after those who traveled them. There is one memorial that differs from all others. Many historians do not recognize this memorial. It's not considered newsworthy by the local media. This memorial is known as "the Lord's Supper." The Gospels provide the details to the final week of Jesus. It seems the biblical record slows down when it comes to this significant event. Only two of the Gospels mention the events of Jesus' birth. Every gospel book records the death, burial, and resurrection of Jesus. No other event was like it. God was being crucified because of the sins of the world. When it came to Jesus' suffering, there wasn't a miracle performed to stop it from happening. There was no supernatural rescue in the garden where Jesus prayed. The cross was Jesus' goal all along. This great memorial is remembered with the bread and the fruit of the vine. It's a strong visual of what Jesus endured in His body. It's a time for us to remember Him.

DEAR LORD, I LOOK FORWARD TO WHEN I DRINK IT NEW IN THE FATHER'S KINGDOM ...

1. Pray to God to remember the body that lived, worked, was beaten, was whipped, was mocked, was cursed, and died.
2. Pray to God to remember the blood that was shed for the forgiveness of sins.

> *"'Take, eat; this is My body.' Then He took the cup, and gave thanks, and gave it to them, saying, 'Drink from it, all of you. For this is My blood of the new covenant, which is shed for many for the remission of sins.'"* **(Matthew 26:26-28)**

Day 284

DEAR GOD, MAY I NOT TAKE FOR GRANTED THE CROSS OR GROW UNAPPRECIATIVE ...

On that dark Friday, three crosses were silhouetted against the sky. Three men were sentenced to crucifixion. Each had to carry their instrument of death to the place of the skull. I look to each cross that stood tall that day. The cross bearing the rebellious thief reminds me of my life without Jesus. My sins are the reason for the innocent One being sentenced to death. "While we were still sinners, Christ died for us" (Romans 5:8). Maybe that is why Jesus died in the middle. The middle cross, bearing the Redeemer, reminds me that my sins are the reason for this event. You see, when it comes to sin, "I" am in the middle. The second or middle cross, bearing the Redeemer, lets me know of the One who paid the price of sin for me. "For He made Him who knew no sin to be sin for us, that we might become the righteousness of God in Him" (2 Corinthians 5:21). The cross bearing the repentant thief reminds me of my new life in Jesus. Have you ever noticed the middle letter in the word "faith"? It is the letter "I." Before Christ, I'm in sin. With Christ, I'm in the faith. This transformation should move us all in Christ to proclaim, "Precious feast, all else surpassing, wondrous love for you and me."[4] It's at this time that we remember our Lord's word: "Do this in remembrance of Me" (1 Corinthians 11:24).

DEAR LORD, I'M THANKFUL FOR THAT MIDDLE CROSS ON THAT DARK FRIDAY ...

1. Pray to God when you struggle to wrap your mind around Him not knowing sin but being sin for you.
2. Pray to God to examine your faith daily as you reflect on the cost for your salvation.

> *"Let a man examine himself, and so let him eat of the bread and drink of the cup."* **(1 Corinthians 11:28)**

Day 285

DEAR GOD, I THANK YOU FOR AN IMPORTANT LESSON ...

My wife came across a school project from March 2015. It was a collection of our middle son's poems in first grade. They had a poetry café for parents to come and select a poem to be read to them. I was at home, recovering from my first brain surgery. I never saw the poem that I'm writing about until recently. The title is "Guess Who????" He wrote, "Is at home; Is nise; Is a pecher; Is relly hart; Is relly sick; Is the Best Friend." I wanted to cry after reading his innocent words from a big heart. He was processing what his dad was going through in first grade. It made me think of the family of a patient. We can focus so much on the one who is sick and rightly so. However, it also affects every family member as well. I sometimes think of caregivers. I know so many people who care for their spouse or parent. Many calls and cards are sent to the sick one to encourage them in their battle. What about the caregiver? The one who watches and helps daily. What about the children? What do think and feel? They are hurting as well and attempting to process it the best they can at their age. I try to be mindful in prayer and in conversation of everyone. I realize as a patient that my family needed just as much encouragement and love from everyone. When you pray for the sick, think of the family as well. They are going through a tough time as well.

DEAR LORD, I WANT TO PRAY FOR ...

1. Pray to God, confessing your need for His healing and His grace today.
2. Pray to God for the peace and joy that only come from Him during this difficult time.

"Now may the Lord of peace Himself give you peace always in every way. The Lord be with you all." **(2 Thessalonians 3:16)**

Day 286

DEAR GOD, I PRAY TO BE SINCERE ...

You wouldn't know it at first, but their home was nothing but a set. One side looked beautiful, an eloquent home with brick and siding on the exterior, while the other side was nothing but two-by-fours propped up with pulleys. The family who lived there didn't exist, except for thirty minutes each week on television. It's amazing the detail that set designers put into a television studio. It has the appearance of being real. However, we know there is another side where there are no cameras or audience. If we put cameras "behind the scenes" of your life, what would we see? On a hot summer day, the mom asked her son to bless the food. "I don't want to say it!" said the boy. "Son, just say what you hear me say," said the mother. The boy bowed his head and mumbled, "Oh Lord, why did You invite these people over on a hot day like this?" What's behind the face we see? What do you do and say when no one is around? Am I guilty of wearing a Christian mask? Jesus warned about hypocrisy. "And when you pray, you shall not be like the hypocrites. For they love to pray standing in the synagogues and on the corners of the streets, that they may be seen by men" (Matthew 6:5). We need to be genuine people who are transparent by our faith and love. Our prayer lives are not flashy or showy, but genuine and sincere. Remember we are praying to God and not people.

DEAR LORD, I WANT TO BE MORE AUTHENTIC IN MY RELATIONSHIP WITH YOU ...

1. Pray to God, realizing everything you say and do carries tremendous weight and influence.
2. Pray to God that if you're wearing a mask, you would be genuine.

"The purpose of the commandment is love from a pure heart, from a good conscience, and from sincere faith." **(1 Timothy 1:5)**

Day 287

DEAR GOD, I PRAY FOR COURAGE ...

You wake up one night to get a glass of water, and you notice that your neighbor's house is on fire. You calmly wipe your eyes to make sure you are actually seeing what you are seeing. You then go back to bed. Is that you? You have a good friend that you love. This friend has always been there in your life. If something is wrong, this person would be the first one to help out in any way. This friendship is only temporary because you have shown no concern for extending this friendship in the next life. There are no plans of spending eternity together. Is that you? Jesus said, "Go therefore and make disciples of all the nations, baptizing them in the name of the Father and of the Son and of the Holy Spirit" (Matthew 28:19). What do you think about when you hear Jesus' command? When it came to evangelizing, Jeremiah, the prophet, said, "His word was in my heart like a burning fire shut up in my bones; I was weary of holding it back, and I could not" (Jeremiah 20:9). Jeremiah could not keep his mouth shut because of the importance of the word. He compared the message as a burning fire shut up in his bones. It has been said that people will respond more quickly to help when someone cries "fire" rather than "help." God used fire to show His power and presence to Moses. Do we have a fire within us? Do we have a fire to share the greatest message ever? Our only hope is in the words of Christ.

DEAR LORD, I WANT OTHERS TO KNOW WHAT I KNOW IN YOU ...

1. Pray to God, knowing there is no other place to go for salvation and hope.
2. Pray to God to teach the truth in love and help the hurting.

"Simon Peter answered Him, 'Lord, to whom shall we go? You have the words of eternal life. Also we have come to believe and know that You are the Christ, the Son of the living God.'" (John 6:68-69)

Day 288

DEAR GOD, TEACH ME TO PRAY LIKE THOSE BEFORE ME ...

"He said to them, 'When you pray, say: Our Father in heaven, hallowed be Your name. Your kingdom come'" (Luke 11:2). The disciples had asked Jesus to teach them to pray. His answer was this model prayer. The beginning of the Lord's Prayer is a statement of complete and ultimate reverence toward the Father. The Jewish people so revered the commandment to "not take the Lord's name in vain" that they would not pronounce the name of God unless reading from the Torah. We have swung the pendulum to the other side with the abuse and misuse of God's name. We even use God's name with profanity. How can we pray to God one minute and misuse His awesome name the other? The word "hallowed" refers to "making something holy." It's God's holiness that Jesus mentioned, not His love, in this model prayer. We are heard when we submit to God's will. We learn to ask for the same will to be done on earth as in heaven. This can be difficult since most of our lives has been centered on us. We get older and learn that there is someone else who deserves more recognition and praise than us. Jesus' answer to the disciples' question helps us when it comes to our approach to prayer. May we learn to pray like Jesus and live like Him.

DEAR LORD, I'M GRATEFUL FOR YOUR TEACHING ON PRAYER ...

1. Pray to God that you may live and pray with reverence and respect for the relationship He has with you.
2. Pray to God that you will take the words you pray and apply them to your daily life and talk.

"When they heard that, they raised their voice to God with one accord and said: 'Lord, You are God, who made heaven and earth and the sea, and all that is in them.'" **(Acts 4:24)**

DEAR GOD, I PRAY THAT MY FAITH IS IN YOU AS THE GREAT GIVER OF ALL ...

I'm constantly amazed by the surrender of Abraham with Isaac. I'm a father of three boys, and I cannot think of giving one up. Isaac was a gift from God. Abraham and Sarah waited twenty-five years for him. Abraham and Sarah had enjoyed years, months, and days with their precious son. Their home was filled with memories of Isaac growing up. We don't know the age of Isaac when God tested Abraham. However, Isaac was old enough to converse and know about worship. The word "test" is the idea of proving the quality of something. What was God testing? Did Abraham love the gift more than the Giver? Do we? God told Abraham to take his only son Isaac and offer him as a burnt offering on the mountain. Abraham knew what a "burnt offering" was. It was an offering where the entire animal was placed on the altar to be consumed by fire. Abraham obeyed God all the way until God stopped him from taking his son's life. Abraham was willing to surrender completely to God without question. God didn't spare His only begotten Son. He had to surrender His life for the Father's will. We are called to present our bodies as living sacrifices to God. We are to surrender our will to God's by presenting ourselves as a living burnt sacrifice. God doesn't want an hour from you. He wants all of you for His glory. Lord, I surrender all to You because You surrendered all for my salvation.

DEAR LORD, HELP ME WITH MY WORDS ...

1. Pray to God, asking for His mercy to enable you to present your body as a living sacrifice.
2. Pray to God, desiring to glorify Him in your body, which belongs to Him.

"And do not present your members as instruments of unrighteousness to sin, but present yourselves to God as being alive from the dead, and your members as instruments of righteousness to God." **(Romans 6:13)**

Day 290

DEAR GOD, I NEED YOU EVERY HOUR ...

One of God's most frequent commands has been "Go!" I think about the children of Israel in the wilderness, the early church scattering because of persecution, and the great commission to go into the world. Think of all the places you have been so far. Some places and moments are pleasant, and others not so much. Where is our journey taking us? Have you ever stopped to think about where you are going? I'm referring to life. Where is your life heading? We know that the Christian life doesn't end in the grave. This journey to be with God takes time for some and not so much for others. It's longer than the journeys we take in a car. It's not any time for us to travel to the end of our state and back. The journey of life takes some time and requires faith and patience. God called Abraham to go when he was seventy-five years old. Abraham was married to Sarah, and they had no children. God was going to establish the Jewish nation with this senior-citizen couple who were past the age of childbearing. What God is able to do and see is something far beyond our comprehension. Abraham was one hundred years old when Isaac was born. When God promises something, He keeps it. We must journey onward and trust and wait on Him. We haven't earned the right for our Creator to wait on us. I don't know where you are right now. I hope you see the need to trust in God and patiently wait on Him.

DEAR LORD, LOOK DOWN ON ME WHEN I KNEEL IN PRAYER ...

1. Pray to God, hoping to meet Him there so blessed Jesus can hold your hand.
2. Pray to God to help you travel in His divine light so that you may know the blessed way.

"Let us therefore be diligent to enter that rest, lest anyone fall according to the same example of disobedience." **(Hebrews 4:11)**

Day 291

DEAR GOD, HELP ME TO KEEP MY ANGER IN CHECK ...

"See that no one renders evil for evil to anyone, but always pursue what is good both for yourselves and for all" (1 Thessalonians 5:15). The two words that make this verse hard to follow are "anyone" and "always." It's easy never to do evil to someone we love and care about. It's difficult to do good to someone who betrayed our trust and hurt us. I can do good to those who love and care for me. However, it hurts to seek to do good to someone who did me wrong. I forgive, but I cannot forget what someone did to me. I don't like writing about it, but it may help someone. It was a breach of friendship and trust. This person did the most unthinkable thing to me. I was shocked and stunned when I found out. I wanted to hurt the person. This was how I felt at first. I was given some time to think about what happened, and I prayed about it. It required a lot not to hold on but to give it to God. In time, I did the one thing that I didn't think I could do. I forgave. Our friendship was ruined, and we wouldn't be the same again, but I forgave him. I see the wisdom in not doing evil but good. I know why God wants us to pursue good. If we don't, the negative feelings will consume our hearts. Praise be to God for the example of Jesus. He loved us at our worst while He died for our sins.

DEAR LORD, HELP ME GET TO A PLACE WHERE I CAN LET GO AND GIVE IT TO YOU ...

1. Pray to God to give you the strength to forgive and move on from what the person did to you.
2. Pray to God to be mindful of your own forgiveness of the wrongs you have done against Him.

"Repay no one evil for evil. Have regard for good things in the sight of all men. If it is possible, as much as depends on you, live peaceably with all men." **(Romans 12:17-18)**

Day 292

DEAR GOD, I KNOW MANY WHO STRUGGLE WITH PAIN AND SUFFERING ...

In the ancient East, a prince was born into a life of royalty in present-day Nepal. His name was Siddhartha Gautama. He was young, wealthy, and believed to be happy. One day, he left the palace and went into the world and saw something he had never seen—suffering. He realized that all people suffered, whether rich or poor. He left the palace to live as a monk. He came up with the Four Noble Truths, which is the basis of the Buddhist religion. People in early history, prior to the birth of Christ, were struggling with suffering. A prophet of God also struggled with how God allowed evil and wrongdoing. Do we struggle with the same? Is it possible that God and suffering are not polar opposites but can exist together? Jesus proved that God and suffering can coexist. When God became one of us, He suffered many things. Did His pain, suffering, and agony on the cross lead to a greater good? Was His death in vain? "To this you were called, because Christ also suffered for us, leaving us an example, that you should follow His steps" (1 Peter 2:21). Our life in God wouldn't be possible if not for Jesus suffering on the cross.

DEAR LORD, I PRAY YOU WILL REVEAL YOUR PURPOSE AND WILL IN TIMES OF SUFFERING ...

1. Pray to God, falling to your knees in your weakness and looking to Him for your strength.
2. Pray to God, asking that all you do today would bring glory and honor in your suffering.

"For Christ also suffered once for sins, the just for the unjust, that He might bring us to God, being put to death in the flesh but made alive by the Spirit." **(1 Peter 3:18)**

Day 293

DEAR FATHER, THANK YOU FOR LOVING ME ...

"In this manner, therefore, pray: Our Father in heaven" (Matthew 6:9). Jesus taught us to whom we pray. Our direction is to God. It starts with God. If you think of a conversation, we get the person's attention by calling their name. We address them by the name given. What is the name given in prayer? He is "our Father." Jesus taught us to regard God as the Father of us all even though God could rightly be a severe judge over us. What if Jesus had said, "When you pray, say, 'Our Judge in heaven'"? We would approach prayer as someone on trial, awaiting the verdict from the almighty Judge. God is a Judge, but He is also our Father. As our Father, we go to Him in prayer to discuss family matters. I appreciate this even more as a parent. I sometimes know what my children are going to say. I want to hear them say it, especially if they want money. Our heavenly Father wants to hear from His children. Where is our Father? He is in heaven. Christianity is a heaven-centered religion. Jesus came from heaven, and He returned to heaven. Jesus told His disciples to "rejoice because your names are written in heaven" (Luke 10:20). He challenged us all to "lay up for yourselves treasures in heaven" (Matthew 6:20). Thank You, Lord, for teaching me to whom I'm praying.

DEAR LORD, I'M GRATEFUL FOR YOUR TEACHING AND EXAMPLE IN PRAYER ...

1. Pray to our Father, thankful for the relationship you have because of your life in Christ.
2. Pray to our Father, thankful that as a good parent, He is there to listen and consider what is best for you.

"Father, if it is Your will, take this cup away from Me; nevertheless not My will, but Yours, be done." **(Luke 22:42)**

Day 294

DEAR FATHER, HOLY AND AWESOME IS YOUR NAME ...

"Hallowed be Your name" (Matthew 6:9). The first petition reminds us that we are talking to our Father in heaven. "The Lord has established His throne in heaven, and His kingdom rules over all" (Psalm 103:19). God deserves more than respect. We are to regard Him with reverence and holiness. We don't make God holy with our prayerful words. He is holy. Jesus is teaching us not to dishonor the name with which we are called. Our view of God influences our attitude in approaching and communicating to Him. God is not some buddy that I can talk to how I want. My children help me better understand the teaching of Jesus in prayer. I want my boys to love their mom and dad. I want them to be comfortable with us. However, I don't want to be their friend or buddy. I'm their father. They will make friends. However, I'm their one and only father on earth. I don't want them to talk to me like a friend from school. As we develop our relationship with God, we need to be reminded that He is God, and we are not. He is holy, and we are only holy because of Jesus. King David had a close relationship with God and leaned on Him for many years. However, He didn't forget the fact that God is above us, and we are below Him. When you pray, remember whom you are talking to.

DEAR LORD, I'M THANKFUL FOR YOUR TEACHING IN ADDRESSING OUR FATHER ...

1. Pray to our Father with reverence and respect for Him as God.
2. Pray to our Father with humility, knowing that you have done nothing to deserve His grace and mercy.

"So when they heard that, they raised their voice to God with one accord and said: 'Lord, You are God, who made heaven and earth and the sea, and all that is in them.'" **(Acts 4:24)**

Day 295

DEAR FATHER, I STRUGGLE WHEN IT COMES TO MY WILL AND YOURS ...

"Your kingdom come. Your will be done on earth as it is in heaven" (Matthew 6:10). I believe this statement would have appealed to the original audience. The Jews were awaiting the Messiah to free them from the Roman Empire and restore the land of inheritance to them. The Messiah didn't come as a warrior, but He came as a suffering servant. The "kingdom" is not a physical one, but a spiritual one. "But seek first the kingdom of God and His righteousness, and all these things shall be added to you" (Matthew 6:33). Our primary goal should be His will because everything else will fall into place. The spiritual kingdom is the relationship we have in Christ. In connection to God's kingdom, His will is done in heaven with the angels and archangels before the throne of God. His will is done on earth but not fully like in heaven. There are many who choose to do their own will. They follow the will of self, of greed, of power, of beauty, and the list goes on. The only will that will be done is God's. Do I seek God's will in my prayers? What do I talk about the most to God? Is it about my life and my day? Am I searching and leaning on God's will to be done in my life as it is in heaven? May God's will be done and not my own.

DEAR LORD, I'M THANKFUL FOR THE ESTABLISHMENT OF YOUR KINGDOM ...

1. Pray to God that in your life today, you will seek His will to be done.
2. Pray to God to help you set your priority with Him first and you second.

"Therefore do not cast away your confidence, which has great reward. For you have need of endurance, so that after you have done the will of God, you may receive the promise." **(Hebrews 10:35-36)**

Day 296

DEAR FATHER, I ASK FOR MY DAILY BREAD AND NOTHING ELSE OR NOTHING LESS ...

"Give us this day our daily bread" (Matthew 6:11). This is not a reference to a whole loaf of white or wheat bread. It's not for a filet mignon or prime rib, but for bread. It's not to fill my refrigerator and pantry with a month's supply of food, but enough for the day. The "daily bread" can be a metaphor for necessities rather than luxuries. This prayer challenges us to be content with the necessities of life. "Remove falsehood and lies far from me; give me neither poverty nor riches—feed me with the food allotted to me" (Proverbs 30:8). Aristotle was a well-known Greek teacher and writer. He taught the "golden mean," which is life between the two extremes. The two extremes are excess and deficiency. It's interesting to see, with other cultures, the teaching of contentment with not too much or too little. God is the source of our daily bread. Jesus was teaching us to be thankful for what God has done. Everything we have we have picked up along the way. The One who put it there for us to pick up was God. We work for our daily bread, but we still recognize that God is the source of every blessing. I believe this old proverb still applies: "Back of the loaf is the flour, and back of the flour is the mill; and back of the mill is the wheat that waves on yonder hill; and back of the hill is the sun and the rain and the Father's will." Be thankful for what you have.

DEAR LORD, I THANK YOU FOR TEACHING NECESSITY RATHER THAN LUXURY ...

1. Pray to God that He will supply you with all your needs.
2. Pray to God to be satisfied and grateful with what He gives you.

"And my God shall supply all your need according to His riches in glory by Christ Jesus." **(Philippians 4:19)**

Day 297

DEAR FATHER, I NEED YOUR FORGIVENESS ...

"And forgive us our debts, as we forgive our debtors" (Matthew 6:12). The Greek word for "debt" refers to that which is owed. It is used to point to an offense, fault, or sin. In Luke's account, it says, "forgive us our sins" (Luke 11:4). This petition challenges our pride and tests our spiritual awareness. We may not want to confess or repent of sins. We may think that we are all right compared to other people. However, our sins stand out as we stand before a Holy God. Jesus linked our relationship with God to our relationship with others. If we are unwilling to forgive or resolve the situation, we have a God problem. He will not forgive us of our sins. We realize that, but we still struggle to forgive. How do we forgive someone who has wronged us? We must redirect our focus to the love that was shown on the cross. Jesus demonstrated the attitude of forgiveness for those not asking for it. We need to confess those strong feelings we have about someone. Our relationship with that person may be strained, but the greatest concern is that our hearts hold no animosity. I cannot say it better than Jesus: "For if you forgive men their trespasses, your heavenly Father will also forgive you. But if you do not forgive men their trespasses, neither will your Father forgive your trespasses" (Matthew 6:14-15). May I forgive others as You have forgiven me.

DEAR LORD, THANK YOU FOR ADDRESSING MY RELATIONSHIP WITH THE FATHER ...

1. Pray to God that you can cast your anger, bitterness, resentment on Him as He cares for you.
2. Pray to God not to let any event or situation keep you from God's forgiveness.

"... bearing with one another, and forgiving one another, if anyone has a complaint against another; even as Christ forgave you, so you also must do." **(Colossians 3:13)**

Day 298

DEAR FATHER, YOU KNOW THE TEMPTATIONS I MAY FACE TODAY ...

"And do not lead us into temptation, but deliver us from the evil one" (Matthew 6:13). Let me first tell you what this doesn't mean. We cannot constantly pray "lead us not into temptation" and then knowingly go into a situation in which we know we will be tempted. It also doesn't mean that God "leads us into temptation," for God "cannot be tempted by evil, nor does He Himself tempt anyone" (James 1:13). What it is saying is that we should not be brought or led into temptation. The responsibility is not with God but on us. Maybe we could say, "Help us not to be led into temptation." In regard to "the evil," it has a definite article before it. It refers to the evil one, the devil. Jesus demonstrated strength in refusing to be led by the evil one in the wilderness. Satan tried many times to get Jesus to do his will. Jesus reminded him of the powerful words of God with "it is written." Satan was denied victory in the wilderness, but he would wait for an opportune time. We don't have to go where temptation is. It can sometimes come to us. We need to be prayerful for God to help us not be led into sin. If we just asked for forgiveness, we need to stay away from what leads us to sin. Don't let Satan win a battle with you when you know he lost the war!

DEAR LORD, I THANK YOU FOR THE VICTORY WE HAVE THROUGH YOU IN THIS LIFE ...

1. Pray to God to help keep your spirit fed well with the words of the Holy Spirit.
2. Pray to God that you overcome Satan's temptation and understand your struggle.

"For whatever is born of God overcomes the world. And this is the victory that has overcome the world—our faith." (1 John 5:4)

Day 299

DEAR FATHER, THANK YOU FOR YOUR KINDNESS …

Our church family puts together care packages for people in need. It's a gallon-size bag with nonperishable food, lip balm, a washrag, a toothbrush, toothpaste, a rain poncho, and other items that we use daily and don't really give much thought about. I have a few in my car in case I see someone with a sign asking for help. It's interesting that since having the bags, I've seen opportunities. One evening, I was getting on the ramp onto an interstate. I noticed a man in an army outfit on the curb, holding a cardboard sign. I pulled to the side with my blinker on. I knew that wasn't the best approach with oncoming traffic. I made sure no cars were coming so I could get out and get the care package. He saw me, and we met in the middle. I said, "I have a care package for you." He thanked me and said, "No one has shown me kindness until now." I asked for his name. He said, "Jeffrey." I gave him my name and extended my hand to shake. I told him, "God bless," and we departed ways. Of all the items in that gallon bag, I hope he values the scripture verse on a piece of paper. "[Cast] all your care upon Him, for He cares for you" (1 Peter 5:7). I can easily say, "This guy has lots of problems. I don't trust him." I have problems myself. We could all use some kindness and a reminder of a God who cares for us.

DEAR LORD, I CAST ALL MY CARES, WORRIES, FEARS, AND ANXIETIES ON YOU …

1. Pray to God to do a little extra to show the kindness and goodness of God.
2. Pray to God that someone can come to know Him today because of His care.

"May the God of hope fill you with all joy and peace in believing, that you may abound in hope by the power of the Holy Spirit." **(Romans 15:13)**

Day 300

DEAR FATHER, I CONTINUE TO BE AMAZED BY WHAT YOU DO WITH SO LITTLE ...

We serve a God who can do much with little. He used a teenage boy and a few stones to defeat the mighty giant. He took a shepherd and his staff to lead His people through the mighty Red Sea. He took twelve ordinary men and sent them out with His mighty word to change the world. An Angel of the Lord came to Gideon under a terebinth tree and told him to save Israel from the hand of the Midianites. Gideon said, "Indeed my clan is the weakest in Manasseh, and I am the least in my father's house" (Judges 6:15). It doesn't matter on this side of heaven how little we have. If God is for us, who can be against us? The Midianites and Amorites had an army so large that it was described to be "as numerous as locusts" (Judges 7:12). God had Gideon, through a test, whittle down his army to three hundred. The three hundred broke off into three companies in the middle of the night. They had pitchers, torches, and trumpets. They blew the trumpets and broke the pitchers and held the torches in their hands. God took three hundred men and defeated an army too big to count. On this three-hundredth day, what can God do with you? There is no doubt that He is at work. He is working things together for the good for those who love Him. May you glorify God through your one life on this three-hundredth day!

DEAR LORD, THANK YOU FOR THE POWER OF THE RESURRECTION ...

1. Pray to God that you can demonstrate the power of God in your small ways.
2. Pray to God that you don't allow what the world sees to determine how God sees you.

> *"Yet in all these things we are more than conquerors through Him who loved us."* **(Romans 8:37)**

DEAR GOD, THE FAMILY OF JESUS REMINDS ME OF YOUR LOVE, GRACE, AND MERCY ...

You may skip a chapter like Matthew 1 because of the strange names. "Ram begot Amminadab, Amminadab begot Nahshon, and Nahshon begot Salmon" (Matthew 1:4). The family lineage of Jesus demonstrates God's love and grace. If you think His family tree was clean, you're wrong. There were some "skeletons in the closet" with people who had problems. Every name mentioned in Matthew 1 was a sinner. If your family has problems, you share that with the greatest family ever. Tamar is named in the genealogy. She tricked her father-in-law into sleeping with her by disguising herself. David is mentioned along with "her who had been the wife of Uriah" (Matthew 1:6). We are reminded of the sin of adultery and the death of Uriah. Rahab is named, and she was a Canaanite and a prostitute. What do people like this mean? It doesn't matter what you have done. We need to stop beating ourselves up. We have the beauty of God's love to forgive us if we are willing to come to Him. We are all in the family of God because of the grace of Jesus Christ. In Christ's family, a prostitute and king, male and female, Jew and Gentile, one ethnic race and another one, moral and immoral, all sit down as equals. We are equally accepted and loved. The list of names in Mathew 1 teaches me that God wants us all to come to Him no matter what. There are no "black sheep" of the family because we all need a Savior.

DEAR LORD, WE ALL NEED YOU TO SAVE US ...

1. Pray to God that you don't allow anything to hold you back from following Him.
2. Pray to God to help you to forgive yourself and be forgiving of others.

"For all have sinned and fall short of the glory of God, being justified freely by His grace through the redemption that is in Christ Jesus." **(Romans 3:23-24)**

Day 302

DEAR GOD, I'M WITHOUT THE RIGHT WORDS WHEN I THINK ABOUT THE COST OF PRAYER ...

We can take a lot for granted. Did you think about breathing today? Did you give much thought about sight, smell, and touch? What happens when we lose the ability to see, stand, or hear? When we lose it, it becomes a constant thought on our minds. I remember in the recovery room after my last surgery talking to my neurosurgeon. We stayed later to have the surgery so that I could be released to go home. The surgery didn't take long. The recovery took weeks and even years. I didn't have the strength or energy just to jump up and do something. It took time and work to get back to where I was physically. That temporary loss makes you appreciate what you have when you are able to gain some of it back. Have you considered the cost of prayer? The only time Jesus prayed to God in the Gospels and didn't call Him "Father" was on the cross. He prayed, "My God, My God, why have You forsaken Me?" (Matthew 27:46). He paid the price so that God could be our Father. That is the high cost of prayer. What do you do with something that costs a lot? You take good care of it. Do you have anything more valuable than a Savior? We should handle prayer with care and not take it for granted. Jesus has opened the way for us to call God "Father."

DEAR LORD, I CANNOT THANK YOU ENOUGH FOR WHAT YOU DID FOR ME AND OTHERS ...

1. Pray to God, lifting up the avenue of prayer with respect and care because of the cost for Him to hear you.
2. Pray to God to help you appreciate and learn more when it comes to prayer.

> *"For Christ also suffered once for sins, the just for the unjust, that He might bring us to God, being put to death in the flesh but made alive by the Spirit."* **(1 Peter 3:18)**

DEAR GOD, YOU PAID IT ALL AND IN FULL ...

The end-of-the-year school trip for sixth grade is to spend two days in Atlanta, Georgia. Some of the things we do are visit the tomb of Martin Luther King Jr., the Ebenezer church building, and an exhibit hall. The tomb of Mr. and Mrs. King Jr. is surrounded by water. The epitaph reads, "Free at last, free at last, thank God Almighty I am free at last." Epitaphs are powerful things. What is said about us when we die is a reflection of what was important in our lives. Ludolph van Ceulen, a Dutch mathematician, was the first to calculate pi. He had 3.14159265358979323846264338327950 engraved on his tomb. Thomas Jefferson's epitaph reads, "Author of the Declaration of Independence and of the Statue of Virginia for religious freedom & Father of the University of Virginia." Jesus' epitaph is the words He expressed on the cross. "When Jesus had received the sour wine, He said, 'It is finished!' And bowing His head, He gave up His spirit" (John 19:30). The Greek word used is *tetelestai*, which according to *Strong's Exhaustive Concordance* means to "bring to a close, to complete, to fulfill." It is finished and will continue to be finished. Jesus paid it in full. He completed what He came to earth to do. His epitaph should encourage us to do the same. "It is finished" when it comes to a day, a career, raising a family, the Christian race. Jesus shows us how to finish what we have started.

DEAR LORD, YOU COULD HAVE CALLED TEN THOUSAND ANGELS ...

1. Pray to God that you can endure through the day or moment as Christ did.
2. Pray to God to be committed to Jesus each and every day.

> *"But now you also must complete the doing of it; that as there was a readiness to desire it, so there also may be a completion out of what you have."* **(2 Corinthians 8:11)**

Day 304

DEAR GOD, MY HAPPINESS IS NOT IN ANYTHING I DO FOR MYSELF ...

It's the "pursuit of happiness" that appeals to us in the Declaration of Independence. We assume happiness is in the abundance of things, comfortable places to live, or steady incomes. One man is described in the Bible as being a "certain ruler" and "very rich." I imagine he had the finest apparel that denarii could buy. He came to Jesus with a question about eternal life. After some discussion, Jesus got to the point with the ruler. "One thing you lack: Go your way, sell whatever you have and give to the poor, and you will have treasure in heaven; and come, take up the cross, and follow Me" (Mark 10:21). The rich man left Jesus sad. All of our lives, we've been rewarded accordingly. You get grades according to your effort and study. You get commended according to your success on the job. The rich ruler didn't need a reward system. He needed a Savior. The first of the Beatitudes is "blessed are the poor in spirit, for theirs is the kingdom of heaven" (Matthew 5:3). If we are to go deeper, we need to change "spirit" with "ego." When we realize how bankrupt we are spiritually, we become poor in spirit. The word "poor" means "extreme poverty." We are in deep poverty spiritually. Happiness is in knowing our deep need for the Savior and receiving what only He can give—forgiveness from God.

DEAR LORD, I AM OPEN TO RECEIVE THE WORD OF TRUTH WHEN IT COMES TO HAPPINESS ...

1. Pray to God, knowing that the pursuit of happiness is in seeking Him.
2. Pray to God, thankful for the peace of knowing that God forgives you because of your life in Christ Jesus.

"... according to the eternal purpose which He accomplished in Christ Jesus our Lord." **(Ephesians 3:11)**

Day 305

DEAR GOD, YOU ARE THE COMFORTER ...

"Blessed are those who mourn" (Matthew 5:4). Children have a way of crying for all kinds of reasons. They may cry because they got hurt or someone was mean to them. They may also cry because they didn't get their way or don't want to go home just yet. I remember my sweet mother's words: "You better quit that crying, or I'll give you something to cry about." What does "mourn" mean? It means to mourn over our own sin. Jesus mourned over sin. "Now as He drew near, He saw the city and wept over it" (Luke 19:41). The word for "wept" means "to cry aloud." He mourned over the unresolved sins of Jerusalem. Jesus took their sin and ours seriously because He died for them. The promise for those who mourn over sin is to be comforted. I've yet to encounter someone repenting and turning to Jesus who afterward said, "I don't feel better." We mourn over the same thing Jesus mourned. When we believe and act as Jesus did, it brings us closer to Him. We are the recipients of God's forgiveness. As long as we are in this world, we will mourn, weep, grieve, and suffer because of it. Happiness is given because our time of mourning will soon be no more. We understand that more with our relationship in Christ. We are addressing the permanent things while in this temporary body. Happy are those who mourn over sin because they will be comforted.

DEAR LORD, TEACH ME TO WEEP FOR ALL THAT BREAKS YOUR HEART ...

1. Pray to God for Him to bring you to godly sorrow as you encounter cultures and attitudes that love what He hates.
2. Pray for encouragement with the truth that weeping may last for the night, but joy comes in the mourning.

"For His anger is but for a moment, His favor is for life; weeping may endure for a night, but joy comes in the morning." **(Psalm 30:5)**

Day 306

DEAR GOD, FORGIVE ME FOR LOOKING AT MEEKNESS AS A SIGN OF WEAKNESS ...

A legend in India tells of a magician changing a mouse into a cat, a cat into a dog, a dog into a tiger. The reason for the changes was the fear of something greater than the animal. As a tiger, the animal still had fear. The magician changed the tiger back to a mouse. He said, "I will make you into a mouse again, for though you have the body of a tiger, you still have the heart of a mouse." Does this sound familiar? We are now adults, but we are paralyzed by fears. The fear of the dark as a child has morphed into fear of losing a job, the unknown, and death. Jesus said, "Blessed are the meek, for they shall inherit the earth" (Matthew 5:5). The word translated "meek," according to *Strong's Exhaustive Concordance*, means to "wholly rely on God's strength rather than our own." The same word is used to refer to taming a wild animal. Will an untamed horse pull a load? A meek person is not a weak person. It's someone who has enough self-control to allow God's will to control his or her life. It takes courage because of fear. Fear wants to take away our courage and dominate our hearts. Jesus wanted us to learn from Him because He was meek (Matthew 11:29). His life was not dominated with the fear of Jewish leaders, Rome, or death. Blessed is the one under the control of God.

DEAR LORD, YOU LEFT HEAVEN FOR US ...

1. Pray to God that the world may see in you the source of your courage and strength.
2. Pray to God to forgive you when you think of yourself more highly than you ought.

> *"Therefore lay aside all filthiness and overflow of wickedness, and receive with meekness the implanted word, which is able to save your souls."* **(James 1:21)**

DEAR GOD, I CONFESS MY HUNGER FOR THE GIFTS OF THIS WORLD INSTEAD ...

I don't think a day goes by in our home where we don't hear, "Mom, I'm hungry. What's to eat?" As they get older, I feel like their stomachs are never-filling reservoirs. They say "hungry," but they don't know what being hungry is. Have you been to a place where leftovers and picking at your food don't exist? Have you experienced a hunger for something? In a world that is predominately lost, what is the first thing we crave? Jesus told us that our hunger and thirst should be for righteousness. "Blessed are those who hunger and thirst for righteousness, for they shall be filled" (Matthew 5:6). We are to have a strong desire for righteousness. This doesn't happen naturally. It's not like craving a juicy cut of steak or nice beach vacation. It's not in something that is temporary. We must develop a spiritual habit for God in prayer, daily reading, and more surrender to His will each day. We are filled in complete satisfaction for God and His righteousness. Have you ever been stuffed from overeating? You may have said, "I can't eat anymore." You were full in that moment but not completely. You had a desire to eat again in time. Can we be completely full in our relationship with Jesus? If you are like me, I have more room to grow in my faith. May we have a daily hunger and thirst for the righteousness of God. We are satisfied but not full.

DEAR LORD, YOU ALONE SATISFY THE HUNGRY SOUL ...

1. Pray to God to stir in you a desire to know and love Him.
2. Pray to God that people can realize the satisfaction for their spiritual craving is in the Bread of Life.

> *"If anyone thirsts, let him come to Me and drink. He who believes in Me, as the Scripture has said, out of his heart will flow rivers of living water."* **(John 7:37-38)**

DEAR GOD, HAVE MERCY ON US ...

Mercy is very much like forgiveness. We don't have a problem on the receiving end. It can be a struggle when we are called to show it. The purpose of mercy is not to inflict pain but to relieve it. Mercy is the desire to help the hurting and needy. Mercy is much more than showing emotion. It's deeper than shedding a tear. Jesus wept over the suffering of others, but He showed mercy in what He did on the cross. If you're summoned to traffic court because of a heavy foot, you are seeking mercy from the judge. If you sinned badly in a relationship, you are looking for mercy from the other. If you sinned, you are looking for mercy from a holy God. Jesus showed mercy. Two blind men came to him and said, "Son of David, have mercy on us!" (Matthew 9:27). What did they mean by mercy? They wanted Jesus to do more than feel sorry for them. They desired to be healed by Him. Jesus demonstrated mercy in healing them. Our situation before God is no different than someone else's. We all are in desperate need of God's mercy. This should help us to be more merciful with someone in need of it. We can relate to being on the receiving end of mercy. If we show mercy, the same will be shown to us. Today looks like a good day to be merciful to someone in need.

DEAR LORD, LET ME BE SLOW TO ANGER AND ABOUNDING IN LOVE ...

1. Pray to God that you may show the mercy that you have received from Him.
2. Pray to God that if He kept a record of all sin, who could stand?

> *"For judgment is without mercy to the one who has shown no mercy. Mercy triumphs over judgment."* (James 2:13)

DEAR GOD, SET OUR HEARTS AND MINDS ON THE THINGS ABOVE ...

I remember when Jay Leno stepped down from *The Tonight Show*. He started the show in 1992 with Billy Crystal as his first guest. In all his years as host, the one guest he could not get was Kathie Lee Gifford. She eventually came on the show. What if you were in the same position to have a celebrity guest on the show? Who would you like to meet? What about God? We are unable to see God fully and completely now. All of our spiritual sight is mediated on the Word, in prayer, and in the works of God's providence. We see images and reflections of His glory. We hear echoes of His voice. There will be a day when God Himself will dwell among us, and we will see Him as He is (1 John 3:2). "Blessed are the pure in heart, for they shall see God" (Matthew 5:8). Jesus calls for us to be "pure" or cleansed. This cleansing is from within and unmixed with the influences of this world. It's to draw near to God so that He can draw near to us. It's to do all in the name of the Lord Jesus Christ. It begins and continues in the heart. We can get so caught up on the outside that we neglect the inside. God looks within and sees our spiritual hearts. The "heart" refers to the mind, will, and emotions. If we desire to see God, we must have a clean heart.

DEAR LORD, THANK YOU FOR COMING AND SHOWING US THE FATHER ...

1. Pray to God to help you to fix your eyes not on the seen but the unseen.
2. Pray to God, hoping that your faith will become sight when you behold Him as He is.

> *"Examine me, O Lord, and prove me; try my mind and my heart."* **(Psalm 26:2)**

Day 310

DEAR GOD, THANK YOU FOR THE PEACE THAT CAME THROUGH JESUS ...

Peace doesn't just happen. We make peace. "Blessed are the peacemakers, for they shall be called sons of God" (Matthew 5:9). It is said that Telemachus lived isolated from the world and dedicated to his life in God. He realized he couldn't serve God without serving people. He went to Rome when the city was considered Christian. However, the churches emptied when it came to the bloody entertainment of gladiators at the Colosseum. Telemachus was horrified by what he saw. He leaped into the arena and placed himself between the two gladiators. The crowd was furious with this stranger stopping their entertainment. They gathered stones and stoned Telemachus to death. Within a week, the emperor declared him a martyr and did away with gladiator contests. This was around AD 401. The days of the gladiators are long past. What about us? Where do we carry on this work of peacemaking? "If it is possible, as much as depends on you, live peaceably with all men" (Romans 12:18). We cannot force someone to come to peace. This shouldn't stop us from making peace. We should be of a mind and heart to want to resolve conflict if possible. At the end of a day, I'm a peacemaker or a troublemaker. Do I seek conflict resolution or not? I can only control myself, and I choose peace.

DEAR LORD, FILL ME WITH WISDOM AND HUMILITY ...

1. Pray to God to keep you from looking to blame others, but rather to get the log out of your own eye.
2. Pray to God, if you're unsuccessful at resolving conflict with someone, to help you use others to resolve it.

> *"Pursue peace with all people, and holiness, without which no one will see the Lord."* (Hebrews 12:14)

Day 311

DEAR GOD, GIVE US STRENGTH WHEN WE ARE SURPRISED WITH AN ATTACK ON OUR FAITH ...

"Blessed are those who are persecuted for righteousness' sake, for theirs is the kingdom of heaven" (Matthew 5:10). It wasn't fair for people to spit on Him. It wasn't right for soldiers to strip off His garments. It wasn't just for the Son of God to hear silence from the Father. The Father listened to the agony in Jesus' voice: "My God, My God, why have You forsaken Me?" (Matthew 27:46). Was it right, fair, or just for Jesus to die for us? No. Was it love? Yes. God knows persecution because of righteousness' sake. He endured the cross so we can know the kingdom of God. Jesus is offering words of comfort to those who are persecuted for their faith. He knows that no one likes persecution, hardship, or difficult situations because of their faith. Jesus wasn't skipping and singing on His way to the place of the skull. We are in a nation that embraces the freedom of religion. This doesn't mean we don't find persecution. We can feel a distance from others because of our faith. We can experience rejection from trying to share our faith. We can experience "no," a door slammed, mocking or laughing at what we believe, and others distancing themselves from us. We can feel humiliated and take it personally. We need to remember the rejection is not with you but Christ. Thank You, Lord, for demonstrating control under intense persecution.

DEAR LORD, I PRAY FOR ALL CHRISTIANS IN THE WORLD WHO ARE PERSECUTED ...

1. Pray to God to give you faith as you endure under a trial.
2. Pray to God, asking these things in the great hope when all knees will bow down before the King of kings.

"Rejoice and be exceedingly glad, for great is your reward in heaven, for so they persecuted the prophets who were before you." **(Matthew 5:12)**

Day 312

DEAR GOD, I WANT TO LIVE THE GREATEST COMMAND ...

I believe our boys have wondered whether I'm crazy, especially when it comes to fall Saturdays. Many times on a Saturday afternoon, you will hear me yell, "Touchdown Bama!" It helps to jump off the couch and do some fist pumps along with some hollering. When our boys were younger, they gave me a funny look. Noah started hollering while running around in a circle. Nathanael would do a hard dash straight for the couch and dive right into it. I felt a stern look from my sweet wife that said, "You're not setting a good example." What gets you excited? Is it a competition with Jesus when it comes to your time and excitement? Imagine telling your significant other, "I'm giving you my heart and want nothing more than to spend the rest of my life with you." Now your significant other says, "I love you, too. I'm willing to commit to you for the rest of my life. I have just one condition. I still want to date other people." Isn't that the same attitude with those who go halfway in their relationship with Jesus? "Lord, I love You. I'm committed to You, but let's not be exclusive." That's going to be a problem. It's not enough for someone we love to be first. We want that person to be our only one. Jesus wants to be Lord of our hearts.

DEAR LORD, HELP ME TO BE COMMITTED TO YOU ...

1. Pray to God to have a love that puts Him first and no one else.
2. Pray to God to forgive you when you say one thing but do another when it comes to your heart.

> *"Keep your heart with all diligence, for out of it spring the issues of life."* **(Proverbs 4:23)**

DEAR GOD, I STAND IN FEAR BECAUSE OF THE DISAPPOINTMENTS IN MY LIFE ...

In 1941, the University of Texas football team was ranked number one. They had to play their conference rival, Baylor, for an undefeated season and play in the Rose Bowl. In the second half, the Texas quarterback dropped back and launched a ball to a wide receiver, Noble Doss. He reached out to catch, and the football slipped through his hands. Baylor rallied to end up winning the game. Doss became a husband, father, and grandfather. He served in World War II. He won two NFL titles with the Philadelphia Eagles. He said that he thought about dropping that ball in the big game every day. The memory of a dropped ball was still great in his mind fifty years later. We are not so different. We can easily allow things in our past to stir up strong emotions. We may have a fear of disappointing God. God's deep well of grace and mercy must have a bottom to it. God must be tired of forgiving me of this. A group brought to Jesus a paralytic lying on a bed. Jesus saw their great faith. He said to the paralytic, "Son, be of good cheer; your sins are forgiven you" (Matthew 9:2). I find it interesting that Jesus mentioned courage in connection to forgiveness (see the NASB). We need to take courage because God hasn't abandoned us. We need to remove disappointment because God's perfect love casts out fear.

DEAR LORD, THANK YOU FOR GIVING US THE COURAGE TO SEEK FORGIVENESS ...

1. Pray to God that His perfect love can cast out your fears.
2. Pray to God that you can let go of yesterday and focus on today.

"There is no fear in love; but perfect love casts out fear, because fear involves torment. But he who fears has not been made perfect in love." **(1 John 4:18)**

Day 314

DEAR GOD, I'M THANKFUL FOR THE REAL SUPERHERO WHO WAS FORETOLD LONG AGO ...

I'm a fan of superhero movies. They remind me when I collected comics. I enjoyed reading about people with special powers, facing unbelievable situations. Each superhero seems to follow the same story line to a degree. The hero faces unusual circumstances. The person faces a crisis, which the hero is the only one qualified to handle. The prospect of doom looms large on the horizon. The hero's story has changed little throughout history. In the eighth century, Isaiah was called by God to be a prophet. Isaiah spoke about a hero who would come to fulfill His divine mission of bringing salvation and peace on earth. The unnamed Servant in Isaiah matches the superhero story. The situation was dire. The people had forsaken God because of their rebellious ways. "I gave My back to those who struck Me, and My cheeks to those who plucked out the beard; I did not hide My face from shame and spitting" (Isaiah 50:6). This unnamed hero accepted whatever came His way. We know this unnamed Servant prophesied in Isaiah. He goes by many names: Son of Man, Son of God, Prince of Peace, Savior, Counselor, and High Priest. His name is Jesus Christ, and He is the greatest superhero this world will ever know. He saved us from the greatest enemy—ourselves.

DEAR LORD, THANK YOU FOR OVERCOMING IT ALL FOR OUR SAKE ...

1. Pray to God that you can live in His image and be heroic by what you say and do in His name.
2. Pray to God, realizing the world needs people to be kind, helpful, and patient and desiring to be that person to those you know.

"'I am the Alpha and the Omega, the Beginning and the End,' says the Lord, 'who is and who was and who is to come, the Almighty.'" **(Revelation 1:8)**

Day 315

DEAR GOD, I EASILY FORGET YOUR WORDS ...

Do you remember the things you learned in school? We learned the concepts of numbers, important events, how to write a paragraph, and the elements on the periodic table. I would cram for a test in school, and afterward, the information was gone from memory. I didn't retain a lot of it because I don't use it in what I do. Jesus expected His disciples to remember things. He wanted them to remember and trust in Him. He wanted them to remember His promises. The disciples didn't believe the women when they said the tomb was found empty. The disciples failed to remember what the Lord said in His ministry about His death and resurrection. It took Jesus appearing to the disciples for them to remember His words. What about us? Do we treasure the words and promises of God? Do we hear them and forget about them? Do we remember that God promised that He would never leave us nor forsake us? What about He who came so that we could have an abundant life? I believe prayer helps us remember the words of God. Have you read a passage and prayed with your heart focused on what you read? I believe prayer helps us bring to mind the things we need to know and remember. May we trust God completely by being mindful of what He has said and promised.

DEAR LORD, HELP ME TO DO THINGS IN REMEMBRANCE OF YOU ...

1. Pray to God for a better understanding and application of what you have read.
2. Pray to God, thankful for the connections you have with God's people because they remind you of His words.

"I remember Your name in the night, O Lord, and I keep Your law." **(Psalm 119:55)**

Day 316

DEAR GOD, I WANT TO REMEMBER OTHERS' NEEDS IN PRAYER ...

The words "remember" and "me" are two simple words that sound strong when put together. When our Lord instituted His supper, He told His disciples to eat and drink in "remembrance of Me." The prodigal son remembered his father's servants and how well cared for they were. His strong memory led him back home. It's encouraging when someone remembers us. They remember a special day in our lives. They remember to pray for us as we have requested. The Bible says, "And let us consider one another in order to stir up love and good works" (Hebrews 10:24). We consider someone by remembering. I remember the last words of someone who passed away. I was able to be with him, not knowing it was his last day. It was a Saturday afternoon, and he was in a hospital bed. He was alert and spoke about when he was younger. This was Howard's final word to me before I left him, what would be his last day on earth. At the end, I said a prayer and reminded him of our worship service the next day. As I was walking out, He said, "Remember me." I said, "I will." I prayed right in the hallway to our almighty God that His will for him be done. I left thinking, have I forgotten anyone who asked me specifically to pray for them? We can agree and go on our day and forget about it.

DEAR LORD, THANK YOU FOR BEING MINDFUL OF MY NEEDS ...

1. Pray to God to be more specific in prayer when it comes to people's requests.
2. Pray to God to connect more to Him as it helps you to remember His words.

"I thank God, whom I serve with a pure conscience, as my forefathers did, as without ceasing I remember you in my prayers night and day." **(2 Timothy 1:3)**

DEAR GOD, FORGIVE ME FOR COMPLICATING YOUR PLAN ...

When I think of summertime, I think of weddings. One of the most memorable weddings was the one at Cades Cove in the Great Smoky Mountains National Park. We all stayed in a big cabin that slept twenty people. We traveled to Cades Cove on a beautiful summer day to the small, white church building there at Cades Cove. The building was not rented. We all gathered in the building while visitors came in to see what was going on. We staged a wedding in the old church building. I loved the simplicity of the service. It was simple and purposeful. We all had the best time, and it was a memorable one. I sometimes think about the simple, small, but beautiful wedding in Cades Cove. I wonder if our lives are hard because we have made them hard. We add too much and take away the purpose of things. Sometimes it's just as simple as a piece of paper to write down our thoughts, a Bible opened, and a prayer. It's a worship service where the attention is on God and not all the stuff that we think we need. It's a Bible and hearts open to praising God. Don't allow the world to clutter your relationship with God. We need to seek Him first. It's as simple as that.

DEAR LORD, HELP ME TO KEEP THE MAIN THING THE MAIN THING TODAY ...

1. Pray to God to live a day at a time and focus on what you can do.
2. Pray to God to trust that He will take the things you cannot control out of your hands.

"... that you also aspire to lead a quiet life, to mind your own business, and to work with your own hands, as we commanded you." **(1 Thessalonians 4:11)**

Day 318

DEAR GOD, I'M THANKFUL YOU TEACH YOUR PEOPLE TO LIVE A DAY AT A TIME ...

Why do we worry so much? We can go through today thinking about tomorrow only. When we do this, we have missed the opportunities and blessings in the day. Jesus modeled one day at a time with His prayer for "daily bread." God gave the Israelites a strong picture of one day at a time. The Israelites had witnessed the mighty power of God. They saw the plagues in Egypt, the crossing on dry ground through the Red Sea, and the collapse of the Red Sea on the Egyptian army. They witnessed one miracle after another. Yet they complained about no food in the wilderness and wished they had perished as slaves in Egypt. God addressed their worry about their present situation by meeting their needs daily. God sent food every day with manna in the morning and quail in the evening. They could only get enough food for the day. The only day they doubled up was on the sixth day for the Sabbath. God demonstrated with the daily amount of food for the people to live a day at a time. What a great visual aid for the grumbling, worried people! What about us? God knows our daily needs. We need to pray more to keep our minds on God rather than our worries and complaints. We should be satisfied with what we need today. How can you better live for the day only?

DEAR LORD, FORGIVE ME FOR WORRYING WHEN YOU SAY NOT TO ...

1. Pray to God to focus more on Him rather than your complaint or dissatisfaction.
2. Pray to God, thanking Him for giving you what you need and asking Him to help you not be dissatisfied when it comes to wants.

> *"Therefore I say to you, do not worry about your life, what you will eat or what you will drink; nor about your body, what you will put on. Is not life more than food and the body more than clothing?"* **(Matthew 6:25)**

Day 319

DEAR GOD, I PRAY FOR PEACE WHEN I DON'T UNDERSTAND MY PRESENT SUFFERING ...

I kept going back into the hospital after complications. I was becoming a regular with the nurses on the floor. In those tough moments in a hospital bed, I was tempted to be angry with God for what I was going through. I was missing out on spending time with my family. We were separated because of the complications with my surgery. I didn't blame God because it wasn't His fault. It was no one's fault. It was the consequence of living in a broken, fallen world. I asked God to be used from all of this for His glory. One of the reasons for me wanting to write this book is to encourage you. I've been on the receiving end of encouragement in every stage and step with my health. What helped me to keep from going to the dark side was focusing on the cross of Jesus. Think about the cross when it comes to your suffering. Christ is with you. This doesn't mean that suffering will go away. The crucifixion of Jesus doesn't answer all questions about suffering and pain. It does help us to see that all suffering is not bad or evil. There was a lot of good that came from Jesus' death. Our present suffering doesn't have to be so great because of Jesus and what He went through. No amount of suffering or pain is greater than the cross and the hope of heaven.

DEAR LORD, I CANNOT IMAGINE THE PAIN AND SUFFERING YOU ENDURED ...

1. Pray to God to forgive you when you complain or point your finger at Him as if it's His fault for your pain.
2. Pray to God to help you have the same mind as Paul when it comes to present suffering. There is nothing greater than the glory that awaits you.

> *"Not only that, but we also who have the firstfruits of the Spirit, even we ourselves groan within ourselves, eagerly waiting for the adoption, the redemption of our body."* **(Romans 8:23)**

Day 320

DEAR GOD, I DON'T HAVE TO GUESS WHEN IT COMES TO YOUR PLAN ...

In 1587, John White led 121 colonists to establish Roanoke Island. White left them to return to England to enlist more help. When he returned several years later, the community was deserted with no sign of struggle and no remains. He saw the word "Croatoan" carved on a wooden post. The settlement is known as the Lost Colony. Amelia Earhart circumnavigated the world by plane. Her plan went down in the South Pacific. Her last transmission heard was in 1931. There are more mysteries in our history. There is nothing greater than the mystery of God's plan for us. In His infinite wisdom, He knew we would rebel and lose Eden. He planned a way to redeem us. One of the oldest thoughts is of God's plan to redeem us through Jesus Christ. This was before the creation of the physical world. Jesus wasn't plan B, C, or D. This great mystery has been revealed through the written record of Jesus' life, death, and resurrection. This great mystery shows how much God cared for us by providing what we needed at the right time. I'm thankful that God knows what I need and when I need it. We are not an accident or a mistake. Today is here for a reason. We are here to receive the greatest mystery by choosing Jesus.

DEAR LORD, I'M THANKFUL FOR YOUR ROLE IN MY SALVATION ...

1. Pray to God, thankful for His infinite wisdom and the revelation of His plan.
2. Pray to God, thankful that what He wants from you is no mystery. He has revealed what you need to do.

"The mystery of Christ ... in other ages was not made known to the sons of men, as it has now been revealed by the Spirit to His holy apostles and prophets." **(Ephesians 3:4-5)**

DEAR GOD, YOU MADE US TO CREATE AND DEMONSTRATE OUR WONDROUS MIND …

The number 3.14 or pi is an irrational number. There are several who have attempted to hold the record in counting the numbers to pi. Some computer programmers have calculated that pi has over twenty-two trillion digits. The world record of memorizing pi was in 2015. Suresh Kumar Sharma took seventeen hours and fourteen minutes to give the first 70,030 digits of pi. Can you imagine memorizing the order of a number for seventeen hours correctly? What about God? Abraham became frustrated that he was still childless. God had promised to bless him with a child. Abraham and Sarah waited and waited and still no child. God brought Abraham outside and told him to look toward heaven and count the stars. If Abraham could count the stars, he would know the number of his descendants. Abraham was unable to count the stars. I've read from NASA that an estimate of stars we know is at least one hundred octillion. In case you are wondering, this is the number one followed by twenty-nine zeros. What we can't do today, God is able to do. "He counts the number of the stars; He calls them all by name" (Psalm 147:4) We serve a wonderful, powerful God. He not only can count and name the stars, but He created them. Yes, God is able to know you.

DEAR LORD, I'M HUMBLED THAT IN ALL OF CREATION, YOU KNOW ME AND LOVE ME …

1. Pray to God to trust in Him and know that He keeps the promises made.
2. Pray to God to let Him be God and you be a follower because of what He knows and is able to do.

"Blessed be the Lord God, the God of Israel, who only does wondrous things! And blessed be His glorious name forever! And let the whole earth be filled with His glory. Amen and Amen." **(Psalm 72:18-19)**

Day 322

DEAR GOD, HELP ME APPRECIATE TODAY ...

I remember my youngest son on my lap while we stopped for a picture on the lawn mower. He would come out on the porch and watch me cut the front yard. When I was done, I would turn off the blade and let him ride with me. He believed he was mowing the yard like his father. We would go around the yard in big circles. The picture of us on the lawn mower was taken on my last day without any known health issues. It would be my last day out of the hospital without any complications. I wasn't ready for the storm that came. Do you have a moment in history prior to a major event in your life? A picture in your mind of the last time you were with someone before they passed. Was it the last day prior to a scheduled surgery? The final day before you were induced into labor? It's amazing to think about how much can change from day-to-day. We can feel invincible and in control one day, and the next, humbled and broken. The picture reminds me that we are not in control of our lives. We think we are. We feel like we have life under control. The disciples were not ready for the storm that sprang up on the Sea of Galilee. Jesus was down in the stern asleep. They woke up Jesus, and He calmed the vicious storm with His peaceful words. He rebuked them for having fear and little faith. We cannot know what will happen tomorrow. We can know that the same Jesus will be with us.

DEAR LORD, FORGIVE ME WHEN I PANIC ...

1. Pray to God that He alone can calm the storms. Look to Him and seek shelter.
2. Pray to God to appreciate the moments, whether good or bad, in a day because you don't know what tomorrow may bring.

> *"But He said to them, 'Why are you fearful, O you of little faith?' Then He arose and rebuked the winds and the sea, and there was a great calm."* **(Matthew 8:26)**

DEAR GOD, THANK YOU FOR THE STUDENTS I'VE BEEN BLESSED TO TEACH AND KNOW ...

I was humbled going to the mailbox in the summer of 2015. I received so many cards with thoughtful sayings, Bible verses, and encouraging messages. Every day was a reminder of someone praying for me. Every day was a letter of encouragement. I was in and out of surgeries and recovering that summer. It was a treat to have the energy to walk to the mailbox to see what was in it. I have kept every card sent to me. Each one means so much. Some of my favorites were homemade cards from former students. One of them wrote, "Hey! I'm so sorry that you have to go through this. I know God is going to take care of you and help you and your family recover from this! Thanks for all you do and helping me through my hard time. We are all here for you! In God, all things are possible." I was humbled with what the student wrote. It amazes me what young people are able to do. We can easily dismiss younger generations. If we do, it's our loss. They have so much to offer. Many want to connect to the needs of others. They are willing to write a card. They want to lend a hand to help someone. Many of them helped me by writing, praying, and encouraging me. They reminded me that I was not alone. They also reminded me of the great and awesome God we serve.

DEAR LORD, THANK YOU FOR SHOWING ME THE IMPORTANCE OF CHILDREN ...

1. Pray to God, thanking Him for the lessons that students teach by their faith.
2. Pray to God, asking that He help the younger generations to see the potential they have in Him.

"Then Jesus called a little child to Him, set him in the midst of them, and said, 'Assuredly, I say to you, unless you are converted and become as little children, you will by no means enter the kingdom of heaven.'" **(Matthew 18:2-3)**

Day 324

DEAR GOD, MY LIFE IS COMPLETE IN YOU ...

Have you ever been dissatisfied with something? Were you built up only to be let down? My wife and I experienced an attraction in Gatlinburg, Tennessee. On the outside, the advertising and props made you believe that you haven't lived unless you go through this attraction. We paid to go experience the attraction. What a disappointment! On the inside, it was ten minutes of outdated props and pictures. The joke was on us for paying fourteen dollars. I felt cheated because of how depreciated it was on the inside. Sigmund Freud is credited with the "pleasure principle." This principle asserts that people will pursue pleasure instead of or to avoid pain. Nowhere can this be seen more than in the advertising and marketing of consumer products. Consider a few marketing slogans: "Have it your way," "Just do it," and "It's everywhere you want to be." It's a big business to sell pleasure and superficial joy. This joy is disappointing and empty. Joy is not in the thrills of life but in the truth. The only joy that is complete and satisfying is in Jesus. I've been a Christian for many years. I'm not tired of the Bible or my relationship with Christ. I continue to learn more each day as I grow closer to God in His word and in prayer. The joy I have is not based on my circumstances. It's in the life, death, and resurrection of Jesus Christ. I hope you have that same joy. There is nothing like it.

DEAR LORD, I CONSTANTLY LEARN MORE FROM YOU AS I CONTINUE TO WALK WITH YOU ...

1. Pray to God for wisdom, better understanding, and happiness as you please Him.
2. Pray to God, thankful for what you have learned from the joyless things in this life. They make you better appreciate what you have in Him.

> *"You have put gladness in my heart, more than in the season that their grain and wine increased."* (Psalm 4:7)

DEAR GOD, MAY I HAVE AN OPEN MIND ...

Imagine that you are a child in Sunday school. The teacher brings in a series of posters, each one depicting a story from the Bible. The first poster is a series of black clouds that darken the top of the poster. The sea is rough with no hint of land anywhere. In the center of the picture, you see a very large barge-like boat. Through the window of the boat, you see a monkey sitting on a giraffe's head. The second poster is a mother standing waist-deep in a muddy river. She is placing her baby into a little handmade basket. A small girl looks on with a worried face. A third poster is a young boy sitting up in bed. He is trying to wake up. His face reflects a state of confusion. He has his head slightly tilted as though he's trying to hear something. The third poster is young Samuel. He lived in a time when it was rare to hear the word of the Lord. God spoke to Samuel. He didn't understand at first because the word of the Lord was rare. The Lord called for Samuel four different times. The first three times, Samuel thought Eli, the priest, was calling him. Samuel did the only thing a young, confused boy knew to do. He ran to Eli. Imagine you are a young person, and the person you are working for says to you, "That's God's voice." When Samuel was willing to hear, God spoke to him. It's hard to hear God when we stay away from His Word. "Faith comes by hearing, and hearing by the word of God" (Romans 10:17).

DEAR LORD, THANK YOU FOR DEMONSTRATING HOW TO LIVE ...

1. Pray to God to be intentional in your day when it comes to reading and hearing His Word.
2. Pray to God to stay committed to your connection to Him in prayer and in the Word.

"Then Jesus said to those Jews who believed Him, 'If you abide in My word, you are My disciples indeed. And you shall know the truth, and the truth shall make you free.'" **(John 8:31-32)**

Day 326

DEAR GOD, HELP ME TO BE INTENTIONAL ...

When I started to date the person who would be my wife, I found every opportunity to be with her and talk to her. We would find moments in-between classes. I would call her. I wrote her letters. I wanted to spend as much time as possible with her each day. She wanted the same. We were in love, and being together made us happy. It was a fun time then and a better time now. I love God. What does that look like each day? Am I just as proactive in finding times to talk to Him? Am I intentional about my day, seeking Him as often as I can? Jesus is the perfect example in teaching us meaningful conversations with God. We should have times in our day when no one else is around. This is important because we are not hurried or distracted about our day. I know of some people whose secret room is in the car. Their phone is on silent, and the radio is off. If we are too busy, then we need to access our love for God. No one is busier than Jesus. His life was filled with demands from this world. He modeled secret places to talk to the Father. He did so early in the morning while it was still dark (Mark 1:35). Other times, He went up on a mountain by Himself to pray in the evening (Mark 14:23). If I love God, I must treat Him the same way. I must make time to talk to Him in prayer each day.

DEAR LORD, THANK YOU FOR SHOWING ME HOW TO MAKE TIME FOR PRAYER ...

1. Pray to God for the commitment to set aside times when you can be alone with Him.
2. Pray to God that you will come to Him willingly with an open heart and in humility because you love Him.

> *"The next day, as they went on their journey and drew near the city, Peter went up on the housetop to pray, about the sixth hour."* **(Acts 10:9)**

Day 327

DEAR GOD, I READ AND THINK I'M NOTHING LIKE THE PHARISEES BUT ...

"And when you pray, you shall not be like the hypocrites. For they love to pray standing in the synagogues and on the corners of the streets, that they may be seen by men" (Matthew 6:5). The religious leaders had made a mess of things. In their pursuit of being right with God, they were wrong because of their pride, trusting in their own works and praying to be seen by others. The Pharisees were polluting peoples' minds by their poor example. Jesus didn't want this for the people. Instead, we go to God in prayer with sincerity, telling Him how we feel. No big words. No great example to others of how spiritual we are or how much of the Bible we know. When was the last time we tested our motives? We can easily look at the Pharisees of the day and see the flaws in them. I can easily read Matthew 6:5 and dismiss it because I don't have a problem like that. I'm not trying to be seen. Right? Do I pray to convince others that I'm a good Christian? Do I tell others about my prayer life so I can appear more mature in the faith? Have my prayers turned into a meaningless repetition? Am I trying to convince God to do things my way? I don't know how you honestly answered these questions and others like them. It's easy to fall into the trap of thinking that "I'm not like them" when in reality we are to a degree. We need to always approach God with respect, humility, and sincerity.

DEAR LORD, HELP ME TO BE MORE LIKE YOU ...

1. Pray to God to be open and honest before Him.
2. Pray to God to help you approach Him with as much humility and respect as you can.

"Draw near to God and He will draw near to you. Cleanse your hands, you sinners; and purify your hearts, you double-minded." **(James 4:8)**

Day 328

DEAR GOD, I DON'T KNOW WHAT TO SAY ...

Have you ever felt something alerting you to pay attention or pulling you in a particular direction? Have you listened to a sermon and sensed God telling you to follow Him? We need the Holy Spirit to live godly lives. The Holy Spirit will never lead us to do anything that goes against Scripture. I felt led by the Spirit when I prayed for God to end my situation for my boys' sake, but I continued to have setback after setback. I wanted it to end and prayed for it because it was affecting my boys. I didn't know what to pray after praying for it to come to an end and it didn't. I'm thankful for the Holy Spirit helping me in my weakness. I was reminded of Paul. He faced terrible situations during his missionary journeys. He was stoned almost to death in Lystra. He was the center of a riot in Ephesus. Have you ever felt overwhelmed by what you were going through? You were tired and physically wanted to give up. Paul continued to trust God, and so should you. The Holy Spirit sees the depths of our struggles and difficulties. He translates our hardships more accurately than you can possibly say yourself. He comforts you with the knowledge that you have come to know and understand. I had comfort and peace despite my setbacks. This wasn't because of what I could do. It was God and the gift of the Holy Spirit. God has given us a tremendous blessing with the gift of the Holy Spirit. Rest assured in what we have in God.

DEAR LORD, THANK YOU FOR THE HELPER ...

1. Pray to God that you may continue to trust in Him and be led by the Spirit's words.
2. Pray to God, thankful for the help of the Holy Spirit to translate your suffering more accurately.

"If we live in the Spirit, let us also walk in the Spirit." **(Galatians 5:25)**

Day 329

DEAR GOD, THE WORLD HASN'T STOPPED CHANGING ...

"While the earth remains, seedtime and harvest, cold and heat, winter and summer, and day and night shall not cease" (Genesis 8:22). In the spring, we see the time change, daylight become longer, allergies, planting, trees blooming, and grass growing. I think of going creek fishing with my father. We would wade upstream or downstream on the Red River. We had a minnow bucket to catch our crawdads. When we felt like we had enough fish food, we would wade through the river. We looked for what we thought was a good fishing spot. Sometimes we were right, and other times not. I learned several lessons from fishing with my father in the spring. I learned it's easier to go downstream than upstream. The same can be true in life. It's difficult to live right with God in a school or workplace that doesn't. It's hard to let your light shine when you have no one to join you. I learned fish would never get into trouble if their mouths were shut. We bait a hook, hoping that a fish will open its mouth and swallow the bait. We, too, find trouble when we open our mouths. I cannot throw a stone because I'm guilty of saying something I shouldn't. The earth continues to rotate and revolve around the sun. The seasons come and go. Be thankful in prayer for your time in spring.

DEAR LORD, HELP ME TO APPRECIATE THE SEASON I'M IN ...

1. Pray to God, thankful for those springtime memories with loved ones.
2. Pray to God that you can leave memorable moments to your family in the same season.

> *"But Simon answered and said to Him, 'Master, we have toiled all night and caught nothing; nevertheless at Your word I will let down the net.' And when they had done this, they caught a great number of fish, and their net was breaking."* **(Luke 5:5-6)**

Day 330

DEAR GOD, I'M THANKFUL FOR THE PEOPLE WHO HELP ME TO BE COMMITTED ...

"While the earth remains, seedtime and harvest, cold and heat, winter and summer, and day and night shall not cease" (Genesis 8:22). The summer of 2000 stands out to me. I made the second most important commitment. I said "I do" to my beautiful bride on the first of July. I don't remember much about that day except how nervous I was. I remember how long it was to walk down the center aisle. I was stunned, seeing my bride in her wedding dress for the first time. I didn't have time to eat any food because everyone was congratulating us. I look back and thank God for giving me the wisdom to marry a beautiful, smart, and godly woman. She has helped me in our marriage. She has given me strength when I felt weak. She has comforted me when I felt defeated. She has reminded me of Christ's love to the church. She is my best friend, and I'm thankful to go through life with her. My marriage reminds me of the importance of commitment. We don't have to be married to be committed people. We should desire to be someone who is dependable, committed, and dedicated. I don't think we see enough of that each day. We see a lot of quitting, giving up, and separating. Be someone whom others can count on. The earth continues to rotate and revolve around the sun. The seasons come and go. Be thankful in prayer for your time in the summer.

DEAR LORD, YOU DEMONSTRATED A COMMITMENT IN YOUR LIFE AND DEATH ...

1. Pray to God, thankful for your spouse and/or friends in your life who hold you accountable.
2. Pray to God, thankful for the One who doesn't give up or quit on you.

"And I prayed to the LORD my God, and made confession, and said, 'O Lord, great and awesome God, who keeps His covenant and mercy with those who love Him, and with those who keep His commandments.'" **(Daniel 9:4)**

Day 331

DEAR GOD, MAY I JOIN AT THE TABLE ...

"While the earth remains, seedtime and harvest, cold and heat, winter and summer, and day and night shall not cease" (Genesis 8:22). In the fall, the leaves are a beautiful painting, school is in session, daylight is getting shorter, and we have holidays, chili, hayrides, and roasting marshmallows on an open fire. I love the fellowship of Thanksgiving. One of my first jobs in the ministry was with a loving congregation in West Tennessee. I had a special place in my heart for the senior group. We met once a month to do different activities. One of them was having a Thanksgiving meal together. One particular year, the Thanksgiving meal was very special to me. I was going to Africa, and I was to be there during Thanksgiving. My wife and I were expecting our first baby. It was a very emotional time. I thanked the members for the occasion, and I was honored to eat this Thanksgiving meal with them. We filled our plates and enjoyed the time together. I needed that time before my temporary separation from my family. I'm grateful for the connections with everyone at the table. We had no electronics, and we enjoyed each other's conversations. We laughed and encouraged one another. I love the memories that come from my time feasting at the table. The earth continues to rotate and revolve around the sun. The seasons come and go. Be thankful in prayer for your time in the fall.

DEAR LORD, YOU SPENT TIME IN PEOPLE'S HOMES AROUND THEIR TABLES ...

1. Pray to God, thankful for the memories of fellowshipping at the table with those who have already gone.
2. Pray to God to show your children the importance of time together at the table.

"And being in Bethany at the house of Simon the leper, as He sat at the table, a woman came having an alabaster flask of very costly oil of spikenard. Then she broke the flask and poured it on His head." **(Mark 14:3)**

Day 332

DEAR GOD, I PRAY THAT I MAY LIVE EACH DAY WITH ANTICIPATION FOR ...

"While the earth remains, seedtime and harvest, cold and heat, winter and summer, and day and night shall not cease" (Genesis 8:22). In the winter, we have cold days and nights, hot chocolate, Christmas, ongoing Christmas music, and New Year's resolutions. My thoughts in winter go to the chance of a snow day. I feel for any school administration that makes the decision to close school due to the weather or forecast. I revert to my childhood days with excitement when it comes to the potential for a snow day. I'm like a child on Christmas morning. I'm constantly looking at every local weather channel. I'm checking my weather apps on my phone. I'm seeing if any meteorologist is going to give a favorable chance for snowy precipitation. Our whole family is involved in school, so it's a family affair. We wait with anticipation, hoping to have a snow day. I realize other people have to work regardless of the weather. I want it to be bad enough for school but good enough for work. When school is called off, we all run around like we just won a major prize. We each are doing our variation of a snow-day dance. I think about the possibility of snow days in the winter. The earth continues to rotate and revolve around the sun. The seasons come and go. Be thankful in prayer for your time in the winter.

DEAR LORD, YOUR LAST WORDS WERE THAT YOU ARE COMING QUICKLY ...

1. Pray to God that the excitement of snow days doesn't compare to the day the King returns.
2. Pray to God to live each day watchful and ready for when Jesus comes again.

"... looking for the blessed hope and glorious appearing of our great God and Savior Jesus Christ." **(Titus 2:13)**

DEAR GOD, MY EYES ARE ON YOU ...

I was in graduate school in West Tennessee when 9/11 took place. I remember the eerie feeling of our nation at a standstill and in shock. We dismissed classes that day, and I could see the same shock in people's eyes driving back home. I noticed people lining up at the local pumps to gas up their vehicles. I didn't know what to do besides pray as a citizen. The next day, I had a counseling class. We met together, and I'm glad we did. My professor addressed the tense situation. He pointed to a verse in the Old Testament. He, too, was shocked and surprised with the chain of events. He read to us a passage that he came across within the day. "O our God, will You not judge them? For we have no power against this great multitude that is coming against us; nor do we know what to do, but our eyes are upon You" (2 Chronicles 20:12). What a gem! It spoke to me strongly in that moment. I didn't have an answer and didn't know what to do. There was someone else who felt the same when it came to a national crisis. Jehoshaphat was king, and a great multitude was coming against him and the people of God. He didn't have an answer to this great problem. He prayed to God and kept his eyes on Him. We are not always going to know what to do. We can, though, be prayerful and mindful of God in every moment.

DEAR LORD, THE WORDS OF MY MOUTH AND THE MEDITATION OF MY HEART ...

1. Pray to God that you can always go to Him regardless of whether you know the answer.
2. Pray to God, thankful that He is wise and knows what is best for you in your life. Trust in Him.

"Let the words of my mouth and the meditation of my heart be acceptable in Your sight, O Lord my strength and my Redeemer." **(Psalm 19:14)**

Day 334

DEAR GOD, I LOOK UP TO YOU ...

When I'm asked what I do, I tell someone that I'm a teacher and preacher. "What do you teach?" "I teach middle school." "Oh, bless you" or "I couldn't do that" is said back. I never thought I would be a middle school teacher. I didn't grow up telling everyone that I aspired to be a middle school teacher. It just happened. I had a student to say, "You're weird." I said, "I have to be weird to teach you." There are great days when students are learning and growing. Then there are days when the best thing I can do is draw a circle on the whiteboard and write in the middle, "Bang head here." Occasionally, there is a moment when you thank God for reaching that person. I was reminded of that recently. I received a text message from one of my co-teachers of a student's work in English. The student had written about me as someone they look up to. The student wrote, "I look up to Mr. Barnett. He is really funny. He gives us chances to learn on our own. He is very nice, and he is very Christian. I need to tell him how much I look up to him." It melted my heart to read that text. I'm actually reaching someone. A person doesn't need to be a teacher to be a person of influence. There is someone watching us and maybe looking up to us. May we take that moment and demonstrate the love of Christ.

DEAR LORD, THANK YOU FOR GIVING US AN EXAMPLE TO FOLLOW IN EVERYDAY LIFE ...

1. Pray to God to take your position and use it to influence others in a positive and encouraging way.
2. Pray to God to help you be mindful of what others see in you each day and be more careful with your words and actions.

"You are the salt of the earth; but if the salt loses its flavor, how shall it be seasoned? It is then good for nothing but to be thrown out and trampled underfoot by men." **(Matthew 5:13)**

DEAR GOD, YOU DESIRE US TO CONNECT TO YOU ...

My smartphone can keep track of how much time I spend on my phone. My average screen time for the past seven days is two hours and forty-three minutes. I'm obviously connected to something. I can catch myself, in-between moments throughout my day, reaching for it and checking my email or Instagram page. It becomes almost a habit. Instead of waiting, we look at the apps on our phones. It's a battle in the classroom. I took a student's phone during class. I asked him why he was on it. He said, "I was bored." As a culture, we are highly connected to people, games, and events through our phones. What if I spent half of my time in a day connected to God rather than trivial things? If we are going to connect more to God, we must disconnect from other things. I'm being transparent because, for me, it's my phone. I need to disconnect from it more and focus my thoughts and concerns on God. I know the only thing that will matter after this life is God. The latest phone, app, or trend will be long forgotten at that time. I'm not dismissing technology altogether. I'm challenging you and me to disconnect from our devices for a time and connect to God more. There is nothing more important than building your relationship with God.

DEAR LORD, YOU CONSTANTLY FOUND TIME ON EARTH TO CONNECT TO THE FATHER ...

1. Pray to God to be more intentional about connecting to Him and disconnecting from your phone.
2. Pray to God not to take for granted the privilege of connecting to Him in prayer.

> *"Let us therefore come boldly to the throne of grace, that we may obtain mercy and find grace to help in time of need."* **(Hebrews 4:16)**

Day 336

DEAR GOD, I'M CONSTANTLY DISTRACTED ...

What are you thinking about? I haven't given you anything to direct your mind toward. That doesn't mean you are not thinking about something. What is it? Are you thinking about food, your cluttered home, a problem, money, stress, or a certain person? Are we so involved that it's difficult to focus on God? We are too busy, too distracted, and too preoccupied. I sometimes tell my boys at nighttime to turn it off in their minds. They struggle to transition from playing to getting in bed. They are still active in their minds because they cannot be still. I say, "Turn that game off!" It's much easier said than done. Do I need to do the same? Jesus was in the home of Mary and Martha. Mary was at the feet of Jesus, and Martha was preoccupied with serving. Jesus said, "Martha, Martha, you are worried and troubled about many things. But one thing is needed, and Mary has chosen that good part" (Luke 10:41-42). Martha was so preoccupied with serving that she was being pulled away from what was better. She was so busy with dinner that she gave Jesus her spiritual leftovers. We do that when God is not first. If your life were recorded for one week and shown to a group of strangers, what would stand out to them about you? I get that we have to get things done. However, we need to devote our days to God because He is our first priority.

DEAR LORD, I CANNOT ALLOW THINGS TO TAKE AWAY MY TIME FROM YOU ...

1. Pray to God to help you spend a portion of your day in prayer and in the Word.
2. Pray to God to give you the strength to demonstrate in your day that He is first.

> *"Continue earnestly in prayer, being vigilant in it with thanksgiving."* (Colossians 4:2)

DEAR GOD, I CAN, BUT REALLY, I WON'T BECAUSE I'M NOT READY TO ...

I came across a poll that revealed some memorable excuses for not working. My mother poisoned my ham. I got stuck under the bed. I broke my arm while trying to grab a falling sandwich. The universe told me to take the day off. The doctor said I needed more vitamin D, so I went to the beach. It seems with every responsibility, there is a limitless supply of excuses. The Roman governor, Felix, sent Paul away for a more convenient time (Acts 24:25). Adam and Eve gave excuses for disobeying God (Genesis 3:12-13). Moses made excuses about his physical inabilities when God called him from the burning bush. Jonah excused himself by getting on a boat to travel the opposite direction from where he was supposed to be. There is no good excuse when it comes to obedience. We are either going to do it or not. There is no in-between with being a follower of Christ. We are not called to give a third of our hearts to Him. We cannot justify being one-half a Christian. We must reach out to Him in complete surrender as He wraps His mercy around us. It starts with being committed in our hearts and minds. May we confirm our decision, beginning with prayer. There is nothing greater than following God.

DEAR LORD, CREATE IN ME A CLEAN HEART SO I CAN SURRENDER ALL ...

1. Pray to God to follow in complete obedience, giving no excuses for what you can do.
2. Pray to God that with all your heart, you would surrender all.

"And do not present your members as instruments of unrighteousness to sin, but present yourselves to God as being alive from the dead, and your members as instruments of righteousness to God." **(Romans 6:13)**

Day 338

DEAR GOD, I PRAISE YOU FOR HUMBLING YOURSELF THE WAY YOU DID FOR OUR SAKE ...

What would Jesus wear today? Would He wear blue jeans or khaki pants? Would He be in a suit and tie, button-up polo shirt, or plain white T-shirt? Jesus was with His disciples at an evening meal before the Passover. He rose from supper without a word and dressed Himself like a household servant to perform a servant's task. Can you imagine the dirty, stinky feet of the disciples? They had walked almost two miles from Bethany to Jerusalem. They had no asphalt streets or concrete sidewalks. The disciples weren't wearing socks or sneakers. When I was in the South Pacific, I wore some Teva sandals. When my time was done, they smelled so bad that I had to throw them away. I imagine the disciples' feet were smelly. The Rabbi served His students. When was the last time your prayer was focused on someone other than you? You began and ended your prayer focused on God and someone else. It's good to have prayers like that. Peter, who had his feet washed by Jesus, said later, "Be submissive to one another, and be clothed with humility" (1 Peter 5:5). We are to be dressed ready to serve others spiritually. Today is a great day to go outside your comfort zone to serve someone.

DEAR LORD, MAY I FOLLOW YOUR SERVANT HEART ...

1. Pray to God to help you focus on others and not stay stuck with you.
2. Pray to God to be clothed with humility in your service to Him and others.

"Let nothing be done through selfish ambition or conceit, but in lowliness of mind let each esteem others better than himself. Let each of you look out not only for his own interests, but also for the interests of others." **(Philippians 2:3-4)**

DEAR GOD, I OPEN MY HEART TO YOU ...

Our youngest of three believed he was the boss. He may still. I remember coming home from work, and he was spouting out orders for me to sit here, look there, watch this, and do that. At the time, he was two years old and stubborn. I tried to sit him down and tell him that I'm the boss because I pay the bills. He looked at me and said, "Sit here!" I sat down. Do you remember the commandments? Moses stood on Mount Sinai and received the Law of God on stone tablets. The Israelites were familiar with a lot of other gods. They had spent hundreds of years surrounded by Egyptian gods. They knew Ra, the sun god in ancient Egypt. What about the God? Jehovah God declared that He was God, and no other gods should be before Him. He was the boss. The issue of idolatry was not related to the Old Testament. Anyone can hammer a hobby or lifestyle into an idol. We can easily replace God with our own creations. A hobby can take up all of our free time. A job demands my devotion. A list of personal accolades makes me feel special and important. Idolatry is a problem because God is jealous for our hearts (Deuteronomy 4:24). He is jealous because of His great love for us. We cannot make Him one of many bosses in our hearts. There is no room for anyone or anything but God. If we love God, may our love sit on the throne of our heart.

DEAR LORD, I WANT TO LOVE YOU LIKE YOU SHOWED ...

1. Pray to God for the strength today to live with your heart consumed by Him.
2. Pray to God for the spiritual stamina to continue to abide in Him and His word with a devoted heart.

"You shall have no other gods before Me." **(Deuteronomy 5:7)**

Day 340

DEAR GOD, THANK YOU FOR MARY'S FAITH ...

A witness is defined as someone who gives evidence. Many claim to be a witness for the Lord, but only a select few were witnesses of the Lord. One of those great witnesses was Mary Magdalene. Mary witnessed to the death and resurrection of Jesus. She is mentioned in all four Gospels in connection to the crucifixion of Jesus. She was the first person Christ appeared to after His resurrection. Mary was able to see for herself. She didn't need a sermon or read Scripture to know. She had personal, empirical knowledge of the life of Christ. Jesus gave Mary a message to tell His disciples: "I have not yet ascended to My Father; but go to My brethren and say to them, 'I am ascending to My Father and your Father, and to My God and your God'" (John 20:17). Mary was a witness to the disciples. She faithfully shared what she saw and what was spoken to her by the Lord. What would this true witness say to us when we get discouraged, doubt, or deny Jesus? Mary knew the truth. Do you believe her testimony? I'm thankful for the feet of those who faithfully carry the message delivered by the Holy Spirit. I'm prayerful for all teachers and preachers of the Word who faithfully teach Jesus of the Bible. I also pray for those who are overseas in a foreign land, preaching the same message but in a different language. I'm thankful for them because I wouldn't be a Christian if it weren't for those who loved God's Word enough to teach me.

DEAR LORD, I PRAY TO BE FAITHFUL ...

1. Pray to God for those dedicated to teaching the Word so that others may know what you know.
2. Pray to God for the seed to germinate and take root in the hearts of the listeners.

"And how shall they preach unless they are sent? As it is written: 'How beautiful are the feet of those who preach the gospel of peace, who bring glad tidings of good things!'" **(Romans 10:15)**

DEAR GOD, I DON'T UNDERSTAND ...

I was a freshman at a community college and working as a janitor at a local middle school when I got the call. I was told that my grandmother had passed away. She had fought ALS for several years. It had left her unable to talk and being fed through a feeding tube. It was difficult at that point in my life to see someone like that deteriorate like that. I was a Christian, but I struggled with prayer. I was nineteen and praying for my grandmother to be spared, but she was gradually going down. Unanswered questions and unanswered prayers (or not the answer we want) about God and health can leave us confused. What do we pray for? I believe we pray what we are feeling in moments of anger, upset, and sadness. The psalms are filled with examples of coming to God with complaints. The Bible doesn't point to a happy earthly ending for everyone. Sometimes people suffer and are suspended in grief. We shouldn't be afraid to go to God with our complaints. It's on our hearts anyway. Life is filled with moments that lead us to struggle. What about a teenager who drains the family finances and shows no appreciation? What about a parent with dementia? Is it a bitter and divided church? Each of these circumstances calls for open, honest prayers that express our feelings. We don't need to feel guilty for being truthful about how we feel in moments that try us the most. Jesus was truthful on the cross.

DEAR LORD, WHY AM I ALLOWED TO EXPERIENCE THIS PAINFUL SITUATION ...

1. Pray to God to always be open and honest with Him about how you feel.
2. Pray to God to build a relationship that conveys all feelings without trying to hide or keep them from Him.

"In everything give thanks; for this is the will of God in Christ Jesus for you." **(1 Thessalonians 5:18)**

Day 342

DEAR GOD, I WANT TO HAVE THE COURAGE TO SAY, "I'VE SINNED" ...

I was bothered by my behavior in high school with someone. I kept thinking back to it as I moved on to college. One day, I got the courage to contact this person and confess my wrongs against the person. I felt like a major weight had been lifted off. I thanked God for forgiveness and the result of confession. The person was surprised but gracious that I called and said what I did. It restored us back after being separated by past actions. Sin can disrupt the relationship between God and us. Confession restores our communication with God. When I struggled with guilt, I resolved with myself to explain my way out of confession and excused my behavior. I would think that the person had forgotten about it. Confession can clear away my rationalization and open me to God. We have confidence that God will always answer a prayer of confession with forgiveness. "And if anyone sins, we have an Advocate with the Father, Jesus Christ the righteous" (1 John 2:1). What should we pray for? We need to pray a prayer of confession for our sins. We need to seek our only Savior to plead our case with the Father when it comes to forgiveness. We need to open up anything blocking our way to the Father, Son, and Spirit. May we never be too proud to say, "I'm sorry for the sins I have committed against you."

DEAR LORD, THANK YOU FOR FORGIVENESS ...

1. Pray to God to make no excuses for what you have done and to own up to it by confession.
2. Pray to God never to let anything that you have done stand in your way with Him.

"In everything give thanks; for this is the will of God in Christ Jesus for you." **(1 Thessalonians 5:18)**

DEAR GOD, I'M REMINDED OF YOUR CARE THROUGH THE LIFE OF JESUS ...

How do you begin your prayers? Do you start with God or with your requests? In the model prayer, Jesus began with God. He started with the Source before asking for something. When I'm praying for someone specifically, I try not to start with the person. I reflect on how God must already feel about the person I am praying for. I know how God feels because of Jesus. The Jews saw, through His emotions, how much He loved Lazarus. I can read about the physical healing Jesus provided to those who asked Him. We can have peace in knowing that we are not praying to a God who doesn't care. I find peace in reading how Jesus cared for humanity. He didn't leave with a calloused heart. We all need the peace that Jesus can give. The church needs peace. Parents of a newborn need peace. College students need peace. Caregivers and relief workers need peace from the front lines of life. We have the gift of the Holy Spirit to help us have peace in taking our words and interceding for us with groaning that cannot be expressed. The Holy Spirit intercedes for the people of God because it's God's will. Why does God will? He cares for us just as Jesus cared for us in His ministry and in His death on the cross. In a world of sorrow and pain, we can be at peace with God because it's a peace that surpasses all understanding.

DEAR LORD, I NEED THE SPIRIT'S HELP ...

1. Pray to God, if it be His awesome will, that you can be at peace with the situation you struggle with.
2. Pray to God, asking for peace from the Prince of Peace, who provided a way for us to make such a request.

"In everything give thanks; for this is the will of God in Christ Jesus for you." (1 Thessalonians 5:18)

Day 344

DEAR GOD, NOT A DAY GOES BY WHEN I DESERVE TO BE UNGRATEFUL ...

"I'm alive! I didn't miss living. That is wonderful enough for me." Who would say something like that? Would it be a person who had a great life? The person who said it was David Rothenberg. As a six-year-old, he suffered third-degree burns over ninety percent of his body. His father gave him a sleeping pill and poured kerosene over him and set him afire. He survived the attempted murder. He underwent more than sixty major surgeries. He passed away at the age of forty-two in 2018. It's amazing that a person like this made a grateful statement. It's not surprising to read that grateful people tend to be happier and more satisfied. Ten lepers approached Jesus on His way to Jerusalem. Jesus gave them instruction, and they went and were cleansed of their leprosy. All ten lepers were cured. Jesus had healed them physically, socially, and spiritually. How many were grateful for what Christ did? Only one came back to show gratitude. Things can happen to us to make us think differently. We can easily say, "It's not fair," or live ungrateful lives. We should be grateful because of the spiritual gift through Jesus Christ. We need to be careful and not fall into the ninety percent of the lepers. We can overlook the blessings we have because of the one thing sucking our time and thoughts. We need to go to God in prayer, thanking Him. We need to praise God: "I'm alive! I didn't miss living. That is wonderful enough for me."

DEAR LORD, THANK YOU FOR SALVATION ...

1. Pray to God with thanksgiving in your heart because you have more than enough.
2. Pray to God to live the day with gratitude for the things you know and have from Him.

"In everything give thanks; for this is the will of God in Christ Jesus for you." **(1 Thessalonians 5:18)**

Day 345

DEAR LORD, RESTORE MY SPIRIT …

A lot happened in the upper room the night Jesus was betrayed and arrested. Jesus instituted His Supper. He informed His disciples that one of them would betray Him. He mentioned that He was leaving. He informed Peter of his denial. In Luke's account, Jesus said, "But I have prayed for you, that your faith should not fail; and when you have returned to Me, strengthen your brethren" (Luke 22:32). Peter quickly said, "Lord, I am ready to go with You, both to prison and to death" (v. 33). What did the Lord mean by "returned to Me"? The devil had asked for Peter. Jesus didn't ask that Peter be spared from trouble. The undergoing of difficulty, failure, setback, and hardship are important steps to becoming a stronger person. Jesus had the assurance that Peter would retrace his steps back to Jesus. We know Peter's shortcomings. What about Peter being restored? In John 21, we have a beautiful scene of restoration. Peter didn't choose to leave in disgrace over what he had done. He made the effort to return to the Lord. Restoration is necessary for us all. We like to think that sin won't happen to us. I'm thankful for the Lord's prayer prior to the events in John 21. He had prayed for Peter. What a touching action by our Lord! He cares for us, especially when we have fallen away from Him. Remember that there is nothing greater than the power of the cross. We must be willing to return to Him. May we be in prayer for one another.

DEAR LORD, THANK YOU FOR THE RESTORATION I CAN RECEIVE FROM YOU …

1. Pray for your heart to be set on Jesus.
2. Pray for the strength and humility to restore your spirit.

"Restore to me the joy of Your salvation, and uphold me by Your generous Spirit." **(Psalm 51:12)**

Day 346

DEAR GOD, THANK YOU FOR COMFORT ...

How does it make you feel to hear "I love you"? What about "It's going to be all right because I will be right beside you"? Has someone said to you, "I forgive you"? Words like these can bring comfort. One day, a minister named Elisha A. Hoffman was calling the destitute of Lebanon, Pennsylvania. He met a woman whose depression seemed beyond cure. She opened her heart and poured on him her pent-up sorrows. She cried out to him, "What shall I do? Oh, what shall I do?" Hoffman knew what she should do, for he had learned the lesson of God's comfort. He said to the woman, "You cannot do better than to take all your sorrows to Jesus. You must tell Jesus." She smiled and said, "Yes! I must tell Jesus." Hoffman was right. What can be more comforting than hearing the words of God? "Let not your heart be troubled; you believe in God, believe also in Me" (John 14:1). "Jesus said to her, 'I am the resurrection and the life. He who believes in Me, though he may die, he shall live'" (John 11:25). "Come to Me, all you who labor and are heavy laden, and I will give you rest. Take My yoke upon you and learn from Me, for I am gentle and lowly in heart, and you will find rest for your souls" (Matthew 11:28-29). We must feel comfortable with telling God. He is the source of all comfort. There is no greater avenue to that than prayer.

DEAR LORD, THANK YOU FOR PROVIDING MY SOUL'S REST ...

1. Pray to God to be open in confessing to Him your cares.
2. Pray to God to realize the power of words and what you say carries a tremendous weight with others and yourself.

"Simon Peter answered Him, 'Lord, to whom shall we go? You have the words of eternal life. Also we have come to believe and know that You are the Christ, the Son of the living God.'" **(John 6:68-69)**

DEAR GOD, I PRAY TO LOOK BEYOND MY ...

I'm so thankful for the phone call I received many years ago from Bob. I had no knowledge of him when I answered the phone. That phone call changed me. Bob was a preacher for nearly thirty years. He was married to a wonderful woman. He was the father of a girl and boy. His life was good until the year 1995. Bob was diagnosed with progressive multiple sclerosis. Four days after receiving his diagnoses, his only daughter of sixteen was killed in a car wreck. His mother died of acute leukemia, and a brother was murdered. These things happened in the year 1995. His debilitating disease kept him confined to a bed the rest of his life. If there were a candidate of a disadvantaged person, it would be Bob. What made his story memorable to me was his attitude and laugh. How could a guy like this find reason to laugh in life? He had written a book called *Don't Ever Give Up*. I was able to visit him in his home in Alabama. I saw him in his room with a computer set up for him to use while bedridden. We laughed and felt sadness together. I left feeling encouraged. If anyone had a reason to complain to God, it was him. He didn't. He accepted what happened and wrote a book to encourage others with his story. Bob passed away a few years ago. I will never forget the impact he had on my life. Can I see the advantage of a disadvantage? Do I believe the pains of today cannot compare to the promise of tomorrow?

DEAR LORD, THANK YOU FOR THE GREATEST GIFT THAT CAME FROM YOUR DEATH ...

1. Pray to God to be open to more than your present circumstances.
2. Pray to God to trust in Him as the only One who can work it all together for the good.

> *"But in all things we commend ourselves as ministers of God: in much patience, in tribulations, in needs, in distresses."* **(2 Corinthians 6:4)**

Day 348

DEAR GOD, I WANT TO GROW IN JESUS' STEPS MORE EACH DAY …

I see a similarity between our path in Christianity and the earthly life of Christ. Jesus' first steps were done in complete humility. He began His walk not standing but crawling. He had to learn how to walk so He could stand. "Humble yourselves in the sight of the Lord" (James 4:10). It takes humility to realize our need for the Father's help. As Jesus grew in wisdom and stature, so did His steps. He matured into fulfilling the Scriptures. His steps to Calvary glorified the Father. It was not until He was lifted up on the cross that Jesus was able to say, "It is finished!" (John 19:30). He knew that all things had been accomplished. His time and reason on earth were finished. Jesus ascended back home, leaving behind very few traces of Himself. He wrote no books. He left no home or even material belongings that could be displayed in a museum. He did not marry or settle down. His brothers and sisters have long passed. Jesus fulfilled His earthly role and left. He left a world still plagued by sin, hindered by disease, and consumed by poverty. He left the world in some ways the same as when He entered it. He did, however, leave a world not lost. He paved a way, provided an absolute truth, and offered a life possessed by Him. Jesus gave us an example to follow. One of the great examples He showed was His prayer life. We need to walk the path that our Lord laid.

DEAR LORD, I'M THANKFUL FOR YOU …

1. Pray to God to better understand how to live because of Jesus.
2. Pray to God always to bear His name in a worthy way and to show people Him by your life.

"And do not be conformed to this world, but be transformed by the renewing of your mind, that you may prove what is that good and acceptable and perfect will of God." **(Romans 12:2)**

DEAR GOD, I CAN LET MYSELF GET OUT OF CONTROL ...

One morning Ralph woke up at five o'clock to a noise that sounded like someone hammering on his roof. Still in his pajamas, he went into the backyard to investigate. He found a woodpecker on the TV antenna, pounding its little head on the metal pole. Angry at the little bird that ruined his sleep, Ralph picked up a rock and threw it. The rock sailed over the house, and he heard a distant crash as it hit his car. In utter disgust, Ralph took a hard kick at a pile of dirt, only to remember that he was not wearing any shoes. Have you ever had a moment like Ralph? A moment when your temper, anger, frustration, or hard-headed pride got the best of you? The Bible gives examples of people struggling in the moment. What would Eve and Adam give for another chance before the forbidden tree in the garden? What would David give to relive that night on the rooftop when he saw Bathsheba? What would Moses give to have another chance to approach the rock in the wilderness? Our lives on earth are really nothing more than a string of moments, one after another. Is any single moment worth shattering our relationship with Jesus Christ? I don't want one moment to cast a shadow over a lifetime of walking with the Lord. I pray for the Lord to keep me safe. I pray that I can learn from my mistakes and be committed to walking closer to God, day by day, hour by hour, moment by moment.

DEAR LORD, I PRAY FOR STRENGTH ...

1. Pray to God not to allow your past to keep you from your future.
2. Pray to God to learn from your mistakes and grow from them.

"Brethren, I do not count myself to have apprehended; but one thing I do, forgetting those things which are behind and reaching forward to those things which are ahead, I press toward the goal for the prize of the upward call of God in Christ Jesus." **(Philippians 3:13-14)**

Day 350

DEAR GOD, I WANT TO BE REGULAR WHEN IT COMES TO MY ...

I'm amazed at the persistence of the lame man laid at the temple gate daily. He had the support of others to carry him daily to the temple gate called Beautiful. He was there to ask for alms. His presence was so regular that worshipers expected to see him there. I have a few regulars near where I live, asking for help. I expect to see them in their spots every day. He reminds me of the tortoise in *The Tortoise and the Hare.* He was slow but steadily at the gate each day. The lame man found salvation in Peter and John because of his regular habit of being at the temple. What if he was there every other day? The probability of being there when Peter and John came by would decrease. What if he showed up on Monday, Wednesday, and Friday? His chances would drop even more. The most important word is "daily." We are to be regular when it comes to our faith. Jesus didn't die for our sins so we could live for Him on Sundays only. He didn't live thirty-three years so we could come Christmas and Easter. Are our prayer lives like our worship? Are they hit or miss? What if we were regular with our prayers? Mary Kidder reminds us of the importance of daily prayer with her hymn "Did You Think to Pray?" "When your heart was filled with anger, did you think to pray? Did you plead for grace, my brother, that you might forgive another who had crossed your way?"[5] I challenge you to be regular with your prayers.

DEAR LORD, YOU LIVED EACH DAY ON EARTH FOR US, AND WE NEED TO ...

1. Pray to God to be committed each day in your prayers and actions.
2. Pray to God to develop the habit of leaning on God each day.

"Give us day by day our daily bread." **(Luke 11:3)**

Day 351

DEAR GOD, TO EVERY SEASON THERE IS A PURPOSE UNDER HEAVEN ...

There is a positive message hidden in a negative word. The word is "depression." The message is "press on." Our lives can feel like a string of seasons. We have random days connected to our calendar. It's easy to overlook God in each season of our lives. The season of change has nothing to do with weather, time, or daylight. It's changes we can control or make. In Ecclesiastes 3, there are twenty-eight activities or seasons we can experience in this life. There are fourteen lines of favorable and unfavorable moments of life. These events are a snapshot of what people face. Some are easy to identify like "life and death" and "war and peace." Some are less noticeable like "mourn and dance" and "break down and build up." It's important for us to know what season of life we are in. It helps us to simplify our lives, to notice God more, and to see what lesson we can learn from Him. It helps us to press on to the next one. Have you ever felt like God was trying to get your attention? Was it a verse you read that spoke to your current season of life? Did an event cause you to think more on the things you put off? In all seasons of life, are you prayerful to discern what is right and best for you? Are you able to press on to the next season of your life? Life is not meant to stay unchanged in the same season.

DEAR LORD, I PRAY THAT I CAN DISCERN MY SEASON OF LIFE AND BE READY TO PRESS ON ...

1. Pray to God not to get too comfortable with your life to where you don't grow.
2. Pray to God to appreciate the lesson in each season of life as you grow closer to Him.

> *"To everything there is a season, a time for every purpose under heaven."* **(Ecclesiastes 3:1)**

Day 352

DEAR GOD, FORGIVE ME WHEN I FEEL LIKE LIFE OWES ME SOMETHING ...

The thirteen states declared unanimously on July 4, 1776, "We hold these truths to be self-evident, that all men are created equal, that they are endowed by their Creator with certain unalienable Rights, that among these are Life, Liberty, and the pursuit of Happiness." Our founding fathers wanted citizens to have certain rights. These unalienable rights don't excuse us from personal responsibility. Have you ever stopped to listen to what is said around us? "I deserve a better grade." "I deserve a better job and bigger paycheck." What do people mean when they say, "I deserve"? They believe what is desired is a need. What about "I deserve" with God? We don't deserve God's love and grace, but He extends them because we desperately need them. We don't deserve heaven or forgiveness because of sin. However, God has provided salvation through Jesus Christ because of His great mercy. Instead of "I deserve," we should say, "I'm responsible." It frees us up from sitting and waiting for life to happen to us. We understand that our country and God have given us the freedom to choose. We play the victim, thinking life owes us something. We can be responsible about our decisions and choices in life. "I deserve a good life" is the easy way. "I am responsible for a good life" is much harder but right.

DEAR LORD, I TAKE RESPONSIBILITY FOR THE WAY I LIVE MY LIFE ...

1. Pray to God to be responsible enough to go to Him in prayer and seek His wisdom daily.
2. Pray to God to be responsible enough to know that you reap the consequences you sow in this life.

"For he who sows to his flesh will of the flesh reap corruption, but he who sows to the Spirit will of the Spirit reap everlasting life." **(Galatians 6:8)**

DEAR GOD, I PRAY THAT AS I DRAW NEAR TO YOU ...

I looked up to my grandfather as a child. He would take my sister and me to the store and let us fill up on candy. My grandfather also had a cup he would spit into. It was dark and brown inside with a piece of paper in it. I remember we had stopped at someone's house. I was in the car. I looked at the cup that he used a lot. I thought I wanted to be like him and try it. I took a gulp of what was in the cup and became sick to my stomach. I was miserable for the rest of the day. I don't know what my grandfather thought about dipping after that. I do remember that I didn't want to be near that cup again. My grandfather passed away when I was eight with lung cancer. He was a good man, and he loved his grandchildren. I wished he could have lived longer. This story reminds me of the power of influence. People are not only watching us, but they want to do what we do. It doesn't matter if it's a good habit or not. They want to be as much like us because of their love. I'm constantly mindful of my three boys. I know they are watching my mannerisms, hearing what I say, and seeing what I do. It can be some pressure knowing three sets of cameras are on me at all times. We have someone who looks up to us. The disciples were influenced by what others taught about prayer. They asked Jesus to teach them to pray. If we go to God in prayer often, we can show its importance to those who are watching us.

DEAR LORD, I LOOK TO YOU AS THE ONE WHO HAS INFLUENCED MY LIFE GREATLY ...

1. Pray to God to be salt and light to your family, friends, and neighbors.
2. Pray to God to be led in prayer and to be a better influence for those who know you.

> *"You shall love the Lord your God with all your heart, with all your soul, and with all your strength."* **(Deuteronomy 6:5)**

Day 354

DEAR GOD, I WANT TO USE THIS DAY WISELY ...

"I'm so busy. I don't have time to pray or do anything else." When or maybe where can we pray? We don't need a church building or pew or chair to pray. We find Jesus praying in a home and on a mountain-side. We have more idle time in our days that is wasted on something not meaningful. We don't have to spend hours of our day in prayer. There is no verse in the Bible that mentions how long we are to pray. The Lord's Prayer is brief and can be read or quoted in a minute. I think of quality not quantity when it comes to prayer. You can pray when you wake up in the morning. You can pray when you are getting a shower. You can pray as you enjoy a cup of coffee or tea. You can pray on your way to school or work. What if I spent more of my phone time in prayer? What would be the benefit? We are growing closer to God because of the frequency of our prayers. We are learning to be more specific, open, and truthful in our prayers. We are growing ourselves because it will challenge us to look further in the Word to know more on God's end. You may be busy. You may have a schedule that keeps you going nonstop. We can use those in-between moments to talk to God. There are too many reasons why we should be praying each day and no good reason why we shouldn't.

DEAR LORD, MY BUSY SCHEDULE DOESN'T COMPARE TO THE LIFE OF THE MESSIAH ...

1. Pray to God to be mindful in the downtime of your day to pray.
2. Pray to God to be purposeful in finding times to connect to Him in prayer.

"And when He had sent the multitudes away, He went up on the mountain by Himself to pray. Now when evening came, He was alone there." **(Matthew 14:23)**

DEAR GOD, I PRAY THAT MY ACTIONS SUPPORT MY PRIORITY IN MY SPIRITUAL LIFE ...

What is greater? Is it your physical life or spiritual life? I ask because it helps to see where we stand with the next question. How long would you go without praying because of the consequence of a den of lions? Would it be a day, week, month, years, or as long as the lions are there? Daniel was a man of prayer in a different land, culture, and language. He continued praying under the command of a different nation. Some of the governors convinced the king to set a decree that no one could pray to another god or man other than the king for thirty days. If one disobeyed, they were to be thrown in the den of lions. What did Daniel do when he knew that the decree was signed? Did he go without prayer to save his skin? We can easily go through a day without praying, and it doesn't involve a den of lions. But this new law didn't change Daniel's habit of praying. He continued to pray three times a day on his knees just as he had done before. Daniel's action demonstrated his priority. He served God no matter what. I admire Christians living in places where it doesn't support their freedom to worship God. We are free to worship and pray openly. I pray we don't dismiss this freedom and privilege we have each day. I pray we can be like Daniel, focused on our times of prayer with God no matter what.

DEAR LORD, THANK YOU FOR SHOWING US WHEN YOU PRAYED IN YOUR LIFE ...

1. Pray to God to appreciate the freedom to worship and pray to Him, and remember those who don't have that freedom.
2. Pray to God to get to a point where you care more about your soul than your flesh.

"For if you live according to the flesh, you will die; but if by the Spirit you put to death the deeds of the body, you will live." **(Romans 8:13)**

Day 356

DEAR GOD, I'M THANKFUL FOR MY SPIRITUAL BIRTHDAY BECAUSE ...

I remember being excited about birthdays when I was a teenager. I couldn't wait until the day I turned sixteen because I wanted my driver's license. I was excited to turn eighteen and register to vote. When we get older, we sometimes don't get excited or look forward to birthdays. Children can't wait for their birthdays. Adults can dread their birthdays. They don't want to be older anymore. Our attitude can change with physical birthdays because of getting older. It's much different with spiritual birthdays. I remember when I was "born again." "Jesus answered, 'Most assuredly, I say to you, unless one is born of water and the Spirit, he cannot enter the kingdom of God'" (John 3:5). I don't want to go back to that time because of my knowledge of God and His Word now. I happily celebrate my years as a Christian. I continue to learn more from God, and I'm growing closer to Him. I look up to those who are older spiritually than me. I worship with many who have been Christians longer than I've been alive. I'm thankful and pray for them. They demonstrate a strong faith in God. They have faithfully served God through the ups and downs of life. I pray for them and for their example to me. I hope to show the same to younger generations. When was the last time you talked to and prayed for someone much older than you?

DEAR LORD, THANK YOU FOR THOSE WHO HAVE LIVED MUCH LONGER IN YOU THAN ME ...

1. Pray to God, thankful for the example of older believers because they are a source of knowledge and wisdom.
2. Pray to God for the strength to live dedicated to Him each day.

"As newborn babes, desire the pure milk of the word, that you may grow thereby, if indeed you have tasted that the Lord is gracious." **(1 Peter 2:2-3)**

Day 357

DEAR GOD, I STAND SHACKLED BY MY SINS ...

She stands at 151 feet. She weighs 225 tons, which is almost equivalent to the weight of forty-five African elephants. Her index finger is about eight feet long. Each of her hands is 150 square feet, about the size of a small classroom. It takes 354 steps to reach her crown. She is named "Liberty Enlightening the World." She is more commonly known as the Statue of Liberty. What began as a gift of international friendship soon became an enduring symbol of freedom. The broken shackles at the statue's feet stand for freedom from tyranny. The law tablet in her left hand represents the Declaration of Independence and the American ideal that "all men are created equal." On the statue's 100th birthday, President Ronald Reagan stated from the monument: "We are the keepers of the flame of liberty; we hold it high for the world to see." I've been on the ferry to go by her. It's impressive to see from the water. It's a symbol of our freedom, and it's iconic as we celebrate our country's birthday. It reminds me of the cost of freedom. There is nothing cheap with freedom of any kind, especially spiritual freedom. There is nothing more sobering than to hear "for the wages of sin is death" (Romans 6:23). We are helpless and hopeless in freeing ourselves from the shackles of sin. However, Christ has made us free.

DEAR LORD, I COME TO YOU SEEKING FORGIVENESS AND A CHANGED HEART ...

1. Pray to God never to forget the cost of your forgiveness.
2. Pray to God to continue to appreciate your freedom from sin in prayer, life, and worship.

> *"Stand fast therefore in the liberty by which Christ has made us free, and do not be entangled again with a yoke of bondage."* **(Galatians 5:1)**

Day 358

DEAR GOD, I WANT TO APPRECIATE MY FREE GIFT OF SALVATION BY INVESTING …

When I turned sixteen, I wanted a car. My grandmother gave me a generous opportunity. She had a 1983 Ford Tempo. It was maroon on the outside and inside. It had a great feature of going over fifty-five miles per hour and the whole dashboard shaking up and down. It came with natural hydraulics so I could bounce up and down in the car. My grandmother didn't give me this car because I was her only grandson. She sold it to me for eight hundred dollars. I worked and saved to pay it off. I didn't like it then, but I'm grateful now that she required a payment. It taught me to appreciate my big purchase. I changed the oil and oil filter, washed the car, and cleaned the tires. I was invested because of what it cost me. Isn't that a life lesson? The more something costs you, the more invested you are. Does this apply to our faith? The more connected you are, the more invested you become. Which person is more connected? Person one goes to church on Sunday morning and prays every once in a while. What kind of investment has the person established? Will it hold them when trials happen? Person two goes to church more than once a week. Person two seeks God's counsel in the Word and prayer daily. The more you invest in prayer, service, and reading, the stronger you will become.

DEAR LORD, LIFE IS MORE MEANINGFUL BECAUSE OF THE TIME YOU INVESTED …

1. Pray to God to build on a foundation stronger than you.
2. Pray to God to invest each day in your relationship with Him by praying, serving, and reflecting in His Word.

> *"Therefore whoever hears these sayings of Mine, and does them, I will liken him to a wise man who built his house on the rock."* **(Matthew 7:24)**

DEAR GOD, I PRAY THAT AS I GROW CLOSER TO YOU, I BECOME MORE OPEN ...

Who am I? What is behind my smile to people? Am I the same person that people see? I realize we have days we struggle with, and we put on a face just to endure the day. Do we try to be genuine and open as much as we can? If we are not careful, we can get caught up in wearing masks to hide our true selves and feelings. We can put on the "happy and I got everything under control" mask when we don't. We can wear the "I'm confident in my skin" mask when we struggle with self-esteem. Our culture is not receptive to expressing our true feelings. We feel vulnerable when we expose our true selves. What if people reject me? What if they don't understand me? We need to be people of integrity. Job was real and open in his pain and suffering. His friends didn't understand and blamed him for his troubles. God blessed him in the end. I pray that we are comfortable enough in who we are because of Christ. I pray that we have a transparent relationship with Christ. There is nothing to hide because it's all exposed to Him.

DEAR LORD, YOU REVEALED THE IMAGE OF THE INVISIBLE GOD ...

1. Pray to God to be transparent with Him and others.
2. Pray to God to live a genuine life that is open and honest.

"I have been crucified with Christ; it is no longer I who live, but Christ lives in me; and the life which I now live in the flesh I live by faith in the Son of God, who loved me and gave Himself for me." **(Galatians 2:20)**

Day 360

DEAR GOD, I'M STRUGGLING WITH WHAT HAS HAPPENED TO ME ...

Adelaide Pollard was born in Iowa during the Civil War. She struggled with her health. She was drawn to a faith healer in Chicago, who was drawing in large crowds. She then gravitated toward an evangelist named Sanford, who believed the end of the world was soon. Adelaide felt called to go to Africa for mission work. She was unable to raise the financial support to go. She was in a prayer meeting, heartsick and disappointed. An elderly woman prayed, "It doesn't matter what You bring into our lives, Lord. Just have Your own way with us." The prayer struck Adelaide. She went home and reread the story of the potter and clay in Jeremiah 18. When it was bedtime, she had written the prayer, "Have Thine Own Way." This beloved hymn was born from a prayer of disappointment and setbacks. We have heard it said, "If life hands you lemons, make lemonade." I say, "If life hands us lemons, turn to the providential care of God. He is the One who can take the lemons of life and work them together for the good." Can we, in a low moment of life, possess the same attitude as Adelaide? Can we truthfully pray, "Have Thine own way, Lord"? The greatest time to trust in God is in life's setbacks. It's in those moments that we find ourselves and see how strong our faith is in God. Life is not easy. Life is more doable with the Lord. I pray for His will and not mine.

DEAR LORD, I WANT THE FAITH TO PRAY THE SAME PRAYER AS YOU IN THE GARDEN ...

1. Pray to God for His will to be done and not yours.
2. Pray to God that, whatever is brought in your life, He would have His way with you.

> *"'O house of Israel, can I not do with you as this potter?' says the LORD. 'Look, as the clay is in the potter's hand, so are you in My hand, O house of Israel!'"* **(Jeremiah 18:6)**

Day 361

DEAR GOD, I CANNOT FIND A FRIEND AS FAITHFUL AND DEPENDABLE AS YOU ...

Joseph Scriven was twenty-five and living in Ireland when he watched his fiancée pulled from a lake. Their wedding was the next day. He migrated to the United States. When he was thirty-five, his mother was facing a crisis. Joseph wrote her a poem and sent it to her. She had the note published, and it became a popular hymn. Joseph fell in love again. However, tragedy struck him a second time when his soon-to-be bride contracted tuberculosis and died before their wedding. Joseph poured his sorrow into his charitable work in living a simple life. He found out that his poem intended for his mother had been published into a popular hymn. He poured his heart to his mother with no intention for someone else to see it. The words of the hymn speak to the importance of prayer in hard times. Life doesn't always pan out like we want. We can have good intentions to do something, until tragedy strikes. Anything can happen at any time. No one knows the next day or next hour. I'm reminded of Joseph's words and of the great privilege of prayer. We have a God who is present and listening to our struggles. He even wants our cares. Prayer doesn't change what has already happened. It does help us to endure the pain from what happened. If Jesus saw the value of prayer on the cross, we should see its value in our day.

DEAR LORD, I GO TO PRAYER IN ALL THINGS JUST AS YOU DID ON EARTH ...

1. Pray to God for a peace that will surpass the pain in your life.
2. Pray to God, seeking refuge in Him from the pain and suffering of this difficult life.

"Be anxious for nothing, but in everything by prayer and supplication, with thanksgiving, let your requests be made known to God." **(Philippians 4:6)**

Day 362

DEAR GOD, I'M GRATEFUL FOR THE "HAPPY DAYS" IN THE SPIRITUAL WAR ...

Philip's mother had eighteen of nineteen children to die in infancy. Can you imagine the heartache? Her name was Monica, and she dealt with death many times over. She had baby number twenty. His name was Philip, and he appeared stillborn. He was placed on his side, where he started to cry. His mother raised him to know the Lord. He wanted to be a preacher but couldn't afford the education. He was advised by friends to choose another profession. Philip spent a day in prayer. In that day, the postman arrived with a letter from a wealthy benefactor. He had offered to finance Philip's education. Philip's answer was so timely that he resolved to live a life of prayer. He worked on praying without ceasing. He kept praying when doing daily routines like getting dressed and washing up. His prayer life led him to write nearly four hundred hymns. "O Happy Day" takes me back to my first full-time ministry position in Haywood County. When souls were saved, the church would sing this hymn. It was a happy day. We were thankful and prayerful to God as another soul was saved in Him. I love those prayers. I love the prayers of thanksgiving and rejoicing with angels. It's moments when battles over people's hearts are won because of Christ. I pray for more "happy days."

DEAR LORD, THERE WOULD BE NO "HAPPY DAY" IF IT WASN'T FOR YOUR LOVE ...

1. Pray to God, asking to be open for opportunities to lead to "happy days."
2. Pray to God for all lives to come to know His loving Son.

> *"I say to you that likewise there will be more joy in heaven over one sinner who repents than over ninety-nine just persons who need no repentance."* **(Luke 15:7)**

DEAR GOD, I CANNOT THANK YOU ENOUGH FOR SEEING US THROUGH OUR ...

It looked like a beautiful June day from inside the window. I was limited in how far I could go because of all the hookups and wires to my monitors. I was in the neuro intensive care wing of the hospital. I looked outside to the cars going by and watched the sun hit the buildings around the hospital. I wondered what my family and other families were doing that day. I wanted to get outside and feel the sun hit my body. I turned around to the nurses and my wife, knowing I had another week to lie flat on the hospital bed. "What good can come from this?" I thought. I couldn't help anyone, let alone myself. It was a difficult summer and one that will stay with me for the rest of my life. My mind goes back to it from time to time. I didn't see how anything good could come from it then. I continued to pray to God and for His will to be done. It was painful to pray that because I selfishly wanted to be healed and out. I learned more about God in that hospital room than in any sermon or Bible class at school. I learned to endure and wait patiently on the Lord. I learned to pray totally dependent on the Lord. God became more real to me in my pain and suffering. I wanted to use my experience to help others and thank God for seeing me through it. You may not understand why you are going through something painful. I pray your day can turn into a more fulfilled day from what you have gained and learned.

DEAR LORD, I LOOK TO YOU IN MY PAIN AND SUFFERING. YOU HELP ME TO ENDURE ...

1. Pray to God for the patience to wait on Him.
2. Pray to God to be open to what you can learn in the painful days.

> *"And we know that all things work together for good to those who love God, to those who are the called according to His purpose."* **(Romans 8:28)**

Day 364

DEAR GOD, YOU CAN TAKE MOMENTS IN TIME AND PUT SOMETHING WONDERFUL TOGETHER ...

On February 13, 2017, I started to post a spiritual thought on Facebook. I said, "I cannot throw a stone at anyone because I'm a sinner (forgiven but a sinner)." I posted something different, but with a spiritual message the next day. I did this every day for a month. I then decided to continue into the next month. Some days, I would write about what happened to me on that day. Other days, I would write about something on my mind. Each time, I referenced a verse from the Word of God and kept the message positive. I put in my mind the idea to write a positive message every day for a year. I wanted to express my gratitude to God by encouraging others with a positive post. I was tired of all the negative posts. On August 29, 2017, I received a message from a friend who had been reading my daily posts. He mentioned that he was retiring from his job and going to work on a small publishing company. I knew this individual because I used to work with his wife. She was a sweet woman. She eventually died from cancer. She fought hard and left behind a husband and two grown children. My relationship with her at school led to my friendship with her husband. This led to him wanting to talk to me about writing a devotional book. I went back to that day, standing up in the hospital room. I was seeing the good that God is able to do for those who love Him.

DEAR LORD, THE COLLECTION OF YOUR DAYS LED TO THE MOST WONDERFUL ACT OF LOVE ...

1. Pray to God, thankful for the people that He has placed in your life.
2. Pray to God, thankful for the good that has come from those friendships.

"And we know that all things work together for good to those who love God, to those who are the called according to His purpose." **(Romans 8:28)**

Day 365

DEAR GOD, I END TODAY THANKFUL FOR WHAT I HAVE LEARNED ...

The memory of a wife, mother, friend, and coworker continues to touch the lives of people who didn't know her. I want to end where it all began. My relationship with her led me to a door that I hadn't planned or thought about. It brought two guys together for the sake of helping others and honoring the one who brought us together. I hope you appreciate the relationships in your life. You never know where they might take you. I never thought her husband and I would put together a book of daily devotions about prayer. I never thought about it when I was sick in the hospital. I couldn't see at the time how anything good could come from my situation. You may feel that way today. I hope you come away today feeling more connected to the One who makes all things possible. He can do more than what we ask or imagine. What will happen after this day? I don't know. Will you continue praying, reading, and encouraging? Will you be inspired to do something that will help others? Have you grown in your connection to God? There is no greater connection than God. None of this would have been possible if it wasn't for God. I'm thankful for every connection made because of God. I pray that your relationship with God will continue to grow. I pray that you will stay connected no matter what happens. I pray that God will be in your life in a big way. I pray that your struggles and pain will not keep you away from God. May God bless you as you desire to connect with Him.

DEAR LORD, I'VE SEEN HOW MUCH I NEED YOU IN MY LIFE ...

1. Pray to God, thankful for the opportunity to grow more in Him.
2. Pray to God to have the dedication to keep on growing in prayer.

"And we know that all things work together for good to those who love God, to those who are the called according to His purpose." **(Romans 8:28)**

FINAL THOUGHTS OF ENCOURAGEMENT

"Pray without ceasing, in everything give thanks; for this is the will of God in Christ Jesus for you" (1 Thessalonians 5:17-18). This applies to every moment, day, experience, and feeling. It includes the beginning of the year, middle of the year, and the end of it. It involves the start of a day, in the day, at the close of the day. I hope you've come away with a better appreciation and practice in prayer. I wanted to write different experiences to address people at different stages in their faith. I wanted to give moments of my life where life was great and also challenging. Again, I'm not the authority on prayer. I do love God and desire to know Him better each day. I've shared moments of my life to help you think about other times and ways to pray. My stories are no different from yours. You know good times and bad times. You've experienced challenges and successes. Our prayers are not defined by our days, but our days are defined in prayers. Whether the day is going to be good or not, we wrap our attitudes and feelings in our prayers. We seek to know God's will better in our lives. Is there a day in our weeks, months, or years when we don't need to pray? I cannot think of a moment, event, or day when we don't need to seek God in prayer. My experiences happened at different times of the day. I believe our prayers should be throughout our days. We are to "pray without ceasing." We are prayerful in everything we do and what is done to us. I pray that you will continue to grow and develop your conversation with God. I pray that you will come away with a better knowledge of God. Remember, each day you are writing your own story. What will it say to those who read your life? I hope what people can say is how we depended upon God in everything because of our need to pray to Him. Thank you, again, for reading and praying. May God be glorified through our prayers.

NOTES

1. John H. Sammis, "Trust and Obey," 1887.
2. R. A. Evilsizer, "In the Morning of Joy," 1895.
3. Isaac Watts, "When I Survey the Wondrous Cross," 1707.
4. Tillit S. Teddlie, "The Lord's Supper," 1922.
5. Mary A. Kidder, "Did You Think to Pray?", 1876.

Made in the USA
Monee, IL
17 March 2020

23372757R00213